THE LONG, LONG YEARS

The Long, Long Years

GILLEASBUIG MACLEAN

The Pentland Press
Edinburgh – Cambridge – Durham – USA

First published in 1996 by
The Pentland Press Ltd
1 Hutton Close,
South Church
Bishop Auckland
Durham

ISBN 1-85821-398-3

Typeset by Carnegie Publishing, 18 Maynard St, Preston
Printed and bound by Antony Rowe Ltd, Chippenham

Contents

Preface

THIS COLLECTION OF MEMORIES (some blurred, but most entirely crystal clear), has been recorded for my children and grandchildren.

It is my personal memorial to the many millions of children, women and men who did not return to their homes, including those known to me; the boys and girls we left behind who had no opportunity to tell their own stories.

It is intended to acknowledge my debt, and to express my thanks, to the large numbers of children, women and men who, often at personal risk, in different ways helped me to survive; and without underrating any of the others, to mention particularly the children and women of Greece, whose unselfish generosity and courage shone brightly in our darkest hours.

Set down at distances of up to 7,000 miles in space, and up to 70 years in time, there may well be some minor errors due to tricks of memory.

Some names have been changed and many incidents have not been recorded.

G MacLean

CHAPTER ONE

Ancestral History

GENEALOGICAL INFORMATION back to the beginning of the nineteenth century comes principally from census records. Full information is contained in a letter in the bookcase; but the main source of information for older times is the book, *The MacLeans of Boreray* by Hector Hugh MacKenzie. Also in the bookcase is a significant amount of knowledge from American relatives.

Census sources cover back to about 1806, the 1841 census stating that Peggy Cameron was then thirty-five. It should be noted that dates recorded in earlier censuses are accurate only to about five years.

My father's name – Captain William MacLean – is recorded in Mr MacKenzie's book.

There are many references to other ancestors in other clan records – for example in the histories of clans Gunn, MacDonald, MacKenzie, and Cameron – and these date back to the first recorded MacLean – Gillean an Tuath, Gillean of the Battleaxe – the year being 1210.

Working backwards from the present day I have scribbled out a very rough record; starting with my own family, William, Nancy, and Iain; then to my father's family, Reginald, Archie, Janet, myself and Donald. My father was born on 13 October 1864, and died February 1927. His father was Archibald MacLean (1831–1888), Ground Officer, Grimsay. My father's mother was Margaret MacDonald who was born about 1839. My great grandfather was another Archibald who was a cousin of Flora MacDonald; he was married to Peggy Cameron who was born c. 1806. Next in line backwards was another Archibald MacLean who held lands at Scotvin on Grimsay; there is no record of his wife. Next was Neil Ban the Third, (fair-haired Neil) who died about the year 1773, at Kallin, Grimsay. He was the Tenth of Boreray, was grandfather of Flora MacDonald, and was married to Marion MacDonald. Her father was William MacDonald, Tutor of Sleat.

Neil's father was Archibald MacLean, Ninth of Boreray, (all these Archibalds would be called Gilleasbuig in their native Gaelic). Archibald was Baillie of North Uist in 1700, and was married to Mary MacDonald, who was the daughter of Somerled MacDonald the First of Sartle. Next was John MacLean, Eighth of Boreray, Sheriff of North Uist 1644, Chamberlain of

North Uist 1657–1700 and also Baillie of North Uist. He was married to Marion Campbell, daughter of Kenneth Campbell, whose wife was a daughter of John MacLeod of Watternish.

Next was the Seventh of Boreray, Neil Ban the Second, whose wife was Ann MacKenzie, a daughter of Alexander MacKenzie, first of Kilcoy. Neil's father, Donald MacLean, Sixth of Boreray was married to a daughter of McNeil of Barra, who in turn was descended from Neil of the Nine Hostages, King of Ireland. Next in line was the Fifth of Boreray, Gilleasbuig an Aslingiche (Archibald the Dreamer), who masterminded the defeat of the MacDonald federation in Mull, and who was married to a MacDonald, the daughter of Donald Gruamach MacDonald, Fourth of Sleat; he married a daughter of MacLeod of the Lews. Donald Gruamach was a direct descendant of Bruce.

The only record of the next one, Alexander the Fourth of Boreray, states that he was killed in battle. The Third, Allan na Tuagh, died unmarried. The second was John More MacLean, Baillie of North Uist who was married to a daughter of MacDonald of Griminish. At last we come to the First of Boreray, Neil Ban MacLean who was the second son of Donald, First of Ardgour. He was married to a daughter of Norman O'Beolan, the son of Patrick O'Beolan Abbot of Applecross whose lineage goes back to the Earls of Ross.

Now we are back at the Ardgours; Donald MacLean, First of Ardgour, was married to Evere Cameron who, according to the book, was a daughter of Ewen Cameron, 13th of Locheil; but there appears to be a bit of an anachronism here, and I think it more likely that she was a daughter of Ewen the Tenth.

Next was Lachlan Bronnach, 7th of Duart. He was married to Fionghal, a daughter of John Bord MacLeod of Dunvegan and Harris. His second wife was Janet, daughter of Alexander Stewart, Earl of Marr. He was born about 1393. There is a certain amount written about him in the clan histories. Next in line was Hector (Red Hector of the Battles), Eachan Ruadh nan Cath. He killed the Norwegian champion, in single combat, at Salen. He captured Dublin with a large fleet in 1400. At Harlaw he and Irvine of Drum killed each other. His friends carried him on their shields and buried him on Iona. He was married to a daughter of the Earl of Douglas.

His father, Lachlan Lubanach (Wily Lachlan), the Fifth of Duart, was Lieutenant General to the Lord of the Isles. He was appointed hereditary 'Right of the Clans' in battle, and was married to Lady Margaret MacDonald, daughter of John, First Lord of the Isles whose lineage goes back to Somerled, thence to Conn of the Hundred Battles, King of Ireland.

Next was the Fourth Chief of the MacLeans, who died during the reign of Robert the Second. He was known as John Dubh and was married to a Cumming, daughter of the Lord of the Braes of Lochaber. His father was Gillicallum, (Malcolm), who led the clan at Bannockburn and was married to Rena, daughter of the Lord of Carrick. The Second Chief was called Gilliemore or Big Lad. He fought at Largs and died about the year 1300. There is no record of his wife. His father, the first chief, was Gillean na Tuagh who was killed in battle about 1210.

Before Gillean Na Tuagh there was a long line of ancestors who are not so well authenticated in recorded history, and I intend to say something about them later.

Before that I will interject a little bit more about Archibald the Fifth of Boreray. His first wife (MacDonald) was descended from Crowner Gunn; but I have lost the record saying from which of the wives we are descended. I did have a reference which pointed to Gunn ancestry, but I am afraid it has been lost. Nevertheless, several of the lines of descent go back to Robert Bruce. Bruce's genealogy is apparently based on the Orkneying Saga, it is set out in the book *Tramp Royal* by Bruce of Stenhouse. Bruce's known remote ancestors are the same as those of Clan Gunn.

Now for the Macraes – my mother, Catherine Macrae, was born on 18 October 1880. Her father was Donald Macrae, Domnnhal Mhor (Big Donald) who was married on 5 April, 1870 to Jane Maclennan, who was the daughter of Thomas McLennan. Domnhal Mhor's father was also Donald Macrae, Domnhal Ban (Fair-haired Donald), 15/1/1808 – 3/4/1888. He married, on 21 January 1845, Margaret Matheson who was the daughter of Murdo Matheson. Next was Duncan Macrae who died on 13 February 1860. He was married to Christina MacKenzie daughter of Murdo MacKenzie of Braintra, who was descended from Dougal MacKenzie, Prefect of Kintail. Dougal was murdered in 1539 by Donald Gorm MacDonald at Eilean Donan. According to my grandfather, Duncan was 102 years old when he died, and he cut down a tree on the day of his death. That would make the year of his birth 1758. He was a sergeant in the Fraser Highlanders, who were also known as the Ross-shire Highlanders. There were many stories that almost certainly came from him and I will give you what I remember of these later.

His father, Alexander Macrae, was known as Alasdair Donn (Brown-haired Alasdair). He was born c.1725 and died June 1832. Information from my grandfather was to the effect that Alasdair was 106 years old when he died. The Macrae History says that both of these men were the oldest men in the parish for several years before they died. Alasdair was married to Isobel Macrae, who was descended from Macrae of Inverinate. Her lineage goes back to Edward First and James First of Scotland via Jane Beaufort and Margaret Drummond.

Alasdair's father was Donald Macrae, known as Domnhal MacAlasdair, who was drowned in Kyle Rhea. He was married to Flora MacKenzie, daughter of Kenneth MacKenzie, of Culdrein, Attadale. The MacKenzie line goes back to John MacKenzie, Second of Applecross and to Kenneth MacKenzie, Sixth of Gairloch. Both of these lines come directly from Bruce.

All the Macrae genealogy is in Macrae histories. Donald Macrae of the Inverinate branch has published a little book which gives a great deal of information about Macraes who emigrated to North Carolina.

Alasdair Donn's grandfather was Donald Macrae. Little is known about him and there is no record of his wife. His father is Duncan Macrae who lived at Coilrie.

Duncan's father was John Macrae, who was known as Iain Breac (Freckled John). It is not certain who was his wife but the probability is that she was a daughter of MacKenzie of Hilton. The Hilton lineage can also be traced back to Bruce.

John's father was the Revd. Farquhar Macrae, about whom a great deal is known. He lived from 1580 to 1662, was chief of the clan, and married in 1611 to Christina McCulloch, who was eldest daughter of McCulloch of Park. Park is a few miles from Strathpeffer.

His father, Christopher Macrae, was Sixth of Eilean Donan, and was married to a daughter of the Revd. Murdo Murchison.

Christopher's father was Duncan Fifth of Eilean Donan. This was the man who was well known for killing the attacking Donald Gorm MacDonald with an arrow from the castle. He was married to a Mrs Matheson (formerly Mrs MacKenzie – she must have been a beauty). Duncan was the second son of Christopher, the Fourth of Eilean Donan, about whom not a great deal has been recorded. His father was Finlay Macrae, Third of Eilean Donan, and next in line was Christopher, the second chief.

The first Macrae recorded in Lochalsh was Christopher's father who was Finlay Dubh McGilliechrist. Dates are uncertain but the family gravestone in Lochalsh Kirkyard gives the date 1410.

Finlay Dubh was descended from Finlay, the fourth son of Macrae of Clunes who was married to a MacBeolain (a name linked to the McKenzies). Two or three generations before that there was 'a man who came from Clunes'. Who or what he was I do not know; but he must have been a MacRa or a Macrae. He was descended from 'Gillian of the Aird'. Which Aird that was is not recorded but my guess is that was another name for the Black Isle. There was a King McRa in the ninth century (this was apparently another name for Gregory the Great). There was a McRa in the house of St Patrick in Ireland; there may be some connection.

From the first documented MacLeans to the present date there are some 22 generations, this works out at over 2,000,000 possible forebears at AD 1210. The total population of Scotland at that time would be a small fraction of that number. Even in the very small number of progenitors to whom we can give names there is a great deal of duplication, many of them marrying known relatives.

The unwritten MacLean history, that cared for by the *seanachies*, goes back to Angus of Tara, High King of Ireland.

My mother, Catherine Macrae, who was better known as Kate, was a teacher, qualified by training college in many subjects. Her favourite subject was French. She often said that she was no good at maths but I found a notebook of hers which showed clearly that she had little difficulty with calculus, so I think that she simply did not like maths.

She was a member of a large family, most of whom died young. Four sisters and a brother reached maturity. The oldest sister was Maggie who was my mother's favourite. She died around 1930 and our grandfather then came to stay with us. He had some very harsh things to say about Maggie's husband; whether or not they were merited, is not known. The next sister was Jean who was married to a carpenter who worked in a Greenock shipyard. They stayed in Gourock. I quite liked the husband but he too was not popular with the relatives. When Jean was young she was very severely scalded in a kitchen accident, so badly that her life was endangered, and she was never quite the same thereafter.

One day my grandfather took my mother aside and made her swear on the Bible that she would take care of her sister as long as she was able. This I found out after the Second World War. My mother became friendly with Alex Thomson's mother and confided in her. The explanation was very welcome when eventually I heard it but I could have done with it fifteen years earlier.

The next sister was Jessie who was married to Adam Collie, a warder in Duke Street prison. One day the husband found a boil on his neck and squeezed it. He was dead a day and a half later, leaving twins; a son and a daughter. Shortly after this the girl took TB which was called consumption at that time, and she died in a month or two. As if that were not enough the mother was knocked down and killed shortly afterwards, I think by a taxi. This left the lad on his own. He had lost his whole family in under a year. I believe he now resides somewhere south of London.

Jean had no family, but Maggie had a large family and there are cousins or their families surviving. There was a set of relatives in Orkney.

My mother had a very hard time after the death of my father. She gradually went downhill, being faced with the impossible task of trying to raise a family of five without resources.

My mother did not like Glasgow. She was born and brought up there but having escaped she did not wish to return. She had taught in a school in the Gorbals for quite some time, and married my father when she was twenty-nine.

Now back to her father, Donald Macrae – Domnhal Mhor (Big Donald) – who was with us for some years. I knew him very well eventually. He came to stay with us when he was beyond looking after himself. Only one of his sons reached maturity; this was Frederick Donald, who was a bit of a tearaway, according to his father. Frederick joined the army and was in it for several years before the First World War.

After nine years' service he was posted to the reserve in 1914. He was recalled fourteen days later and was posted missing in October 1914. His name is in the clan book *The Clan Macrae Roll of Honour*, also on the war memorial at the castle, the memorial at Balmacara, the National memorial and I would think he would be noted on the Portree memorial. He was in the Argylls.

Fred was named for his uncle Frederick who was lost at sea in 1882. My grandfather went to the quay at the Broomielaw to see him off. The ship had only 1′6″ of freeboard above the waterline when she sailed. It was never seen again. A wooden bucket with the ship's name was found on the West Coast of Ireland. There was talk of wreckers but there was no evidence. My grand-uncle's full name was Frederick George. He was 29 when he was drowned at sea. He was on my grandfather's mind most of the time, together with the son carrying his name. There is a copy of the wreck chart of the British Isles for 1879–1880 in the book *Sea Pictures*, and this chart shows a disgustingly large number of vessels lost. The book was presented to my eldest brother in 1924 by a lady who was resident in the Chateau de Thorenc, in France. There was a boatbuilder's yard at Dornie. It was to the east of, and not very far from, the castle. It is likely that it was from here that my great-uncle picked up his ship. It is known that one of the teachers who taught at Inverinate in 1870 went to sea from there, he being a sea captain also.

My grandfather was the eldest son of a large family – he had one older sister, and was born in 1847. He left Lochalsh to look for work in Glasgow around 1870. He worked first of all as a warder in Gartnavel Asylum for a few years before joining the police force, where he remained for the remainder of his working life. He married, in 1870, Janet, the daughter of Thomas MacLennan. The marriage took place against the clearly expressed wishes of his father. He was told that if he married this girl he would not see his father's face again, and after the wedding his father wrote asking for the return of his watch, which he had earlier given to my grandfather. We know very little about Janet. My mother never spoke about her, and I have been unable to discover any reason for her father-in-law's apparent hatred. When my grandfather was very old and very forgetful he told the late Captain McGillivray, in my hearing, that his wife was a drunken so and so. There was a certain amount of evidence that things were not going too well. The same gentleman was told that my grandfather would come home from work to find a cart and a flitting at the door, preparing to go to another house. Apparently this kind of thing happened more than once. It seems that the wife could not manage on what she was given; whether or not she was given sufficient I don't know. Most of the time he was in the 'force' he was a sergeant, so money should not have been a problem.

Janet had a brother, Duncan, who went to Canada. He was known to us as 'Uncle Duncan' and really did very well. He was originally in the North West Mounted Police. He and another officer captured a dangerous criminal after a hard and dangerous chase. They both received commendations for bravery. After this he went into business and prospered; in today's terms he would have been a millionaire. He was very good to us, and sent us a very handsome present every Christmas. A close relative of his, a teacher, came over in the 1930s and told us a great deal about the Canadian relatives. That was the last contact that I can remember.

It is apparently recorded somewhere that my grandfather was born in Avernish and I am not at all sure that this is correct, because he lived at Inverinate until he was seven and received all his schooling there; his great-grandmother was a Macrae of Inverinate. He had many stories about this school. Every pupil had to carry a peat to school each day to keep the fire going. Speaking in Gaelic was forbidden, although the majority could speak nothing else. They were drilled to say, 'Good morning, Mr Forbess,' on the first entry of the teacher, and they would frequently say 'Good Forbess, Mr morning'. Speaking in Gaelic was punished with the tawse. Occasionally they would shout out that this boy or that girl was 'Speaking Gaelic here' and some poor innocent soul would receive two or three of the best. The teacher's name was pronounced as I have written it, how it was spelled I do not know. This teacher was the gentleman who later became a sea captain; perhaps he was worn down by his flock.

There were many stories about when Grandfather was young, and one in particular that he told many times. All the boys would go out walking on a Sunday and to amuse themselves one Sunday they caught a number of sea trout and salmon by 'tickling' them in a pool they knew about. They would have made expert poachers. They collected them to take home, when they remembered what day it was. Then they stacked them back in the river with a large stone on top. They returned on the Monday morning, and took the fish home expecting great praise from their father. Instead of praise they had their behinds tanned. Apparently there was a little white mark on each fish where it had had contact with other dead fish.

Another form of amusement was to climb the steep hill at the back of the house and roll boulders down from the top of the rise. The rocks, when they hit an embedded boulder, would usually at some point bounce fifty or a hundred feet in the air. One time they were at their usual amusement when they noticed a coach on the road below, directly in line with a very fast-moving boulder. Fortunately it bounced over the coach and splashed straight into Loch Duich, and no one else was any the wiser. After that particular ploy they looked elsewhere for their amusement.

He told me that he went to Avernish when he was seven, that would be about 1854, and would be I think when his father was given the croft. There were stories about the establishment of the crofts also. A piece of land would be given to two people to divide to their mutual satisfaction. The usual practice was that one would be appointed to divide the land and the other would then have his choice. At Avernish my great-grandfather had the pick of the land, the other crofter having divided it. He chose the best land although it was further from his own house and nearer the other crofter's home. He was convinced that the other lad had tried to cheat him. They were there until my grandfather's family died out in the Thirties. The new house they built lasted much longer but is now a ruin.

There were many stories about his adventures in Glasgow. For example, he and another policeman were on night patrol, I think he said in West Nile St, when they heard a great commotion that seemed to come from a top flat in one of the tenements. A female voice was screaming blue murder and there was a noise sounding very like 'smack, smack, smack' on a bare behind. It being too high to reach quickly they took a stone and threw it into the window, they then went round the block and came back down on their original beat. The street was now silent but they met an Irishman and his wife in their night attire with a strong complaint. 'Sure, officers, we were sleeping peacefully in our bed when two big blackguards threw a stone into the window.' We heard that story many times.

Another time two of them were sent down to investigate a disturbance at Glasgow Green. A shipload of 'tattie-howkers' had arrived from Ireland and a big woman was holding forth in the middle of a large crowd: 'I'm 58 years of age, and I haven't had a shoe on my fit since I was borrn.' 'And I don't think she had washed them either,' said my grandfather. She continued, 'And I have here a bottle of Calum Cille's water and no policeman in Glasgow daar lay a hand on my shoulder.' I should explain that Calum Cille, who was named by the Irish 'Tattie Howker' is the Gaelic name for Columba. Grandfather said, 'I laid a hand on her shoulder right enough; I put her in the cooler for the night.'

The officer in charge came to him one day and said that there was trouble in the cattle market; a bull had escaped and was causing problems. He said, 'You understand about cattle so you go down and sort it out.' When he arrived at the mart he found a very angry Braman bull running about. It had the hump all right. He expected no trouble but the bull did not understand Gaelic, and it nearly killed him. I don't think that he was ever off work but he took quite a fair knock and he used to say that he could still feel it in his eighties.

Occasionally they had English officers in the force. There was one with whom he was very friendly. At that time, for some reason, they patrolled in threes; this would be a Highlander on each side and Bridges in the middle. Bridges would look up at the men on either side and complain: 'Where I come from they call me Big Bridges, up here you call me Wee Bridges.'

My mother was the only one in her family who did anything scholastically, although the others were not stupid. I had doubts about Jane but when I found out what had happened to her I realized that there were good reasons for everything. As for Janet McLennan, any person who left Kintail to live in the poorer parts of Glasgow in the 1870s would require some cheering up. That could be the reason for taking to the bottle, if indeed she did so.

My grandfather was in all the Highland Societies in Glasgow. He used to sing at them. When, in his old age, he stayed with us he was always singing. He sang Gaelic songs and hymns in Gaelic and English. He had a book which he prized greatly. It was inscribed 'Ealasaid NicConnich' that is Elizabeth McKenzie, and is called *Clarsach nam Beann − The Harp of the Mountains* by Evan McColl. A similar book in English has been published called *The Mountain Minstrel*. I have found another book signed Elizabeth MacKenzie: this is a book of poems by James Hogg, which I think belonged to my mother, and I have come to the conclusion that it is not possible to find out who was the original owner but it could be my mother's grandmother or a relative of hers. Evan McColl's book was published with the help of a large number of subscribers, many of whom are listed at the back. There is a surprising number from Caithness and from the east coast of Sutherland.

One day Sgt Macrae was to escort an 'upstart troublemaker' who was to speak in some public place, and the police were to ensure that there was no trouble. The man's name was Keir Hardie and he was, according to my grandfather, 'a thorough gentleman and no trouble at all'. The man was the first socialist MP.

Being bored one very quiet night, and looking for amusement, one of the patrolling constables caught a stray dog. They tied four or five tin cans to its tail and let it go. The animal was terrified and disappeared like quicksilver. They could not undo what they had done but they were thoroughly ashamed of themselves and never again treated an animal like that.

Now a tale from Macrae country – a soldier returning from fighting the French walked from Strome Ferry over the hill towards Auchtertyre. He happened on a man who had been cutting a patch of oats and had fallen asleep in the hot sun, he lay on his back with his right hand outstretched and open. 'Donald lifted his kilt and he shit in the hand. He then found a long straw and began to tickle the man's moustache. After twitching once or twice the sleeper slapped his hand over his mouth, while Donald went off down hill at speed. That,' said my grandfather, 'would be a typical ceilidh story, the truth of which can not be vouched for.'

While in her teens my mother was knocked down by a drunken cabbie and received a severe blow to the head. I have forgotten whether it was the horse or the vehicle which struck her but she was left with a touch of deafness in one ear and a punctured eardrum.

Now the police again – at one stage in the police force development, someone decided that the steady flatfoot beat patrol was slovenly, and it was decided to do something about it. The service of a retired Irish RSM was obtained to teach the teuchters how to walk. There were drilling sessions for an hour a day for a considerable time. The parade ground was Glasgow Green. Neither the training nor the trainer were popular. 'If I had you down in the barrack yard, with a full pack, and 66 rounds of ammunition in your pouches, sure I would warm you.' 'And no doubt he would, too,' said my grandfather. One day he had them just about done, they were back and forward, up and down, right incline, left incline; form fours, form two deep, and so on. Eventually he had them in revue order, a thin blue line, all facing the RSM. Then he was at it again, 'By the centre, quick march, left, right, left right': he walking backwards, and the long blue line marching forwards.

There was a ragged old lady lying sleeping on the ground, recovering from the effects of the previous night's drinking. Eventually the RSM reached her, tripped over her, fell on top of her and 'nearly burst her'. That was the end of the day's exercise.

Most of the time the police left their stations in large groups for street patrol. There would be perhaps 50 officers in pairs, marching along the street. The last pair would fall out and start their patrols as they reached the various beats. They would be accompanied by jeering youngsters chanting,

'Hens march to the midden, do whatever you are bidden,' and so on. My mother had an oft-repeated recollection of military drilling which went like this, euphemistically put: 'Left incline, you beggars, LEFT INCLINE. You may have broke your mummy's heart but you won't break mine.'

Fred, my mother's brother, was reported 'missing' at Mons in October 1914. From as early as I can remember she still expected to see him come home. Then one day, in the early 1930s a letter came from the War Office containing a scroll recording his grave and the war cemetery. Possibly they had just recently found him, but it was quite a shock to my mother. I think Archie may still have the scroll.

When he was in his teens my grandfather climbed the hill above Inverinate where he found a deer trapped in a snowdrift. He said that he killed it with a stick, and then stood trembling beside it, shocked at what he had done. He was afraid of being transported, and if he had been discovered that is what would have happened. That was in 1865 or thereabout; today he could kill the gamekeeper as well and he would be told to be a good boy and sent home.

Even in the nineteenth century Glasgow was a very cosmopolitan city and many foreign sailors stayed for short or long periods. The largest number of incomers were the Highlanders, closely followed by the Irish. It may be that later the Irish had the largest number.

My grandfather became friendly with a sailor from the Levant. Whether he was Turk, Syrian, or one of those peoples who have been almost wiped out, at this moment I forget; but he was a stranger in a strange land and had a pretty young wife. He was very fond of the girl so, before leaving for a rather long voyage he asked my grandfather to see that she was not harassed. He also asked a friend from the same people as himself to look after her. When he returned he met his friend on the street as he was nearing his home. After the usual pleasantries he said, 'How did you get on with my wife?' 'Oh,' said the 'friend', 'I got on very well with her; I slept with her every night.' 'In that case,' said the sailor, 'you'll never sleep with another one,' and with that pulled a knife from his sleeve and stabbed his former friend on the chest, who clasped his hands to his breast and ran into an adjacent police station screaming repeatedly that he had been murdered. He was jumping about and with difficulty the police managed to get him down and removed his upper garments, only to discover that he was so well padded that the knife had not penetrated. None the less there was by this time a sizeable pool of blood on the floor, and further inspection revealed that he now had two openings in his stern – the wronged husband's parting shot.

On another occasion two people were having themselves a fight. They were rolling about in the middle of the street making a great hullabaloo, again right in front of the police station. They were immediately pulled into the station and charged. One of them was quite articulate and the other would not open his mouth. Suddenly the silent one put his hand in his pocket and put a circular piece of his tongue, 'about the size of a florin', on the desk in front of the officer. Evidently when they were rolling about he had put his tongue out at the assailant and had it bitten off.

Stories about the 'Wild Macraes' were common in Lochalsh. They had turned to smuggling, probably when they had lost their land and before they were given their crofts. It was said that they would really stuff food into themselves for a full day, before setting off on an expedition. The food would keep them going for a fortnight, then they would sail home and store their ill-gotten gains in the underground house. It was known as the smuggler's cave to those involved and their families. When we were boys it had a stone front about four feet each way, with a circular entrance about two feet in diameter, which was unfortunately blocked by a stone about ten or fifteen feet in. It appeared to have slipped and as boys we were unable to move it. When I returned for the first time some 25 years ago the stone front had been removed and the entrance filled in with earth a few feet back. On a later visit the entrance had been again filled in, and above the cliff face, a little way back from the edge there was a deep conical depression in the ground, as if the chamber had collapsed. I always had a desire to excavate this souterrain but the opportunity never came and it is now physically impossible.

There is, in my possession, a six-inch map which shows the positions of the croft boundary walls. The survey was carried out in 1875 and revised in 1902. I have pencilled on it the position of the souterrain which was known as the smuggler's cave. There are two bowl-shaped small sinkings in the rock on the shore in front of it, and it may be found by means of these.

Another of my grand-uncles, John, was journeying from Avernish to Balmacara on some business: he failed to arrive; the boat was found but no trace of John was ever found. I had the weird notion that we might find some answers in the earth house. John was responsible for cutting some of the names which are on the family tombstone at Kirkton of Lochalsh. He built the little church at Dornie, and some other places round about.

The best-known of my grandfather's brothers was Farquhar who rebuilt Eilean Donan castle. Him I remember very well. There is a great deal of information extant about him. There is a letter from him slipped into the war memorial book. He spent over twenty years of his life rebuilding the castle; in his time off he was rebuilding the family house. He completed the castle but did not finish the house: there was a small part of the roof left undone. He had a wonderful hand-carved stair which has disappeared. The estate owner removed the slates and everything fell in after that.

On my first return visit to the area I dug down into the ruins and located the remains of his tool chest. He had a lovely set of tools of which I was very envious. There was a complete set of beautiful moulding planes which had rotted away. Some of the wood was left, but the irons were gone; all that was left of them was strips of rust. I think it possible that the staircase also rotted away, but I hope that someone did remove it, it was a wonderful example of craftsmanship.

There is a memorial tablet to him just inside the door of the castle. All it says is, 'Fearchar a Casteal, 1858–1932'. He was interred in the family plot at Kirkton Churchyard. His sister Kate is interred there also although neither is recorded on the stone.

Copy of letter to Margaret Nicholson, Grimsay, N. Uist. from Hattie Hitchmough, Lexington, Nebraska, dated 19 January 1985.

published with Mrs Nicholson's permission

Dear Margaret, Your letter of 1–1 came today after going to another town in Nebraska. It really is necessary to put the zip code number on the address as the postal Dept rely on that for quick delivery. Mine is 68850. I will try to give you a bit of history as we know it, as the grandparents did not talk much about their life in Scotland and we younger ones, at that time, were not genealogy minded to ask questions, and what a mistake, as when the older generation is gone their knowledge is gone too.

Now as we know it:

Some time in the early fall of 1874, a group, consisting of John and Mary MacLean, their children, Archie and his recent bride, wife Annabelle Nicholson, and her mother Rachel Nicholson; another son William: daughters, Mary, Maggie, Christina. Oh yes, son Malcolm. They came direct to Plum Creek, now Lexington, on the train from where the ship docked, I don't know where that was. They were met here by Hugh MacLean, who had been here some time, and had a tree claim and homestead eight miles north of town. The group stayed with him until they could file on a homestead, that was 160 acres of land which they had to improve and live on for two years before they received a deed to the land. This was good farmland which is now worth about $2,000 per acre, but they were not satisfid with that and gave it up to go farther north in the hills, (about nine miles) which was much like the country they had left in Scotland. Raising cattle was more to their liking than farming. They homesteaded there, improved the place by building a sod house and barn. As time went on they filed on more homesteads near there and in 1894 my Grandfather Archie bought 160 acres from the railroad, and built a frame house and other buildings. It is still hill land with some farming and pasture. I own that parcel of land now. I will tell about Archie's family. Archie's wife Annabelle was pregnant when they came here and my mother Mary was born 2 January 1875. Then in succession came Anna, 14 April 1876; Marion 14 August 1879; Donald 10 November 1881; Ella, 14 May 1884; Johnny 23 March 1886 and died 23 November 1886; Kate 25 October 1887; George 29 May 1890; Archie 4 April 1893; Rachel 15 July 1897 and died 28 January 1910.

The nearest school was six miles away so the oldest three didn't get much schooling; they herded the cattle, they would take a sandwich and water and stay with the herd all day and drive them home in evening. The hills were full of rattlesnakes and prairie dogs and the children were so lucky that they were never snakebitten. As the oldest ones were old enough to work as a 'hired girl' they were farmed out to someone who needed help and could pay them a small wage. In later years they moved closer to the valley and the schoolhouse so from Ella down they attended school. Ella and Kate graduated from high school and then taught school until they were married. All the children are gone now and at 82 I'm the oldest grandchild. The other cousins are scattered throughout the US from Pennsylvania to California and south to the Gulf of Mexico.

So now I can't tell anything about Great–grandma Rachel N except she married Hugh MacDonald who came from Canada about 1900. All the papers of hers that I have here are her homestead application and notes she repaid at the bank.

I have 28 descendants and 24 were here for Thanksgiving, Christmas and New Year, so it takes some planning to care for that many. They all (but 4) live in driving distance so they were here for the days.

I haven't been at Tina's for a while but must make a call soon. I'm glad to hear you have the TV. I sure get enjoyment from it in evenings.

Hope this letter helps you and I will send more in future.

Regards, (signed) Hattie Hitchmough.

Boreray 1980

Sparkle of white sand on the island's lee
The flower-choked machair edging to the beach
White flashing gannets driving to the sea
Spirits of clansmen long beyond our reach

Celtic monks and Spaniards in death side by side
The rotting boat that's lying near the bay
The roofless homes were fulmars now reside
And seagull's chicks where children used to play

Mute swans and cygnets sail the great loch still
Still great grey seals stare at island's shore
Small black-faced sheep still graze the rocky hill
What of the clan, will they return no more?

Five hundred years on Boreray –
Out and far are their homes today

CHAPTER TWO

Boyhood Memories

A T THE BEGINNING OF THIS CHAPTER I should say that the present sent by Uncle Duncan each Christmas was Canadian dollars; I will also record some more stories from my grandfather.

He was called out on a very hot summer day to one of the city tenements. The family on the ground floor was being flooded, there were no complaints from the other floors but water was running out of the close at ground level. He entered and went from house to house until he reached the top. He then entered the roof space and found there a lead-lined wooden cistern, he said it was about 8′ square and about 4′ deep. The young boys from the tenement were using it as a swimming pool. There was an overflow standpipe in the middle which they found to be a nuisance and broke off. The water flowed in at the top, and then flowed out at the break. After some time there remained enough water to paddle in. The sergeant then entered the top floor house and found that when water had come rushing in the tenant had merely taken the poker from the fire and made a hole between the floorboards, and that was their problem solved. The process was repeated in every flat down to the ground floor, where the water flowed out through the close.

There was a particularly gory story about the fighting at Badajoz; unfortunately I have forgotten the details.

However, there was a tale of the American War, this must have been the War of Independence, from the dates of my great, great grandfather's active service. The Highlanders were losing men at night from some unknown cause. They were losing pickets and sentries. When one particular picket began his watch he was told, 'We don't know who or what is taking our men; but if anything comes nearer than twenty feet, shoot it.' Everything went well until dawn was beginning to break and a pig appeared. It was snorting around in the bushes, picking up this and that, and gradually getting closer. The soldier was by this time tired and fed up. He said to himself, 'My orders were to shoot anybody or anything approaching within twenty feet. You have come far enough.' He then shot it, and this wakened the camp. The pig was examined and it proved to be an Indian wearing a pigskin.

A Scottish soldier, a Highlander, at Waterloo, was caught in the open between the squares. He must have been a runner. In any case, a French dragoon came out after him, waving his sabre. Fortunately the Highlander saw him in time to remove his plaid and spread it on the ground. He immediately stood in the middle of it. As the dragoon was approaching near enough to slice him with his sabre, the horse shied away, apparently thinking the dark plaid was a hole in the ground. There was a bit of a stand off but the Higlander's brown bess and bayonet were longer than the sabre and he managed to kill the dragoon.

There was a famous murder case in Glasgow. A man called Oscar Slater was convicted of killing someone and, on appeal, the death sentence was commuted to life imprisonment. He served 21 years and when he was released there was a great deal of publicity about the trial. Some people said that the Crown had not fully proved their case. Conan Doyle took an interest in the case, and Slater finished up with £6,000 compensation. One day someone asked my grandfather what he thought about it. 'Well,' he said, 'while that case was going one of our lads went to see Slater's parents about something, and he asked if they believed their son was innocent. They said that they did not know about the case; but if he had been tried under Jewish law he would have been stoned for half of what he had already admitted.'

Before I forget I will interject at this point a story from my mother. When I arrived home from Austria she told me that one day she had entered the butcher's shop to collect her meat ration. While there she enquired if there were any eggs available. Eggs were 'off ration' and were sold as and when available, and of course they were usually under the counter. She was told in no uncertain terms that there were none; 'Don't you know that there's a war on, woman?' At that time my mother had four sons serving overseas, and I think that Seonaid was in London. Well, I don't know if it was natural nastiness that turned people into column dodgers, or that they were less afraid to display it when the men were away.

My grandfather said that at the last charge at Waterloo the Highland Brigade and the Greys went in together, the Highlanders hanging on to the stirrup leathers of the Greys, and this was a very successful manoeuvre. For a long time I was unable to find any confirmation of that story. The famous picture *Scotland for Ever* does not show the Highlanders. My grandfather's grandfather was not at Waterloo, he was out of the army by that time – but the artist who painted the picture was not there either. I recently obtained a short history of the Gordons, and this describes the charge, exactly as my grandfather had related it. He said also that after the battle Napoleon was particularly complimentary to the Greys, saying, 'How beautifully those grey horses ride. If I had 10,000 of these men I could still conquer the world.'

That reminds me of a long talk I had with an SS officer at Leoben in May 1945. He said, 'If you people, British and Yanks, would stop now and leave us free to fight, we would still beat the Russians for you.'

My grandfather spoke at different times of this one or that one who left Lochalsh to go and fight the French. Sometimes he would say about someone he did not like very much, perhaps a Campbell or a Skyeman, 'He had a face that would frighten the French.' It should be remembered that the last time this country fought the French was 32 years before my grandfather was born.

There were several stories about folk being transported for seven years or for life. They were sent to Botany Bay for various crimes, some indeed worthy of heavy punishment, but many were trifling.

There is some circumstantial evidence in favour of the Waterloo stories in Volume 2 of Colonel Stewart's book *Sketches of the Highlanders of Scotland* – it was printed in 1822, seven years after the battle. It is quite clear that the Highland Brigade was at Waterloo, known then as the 104th Regiment; it is also noted that Napoleon made it clear that he had a great admiration for the Greys, whom he called the terrible grey horsemen, and also for the Highlanders. It is well worth anyone's time and trouble to read Byron's *Childe Harold's Pilgrimage* completed in 1818, not only for the beauty of the language but also for the snippets of history which it contains. Most of the information about Waterloo is contained in the third canto, starting about the eighteenth or nineteenth verse.

Now it is time to say something about my father, if I remember anything more about the Macraes I will note it later.

My father, William MacLean, was born 23 October 1864, at Scotvin, Grimsay. He was the fourth child of Archibald MacLean and Margaret MacDonald. His oldest brother, Archibald, was born 30 July 1860, and died in Southern Rhodesia, October 1899. The next son, Alexander, was born on 27 August 1862 and was drowned on the north ford, when he was caught by the rising tide on 9 January 1904. There is a memorial stone to them in a cemetery on the west side of the island.

The 1881 census states that William was sixteen, born on North Uist. I have no record of when he first went to sea, but being brought up on a rather poor croft, he did very well to get on the way he did. He served abroad in clipper ships for several years. I have no record of the names of individual ships. He rounded Cape Horn at least once, and I think three times in clippers. He was on the china clippers for some time. He was qualified to take charge of an ocean going vessel in sail or steam.

On one particularly long voyage south, the crew to amuse themselves put a hook and line over the stern of the ship and baited it with salt pork to see what they could catch. They caught a shark, and with difficulty got it on board and killed it. They decided they would like to eat it (they were by this time sick of salt pork and biscuits). They cut a large piece off it and cooked it. First of all they tried it out on the cat, which could not get enough of it, then a fair number of them took some. My father said it tasted like ham. There was an Irishman aboard who took a particularly large piece then the remainder was thrown overboard and they went about their business. Later the cat began to act rather peculiarly, starting to jump up and down, trying to get through the little brass rings they had on deck, and finishing the display by jumping overboard. Some time after this it was the Irishman's turn to go on watch and he was nowhere to be found. A second and very thorough search was mounted and eventually Pat was found in the chain locker; if it had been stormy at the time the chains would have beaten him to pulp. His explanation was, 'You saw what the cat did, and I had a much larger piece of the shark than him.'

On one of his early voyages they had shore leave in a port in Portugal. While the crew was preparing the ship for sea my dad and his pal from Uist went for a walk in the countryside at the back of the town. They came to a place where there were orange trees overhanging the road and bearing some very fine looking oranges. They helped themselves filling their pockets and their hands, and at that point, as my father put it, 'the Portugoose arrived.' This man was in a very bad temper, with much gesticulation and fluent cursing in Portuguese. He then removed his jacket and threw it down, then another and another and another, until they had counted twelve or thirteen then. My father said, 'I think that must be the last one, we had better go.' They took off and ran almost the whole way back to the ship. All that was left by that time were handfuls and pockets full of pulp.

He went ashore in Albania with a party of upper-crust characters to hunt wild boar. After the last hunt one of the party presented him with a large pair of binoculars. Archie still has these binoculars, and they still work.

He was very close to his younger brother, Calum, whom he took with him on several voyages. Calum was a first-class craftsman, a ship's carpenter, and an excellent cabinet maker and boat builder, and good at much else besides. He was working in the Liverpool area during the First World War, being well past military age, and of course still had his Western Isles accent. One day, in a shop, a group of Scousers began to nag him with such things as, 'You old German, get away out of here.' He was furious and joined up immediately, although quite unfit for it. My father bought him out; they had many a laugh about it later.

Calum was married to an English girl, a Catholic. The boys, my cousins, were brought up in Liverpool and went to Manchester University. Archie became an architect and for most of his working life was a senior lecturer in the Royal Technical College, Glasgow (now Strathclyde University). He would be about twenty years older than me, and eventually I met him after the Second World War. We lost touch when he left Glasgow and for many years now his name has not been on the architect's register. His brother was older, I think, and became a very successful builder. I never met him. Calum refused to stay in Lancashire; one can hardly blame him. His wife refused to stay in Uist, and she can't be blamed either. Eventually they divorced and Calum married a local lady later. They stayed on the west side of the island.

While I was working in Oban, before the war, we were asked to design a house for the lifeboat mechanic in Barra. When the plans were complete the mechanic was invited to the office to ensure that the house would be suitable. He came to Oban and I had quite a long talk with him. He was a gentleman about twenty years older than me by the name of Alan MacDonald. Some days later I spoke to my mother about him and I was informed that he was my first cousin. That was the first time I had heard about cousins in the Western Isles, and we never met again.

In the late 1920s or early 1930s Mrs Monk, who had relatives in Uist, often came to visit my mother. (There were people named Mannach on Boreray when the island was visited by Martin Martin 300 years ago – 1697 – Mannach may be translated as Monk.) Farming was in a bad way at that time and Mrs Monk would visit the auction mart and buy a sheep for five shillings. They would pay half of the cost each. Then for some time afterwards we would have all sorts of weird and wonderful dishes, some of them very tasty indeed. Five shillings is 25 pence in modern money, so our half sheep would cost us about 12½ pence.

Donald was at one time very interested in unusual cooking, and he decided he would like to try sheep's head broth. A sheep's head was purchased, singed on the fire, put in a big cauldron over the fire, and boiled for two or three hours. I seem to remember that it had to be split first; anyway it was bubbling away in boiling water with its great big eyes looking at us for three hours. The finished article was reasonably palatable; but the staring eyes were very off-putting.

On another occasion he made a 'real' haggis. Where the recipe was dug out from I don't know. The main essential ingredient was 'one sheep's bag and pluck', and it was cooked in the same big pot. The pluck was the heart, lungs and lights; in fact everything attached to the windpipe. This thing was placed in the pot and boiled for three hours with the windpipe hanging over the fire. While it was boiling all the muck came out through the windpipe and dropped into the fire. The gristle, windpipe, and any other undesirable pieces were removed and the remainder minced. This was then mixed with oatmeal and different kinds of seasoning. Then the sheep's stomach was prepared; it stank a bit when it came from the slaughter house, and required a great deal of washing. It was then half-filled with the mixture already prepared and sewn up. It required several hours' boiling and simmering, and was very good indeed.

A relative from Uist arrived one day and there was a great deal of story swapping. At one point the visitor was telling a story about Calum rowing into Scotvin, in one boat and towing three others, when my mother interrupted with, 'Wasn't I there when he arrived?' She had called his mother to the window, and drew from her the immediate comment, 'Amadan gorach'; that is, 'Silly fool.' Apparently he had built the boats on the west side of Uist and towed them home a great distance. The story is still related in Uist.

Another cousin was William Archy MacDonald, who was for a long time in Pretoria, South Africa; and indeed was for some time president of the South African Society of Architects. He also has not been on the RIBA Register for many years.

You may have noticed the frequency with which the Boreray MacLeans used the name Archibald or Gilleasbuig. In our family there are or were four cousins bearing the name, although I am the only one with the Gaelic form. I had thought that the reason might have some connection to the death of my father's older brother, an attempt to keep the name going. I have tried to find out where the name originated, and my best guess is from one of the original Cameron chiefs; the second chief in the unwritten clan history was Gillespic, who lived in the thirteenth century. There were also connections with the Douglas Clan, who used the name frequently, and with the Clan Campbell, but their connection was much later than when the Borery MacLeans first used the name. The clan had several chiefs with the name. The Boreray MacLeans came from the Ardgour branch. There was one Ardgour generation only in the line. The first chief of Boreray's mother was a Cameron of Locheil.

People of the Western Isles saw no good reason why there should not be two children of the same name in the one family, and there were many families where two children of the same name were to be found: that answers the first question I am usually asked about my older brother and myself. Whether I was the lucky one or the unlucky one to get the Gaelic version is a matter of opinion, but I can think of many other names I would like even less than Gilleasbuig, and while it did cause me some problems in my younger days, by the time I was in my teens I was quite proud of my name and would not let anyone within my hearing criticize it without reply.

My mother did not get on very well with my father's people; she said that they were apparently not amused that their favourite son or brother had decided to marry a Glasgow keelie, when there were plenty of fine young women in Uist who would have been glad to marry him.

Now another digression – in the late 1920s and early 1930s there was an itinerant Jewish pedlar who used to call on us. He sold clothes, carpets, and indeed would supply anything that was requested. When my grandfather was in bed, too old to rise, my mother took the pedlar into the bedroom and introduced them. They chatted about Glasgow for a short time, and then parted. When the pedlar, Sammy Meier, had gone, my grandfather asked my Aunt Jean, who had stayed in the room, who he was. Grandfather was very deaf indeed, he was at least 86 at the time. She shouted out, well within Sammy's hearing, 'He's a dew, he's a dew, he's a d-e-w, he's a DEW.' At that I left the room saying to myself, 'I can no longer stay with you.' I don't know why I thought it so amusing.

The earliest recollections I can date are of Donald being born, when I was a month under three years old. Father was away a great deal of the time but he was home at that time. I have some recollections of being in a boat with him in Oban Bay and finding wild ducks' nests with eggs. This was about the same time, at the dawning of my memory. I also remember Seonaid going to school for the first time, about a month after my third birthday. There are memories of a holiday spent on the Iolaire at Roseneath, where we always had tea and toast for breakfast, and there were very comfortable cane chairs to lounge in. We would play with a ball on the deck and we must have been cursed many times when I let it run down the scuppers and they would put a boat out to bring it back to me.

There was a large detached site immediately in front of our home in Oban. It was owned by a man called McGregor who walked with a limp which was probably caused by a war wound. He was a lawyer in the town. The site was like a small farm off which they took a crop of hay every year. Eventually the place was sold to Trustees for the Carmelite Community who made it into a convent. A certain Father McClymont used to visit the convent twice a day, and a stern looking character he was. One day, for no particular reason, I put my tongue out at him as he went past. He came after me. Across the rear entrance was a six feet high trellis fence with a gate in it of the same material. This gate had a strong shootbolt on the inner face. I reached the gate a step or two ahead of him and managed to engage the bolt, then I made off and into the back door of the house. The priest made for the front door, hammered on it briefly and then walked in, meeting my Mother approaching the door from the inside. Next I heard her saying, 'Well if he did that he'll be punished,' and she then came in to the scullery.

We had an old lady there who used to help with the washing, a Mrs McLachlan, and mother said to her, 'Where's Gilleasbuig?' 'He's in behind the tubs here, what's he been doing?' 'He put his tongue out at the priest. Come here till I give him a sixpence.' That was my 'telling-off' and punishment, perhaps because my mother objected to the way he had stormed in, but the whole affair was an object lesson to me. I learned that all people have feelings, and that no one should be attacked without a very good reason.

The causeways between the Uists and Benbecula are of fairly recent construction and before their day there was always the occasional person taking a chance with the tide and getting into difficulties. As I have already mentioned, my Uncle Alexander was lost there; it seems that he had been repairing a window at Scotvin and had crossed the ford to buy glass. On his return he was caught by the rising tide. The glass could be seen for many years and was known as a warning to others.

My paternal grandmother was born at Baleshare, Benbecula. There is a photograph of the remains of the house in which she was born in an album here. Baleshare means the eastern township, the western township having been washed away during a great storm in historical times. It is noted in old records that sections of the west were inundated and washed away, it being mostly sand.

The road down to the primary school in Oban was very steep, the school being built at the foot of the hill on which we lived, the result being that we went to school very quickly and loitered on the way home. During my first year at school I was strolling home one day when I saw Donald at the side of the road ahead. A couple of older boys were speaking to him. When I reached him they said, 'He won't move, he won't shift.' I asked them to leave him and I would take him home. The place he was sitting was where it had been reckoned to be too steep to build houses economically. It was overgrown with trees, bushes, saplings and brambles. The whole area was covered with leaf mould right down to the roadside. There was a spring and a tangle of rasps and thorns where the wren used to nest. This was where he had made himself a slide in the leaf mould. It was about ten feet long and he squatted at the foot of it. He had been sliding for some time until he realized he had slid the seat out of his pants, and he was not going to move. Eventually he was persuaded and he came home with me. He would not be more than 2½ years old at the time.

My mother was coming home past Duart Cottage, and at Gowrie Villa she found Mrs Fraser (Frenchie's wife) in a fierce argument with McGregor the milkman about the accounts for the previous week, in fluent Gaelic. In effect Mrs Fraser was saying, 'Sunday, Monday, Tuesday, Wednesday,

Thursday, Friday, Saturday, SEVEN DAYS THERE,' and McGregor would retort, 'Sunday, Monday, Tuesday, Wednesday, Thursday, Friday, Saturday, Sunday; eight days.' It is not known what was the outcome; but you don't hear much Gaelic in Oban now.

Mr McGregor's horse was a very intelligent animal, a white beast with large hairy hooves; if there were such things it would have passed for a smallish white Clydesdale. It did not like hanging about and if there was too much chatting up of the housewives it would walk away with McGregor running after it and attempting to catch the milk coming from the brass tap. At that time all the milk carts had two large churns at the back fitted with brass taps, and usually a much smaller container with cream. The various milkmen all had their own customers. The railway carriers all had horse-drawn lorries, and after twelve noon the horse would not work until it had been home for its lunch.

The house we lived in was almost at the top of one rise in the road, and there was another very steep road going up to the right from the rise. The railway lorry had a load of special turfs for a garden at the head of the steep part. It was too late, the horse would not move further up the hill. To my amusement the carrier was seen carrying the turfs, about twenty at a time, while the horse stayed at the foot of the rise laughing at him.

Craigroyston, the house we were in to begin with, was semi-detached. On the ground floor there was a dining-room, a very large kitchen, that doubled as a family dining-room, a large scullery that would now be called a washhouse, a coal-cellar that would take at least five tons (I've seen more than five tons in it) and a toilet. In the scullery there were two tubs, a sink, and a boiler heated by a fire with its own chimney. The kitchen had a large open range, with an oven and hotplates, and all sorts of places one could open and put the flue brush in. It was indeed a wonderful apparatus. Beside it we eventually had a gas stove, and gas was the only form of energy we had inside the house, except for fires. There were fireplaces and gas lighting points in every room. The gas was distributed by means of old leaky lead pipes that stank horribly, and I developed a hatred of gas which has stuck with me to this day. Natural gas is not quite so bad but it is often heavier than air and can collect under floors and lie there like an unexploded bomb; if possible I will stick to electricity.

The ground floor of the house also contained a bedroom, and a large walk-in larder, as well as two cupboards. On the next floor were a parlour, two large bedrooms and a slightly smaller bedroom. The top floor (attic) contained two reasonable bedrooms, and a smaller alleged bedroom which might have been good for a hermit's cell, but for little else; there was also a small boxroom and a sink on the landing. Every place was fully furnished.

We went from there to Laurel Lodge which was just a but and ben. There was a small kitchen, about 10′ square, with a small range in the corner; off it there was a bedroom about ten feet by seven The entrance vestibule was approximately four feet by six feet; off it opened a bedroom which was approximately four feet by six feet; off it opened a bedroom which was six feet by, I think, six feet six inches. The living-room, about ten feet square opened off the vestibule. There was a coal cellar about four feet by three feet outside and a toilet the same size, and that was all. There was neither electricity nor gas.

Obviously we had to get rid of a great deal of the furniture, the wonder is that we managed to retain so much. I drew a plan and marked where the things we could keep were to go, agreed it with my mother and she got rid of all the extra things. Then her sister decided to keep much of her furniture and we were in trouble. We got round it. We put tents up and used these until she saw sense. She kept a huge trunk. There was no room for it anywhere so she put it in the vestibule, and we had to climb over it to get to the tiny bedroom, and squeeze past it to get to the other rooms.

Donald particularly did not like this, he was constantly 'girning' about it. Then he came home with a small bottle of nitric acid, which he carefully poured over the brass hinges and lock. When Jean next went to the trunk all the fittings were green, and she got rid of it.

At this point I will add a few stories about Donald. When we lived at Laurel Lodge we would simply hop over the fence and go for a walk. This was good for clearing the head and letting one think, and I used to do this quite often; indeed, any time there was anything bothering me. We could go for miles without crossing a road. It was very good therapy. There was a crofter next to us, Cameron by name, who kept a number of very scabby cows. One day we noticed a very very thin cow, the hip bones were very prominent. We saw it again when we went for our evening stroll next evening. This time the bone had come through the skin and there were flies all over it. Next day there was a patch on it almost like a rubber seal from a tyre. The cow was still grazing away. The next time we saw it the patch had fallen off and the flies were back, and that was the last time we saw the cow.

One time we were upstream from his house, when he came upon us shouting and bawling, called us sheep stealers, and much more besides. Eventually he calmed down and asked us who we were. When we told him, he said, 'You were the boys who used to come up here with kilts on stealing things and causing damage.' By this time we were both furious but I didn't say very much; I had worked out that it was probably Corson and Martin who were the 'criminal' kilt wearers. They were a few years older than us. He then told us he owned everything that could be seen from where we were standing. In clear view was the top of Cruachan and the moon beind it, and of course most of the Glencruitten estate. All the way home Donald was repeating, 'He's not going to speak to me like that, I'm not taking this.'

He came home from school next day carrying a supply of calcium carbide. We took an empty 2 lb treacle tin and an empty mustard tin. He put carbide in the small tin with a lid on it, and put a half inch of water in the treacle tin, and hammered the lid on, and carried it over to see our friend at Pollivinister. The croft house was built on the edge of the road, there were no lights showing: it was dark, it must have been between the moons. We carried it very carefully, being careful not to spill it, reached the place, gave it a very good shake and placed it upside down on the step. We started to walk back the way we had come. We were almost at Colin McKenzie's place when we heard the most terrific explosion; it sounded as if the whole house had gone up. They would find the lid on the doorstep, but many times I wondered where the tin had ended up.

The next day we went out on reconnaisance (it must have been Saturday). There was nothing to be seen at the house so we went further along the road. It was only a cart track with a steep bank on one side, flat ground covered with whins, on the other. We met Mr Cameron. As soon as he saw us he dived as far as he could go up the bank to the fence, saying, 'Good morning, Gentlemen.' We had no more trouble from that source.

My aunt was working as a housekeeper to the parish minister. She went away every morning and came back at night. She came home one night with a large jar of bramble jelly. It was beautiful stuff, she gave my mother a piece of it, and I think we got a lick of it, I'm not very sure, then she carefully put it in her bedrom, hidden. I did not see it again. This did not please Donald at all and two or three days later he obtained a bottle of cascara sagrada, carefully mixed it into the jelly, and came into the other room where I was working at something. The toilet was outside, and one had to pass the window of the room we were in to get to it.

About a quarter of an hour later my aunt ran past to the toilet, and repeated the action several times in the next hour. Altogether it was a rather nasty incident for which I received the blame.

Now here is another police story from my grandfather. He was called out to investigate a complaint from most of the residents, about a putrid smell emanating from one of the houses. Of course it was on the top floor of a tenement. The householder invited him in and he found a very large pig, a huge boar, in residence. He asked, 'How long has that thing been here?' 'Oh, sure, your honour, it was born here; it's been here always.'

Our friend Cameron, the crofter, did not have an easy life. There were many dogs in the housing schemes around Oban that were not kept under control, and some of them were worrying his sheep. Often we took an evening stroll past his cottage. We passed one afternoon and noted a dead sheep lying on the roadside near his place; it may be he was not well enough to bury it. The next time we passed it could be smelled from at least twenty yards away, and the smell was not sweet. We passed again the following night, the smell was even more disgusting, and there was a large animal feasting on it. It ran off as we approached into the bushes. The stink was so bad that we had to run past it. The following night there was no sign of anything, so Donald said, 'It's even eaten the smell.'

Bunty Whyte and 'Skipper' Lay did a bit of poaching, and sometimes took rabbits from the croft. Crofters were usually delighted to get rid of the rabbits. Bunty used an old muzzle-loading shotgun, which had been his father's. His distance vision was poor; but he refused to wear spectacles except when working at paintings in his studio. They were hunting above the cottage when a rabbit got up. Bunty took a shot at it and shot in Mr Cameron's skylight. They went to the door and paid for it. During the war Bunty was killed in an air raid in Southampton. I don't know what happened to Skipper Lay.

Donald was left-handed, and for a long time he was a bit awkward with it, but in his mid-teens he became very good as a bowler (cricket); he had very good control of the ball. One day, during the summer holidays, we were walking to Ganavan Sands. We had just passed Jack's shop when we passed one of the Catholic boys. He made some sneering remark but we just carried on. Then there was a great crash. Donald came running down and went in between us, with his 'hang-dog' look on his face. I said to him, 'What was that?'

He said, 'A window got broken.'

I said, 'Did you throw the stone?'

He said, 'Yes.'

'Why?' I said.

'I'm not letting them make faces at me.'

That spoilt our day; I knew my mother could not pay the cost of the window. We went home and were there about twenty minutes when there was a knock on the door. I opened the door and there was Taylor the policeman, the redfaced one who was known as 'sunset'. He had a notebook and a pencil with an army cartridge case on the stub, an army memento I would think. He then licked the end of the pencil and started his cross-examination. It was: How did this happen, and how did that happen, and the boy says that you threw the stone. I could have told him that if I had thrown the stone I would have hit the boy, not the window.

I was asked if I had intended to kill the boy. Clearly he did not believe that I had not thrown the stone. He said that the insurance would pay for it but that he had to make a report, so the matter cleared up very well.

In my teens my brother and I started to walk around Oban. We tried every road, usually going out one way and back by a different route, until there were no more roads left to try. We then slowly increased the distances and the length of time we stayed out. A favourite route was out by Glen Lonan and returning by Glen Feochan, climbing Ben Glass *en route*. Sometimes we were eighteen hours away. This training stood me in very good stead in 1941 in Greece, several of my companions being much surprised at how well I had stood the pace in our starved and weakened condition.

When my cousin, Adam Collie, lost his family, he came to us for a fortnight's holiday. We took him on the Glen Lonan-Glen Feochan circuit, after carefully pointing out the difficulties; but he was keen to come with us, saying, 'I do a lot of walking, I'll be all right.' I was two years younger than him and I think his idea was, 'anything you can do I can do better'. He began to complain when we were climbing Ben Glass, kept wanting to go back; but by that time we were committed, it being as quick one way home as the other. We had just climbed a very steep slope about 300 yards long, and had reached a point where it had changed to a much gentler rise, when I dropped the small haversack containing our small stove. It rolled right down to the foot of the slope. There was nothing else for it, I had to go after it. As I started down Adam took off up the way, and he had a long start on us by the time I reached the top again. There was about half a mile of almost level moor and a short climb to the top. On another occasion we had climbed the hill and had just started down, when we were suddenly engulfed in a thick mist. We could see perhaps five or six yards. Normally we ran most of the way down.

CHAPTER THREE

Early Working Life

ON THE OCCASION MENTIONED in the last chapter we were sprinting down through the mist when I had a sensation that was almost like a command to stop. Having stopped as quickly as I could, I then moved forward two or three paces, and found myself at the top of the highest cliff on the mountain. It is not a very high cliff, but it is high enough to kill.

Donald and I with a few friends spent many good days on the hills, at different times, and usually on Ben Glass. It was at a convenient distance and not too high. In the two or three years immediately preceeding the war we frequently walked the Loch Nell circuit, going out by Kilmore and returning by Glencruitten. From the top of the hill above the loch we would run down to the Glen Lonan road junction. We did this one night as darkness was falling. It was nearly midnight and as we reached the road junction for the glen, running quite quickly, a young girl, barefoot, burst out from under the bridge and sprinted away along the road to Glen Lonan. We never found out who she was or what she was doing there. We were greatly surprised, and I would think that the girl was terrified.

When I was employed as an apprentice to Falconer in Oban we went one day to see MacDonald of Barguillean about various matters. We went by the main road to Taynuilt, and then by the side road to Barguillean. As we were nearing Barguillean House, I saw a dog run across the road from the hill down towards Taynuilt. It was a winter's day with about an inch of snow on the ground. Shortly afterwards we met two men with guns accompanied by Siki MacDonald. Siki had been at school with me and would at that time be sixteen or seventeen years old. One of the men stopped the car and asked if we had seen a dog. The boss had seen nothing; but I told what I had seen. The man shouted out, 'Siki, run down that road and look for the tracks of a large black and tan dog.' Siki complied, they made after him, and that was the last we saw of them at that time. We went on, took levels for a new fishing loch, checked the byre, had coffee from Barguillean, and set off home. As we neared Taynuilt we caught up with the gamekeepers and Siki. The boss stopped the car and said, 'Well, did you get that dog?' At first the man looked a bit blank, then he said, 'Oh yes, we got THAT dog, but it was the wrong one.'

On one of my earliest recollections of Halloween, I would have been about three and a half, we went into the front room at Craigroyston. Most of the blinds were down, they were wooden-slatted venetian blinds, and my brothers and my father were looking out of the window. I being the smallest around at that time, moved to the front, pulled myself up on my tip toes, and looked out to see what was going on. There were a number of boys about a hundred yards away. One had a long skirt down to the ground. He was a lame boy, and I knew him from the way he walked. My elders were discussing what they were doing and so on. I thought they might be burglars so with my big mouth I said, 'Maybe they're buggers.' Then I learned in about two seconds flat the difference between the two words. My father was at home at the time, so there might be some chance of dating it from that if it mattered.

Now for more little stories about animals. While I was in Dunoon I stayed for some time in a house that was sited near a burn. The landlady was an old lady who had three sons and several grandchildren. Her family were frequent visitors. She kept chickens at the waterside and sometimes waterhens would feed with them. There was a large tomcat which claimed hunting rights on the area, and it was a thorn in the old lady's side. After losing some chickens she managed to catch the cat. One day while we were having dinner she came into the room with the cat in one hand and a sack in the other. It was a very dejected looking cat. She had me hold the sack open while she inserted the cat, tied up the sack and threw it in to a corner. She was talking to the cat all the time, things like, 'Be quiet. Just you wait, George will sort you out when he comes home.' At last Geordie arrived, took the sack outside, and dug a hole in view of the window. The old boy had his back to the window and he kept turning round to have a better look (this was an old gentleman who also had a room in the house). George opened the sack, the cat rolled out, and fell into the hole, and George came in, washed his hands and sat down. After some time the old lad could contain himself no longer and he bagan to ask questions. He said, 'You buried the cat, killed the cat?'

'Yes, that's him away, dead and buried.'

'How did you kill the cat?'

'Oh, I just chapped him on the heid with a hammer.'

Some time after that incident the landlady was presented with a monkey, a fair-sized animal perhaps 2'6" tall. She had a special cage made for it and indeed spent quite a large sum on it. It became a great friend of hers until it disgraced itself one day and bit her finger. She had the answer; in about an hour she had the vet down with his syringe. The monkey was then sent to be with the cat. Altogether, it was a very expensive business for her.

To revert to the story about Siki and the dog, I was told when I came home from Austria that Siki had been lost in Malaya. This may or may not be true, information about servicemen was changing from day to day, and lads were being confused with brothers, cousins, and even mates. There was a boxer named Battling Siki, and that is where the nickname came from. Another scholar from the same area achieved fame in the school for an essay he handed in for his homework. It was excellent, concise, and to the point – this was it: 'Three men were wrecked on a desert island, and a passing trawler picked them up.'

My boss had an elderly relative who was being taken to live with the family. Her house was being run by a housekeeper, and prior to getting rid of it he went to check it. He noticed a few beetles running about – 'clockers', he called them – so he purchased a large supply of Keating's powder, poured it round the skirtings, cupboards and everywhere he could think of, then went home for lunch. He came back an hour later, and found, 'hundreds of beetles lying on their backs, waving their legs in the air. So I just swept them all up, and put them on the fire.'

When I finished active service I worked for two years in Oban for Bob Campbell. He was a thorough gentleman, 55 years older than me. He had a fund of stories of Oban up to 70 years previously. He told me that he had seen the plans of McCaig's Tower. There was to have been another portion in the centre – a circular tower maybe a third diameter of the main tower, but much higher – and the main tower was then to be roofed in to the central one. The thinner tower would have been topped by an observatory, and the mass shape would have been rather like Lutyens' Liverpool Cathedral.

He and his pals were enthusiastic cyclists, in the days when cycles were scarce. They would leave Oban on an expedition in the morning and return in the evening, sometimes after dark. One of them was a baker known as Jahussi because he was afflicted with a stammer, and that was supposed to be how he spoke. He was the only one who could afford a lamp and a bell, so he was elected to lead the way. There would be seven or eight of them behind him. They were entering Oban one night down the Bealach an Righ. As they reached the bend at the top the followers heard Jahussi shouting, 'ck, ck, ck,' and before he got any further six of them were under the cart.

At one of the town elections last century, one of the candidates was a man who was very fond of himself (aren't they all), and he thought he had a very good chance of winning. He canvassed each elector giving his vision of the future. He got about fifteen votes, and the winner had about two hundred and fifty. When the result was declared the winner thanked everyone who had voted for him and said that he would do his best for all. The next one also thanked his supporters and hoped to do better next time, and it went on until they reached the man with fifteen votes. He also thanked his small number of supporters and then said, 'I have found out something today: there are 269 damn liars in Oban.'

One night Campbell said to me, 'We're going up the Ballachulish line tomorrow, will you take a piece with you; we might not get lunch.' So I said 'fair enough' and put the food in a haversack. We left by the 9 o'clock train. It was a beautiful summer day. We got off at Duror, and stood outside the station for some time. At last Mr Campbell said, 'They were supposed to be here with a car. We'll walk towards them, it's down this way.' We strolled slowly back towards Oban while he gave me a lesson on botany, telling me odd things about different flowers; it was a very interesting lesson. We sat for some time at a bridge about a mile from the station, and then started to walk back. When we reached the station he looked slightly shocked, then he said, 'Damn it, we should have got out at Kentallen.' We lost that client; but he was too old to work and too poor to retire.

There is an island called Lismore (it means big garden). It has very fertile land and a very tight community, similar to Keiss; the only people who are really accepted are those whose grandparents are in the local cemetery. It is a few miles north-east of Oban. The postmaster there was also a local shopkeeper, and the piermaster. Having offended someone he was informed, by one in the know, that he was to be sacked and that an official was already on his way to do the job. He asked the piermaster in Oban to let him know as soon as the boat left. He was standing ready on his pier as the vessel approached. As it slowed down he threw the sacks of mail on to the deck, shouted, 'There's your bloody post,' and waved the boat on. It was not allowed to stop that day. The PO official had to go as far as Fort William before he could leave the vessel, hire from there to the ferry at the north end of the island, and hire again to the post office. By that time, the Lismore man's resignation was in Glasgow.

As I mentioned previously, my hill training helped me later in Greece. An English lad spoke to me at the end of the war in St Johann, and congratulated me on the show I had put on above Thermopylae four years before. I have no idea who the lad was. I was unaware at the time of the number of people who were watching me, while I was watching two Black Watch lads about a hundred yards ahead, and thinking they were doing very well.

At this point I would like to say a little bit more about my father. He spent his early working life on commercial ships but as soon as he got his ticket he went on to yachts, many different ones. He was skipper of the *Christine* when he got married. It belonged to the Earl of Home. They were given a clock by the earl, and there was an etching of the earl in the house for many years. The earl took it from the wall and gave it to my father when he got rid of the *Christine*. The next one would be the *Iolaire*, a large vessel, a ton short of 1,000 tons; this was carefully calculated to escape a heavy tax. It belonged to Sir Donald Currie, and was fitted with two 3″ guns and became flagship of the Stornoway patrol during the First World War. My father was skipper, Lt Commander, under a naval commander in charge of the group. He was invalided out of the naval reserve in 1917. I don't know what was wrong but he did spend some time in a hospital at Gosport.

He then bought a boat of his own called the *Isabella and Jean*; what he was doing with it and how he disposed of it I don't know. He oversaw the refitting of the *Iolaire* after the war and later he was employed by a man called Captain Liddel who had been a tea planter. His yacht was called the *Osprey*, and my father served on it the rest of his working life. Capt. Liddell purchased a larger yacht called the *Narcissus* and appointed my father captain, but he died before taking up the job. At one time my father captained another yacht called the *Zingara*; who owned it I don't know. The name came into prominence some years ago when one of the royal children was called Zara, a shortened form of the name.

Most of the time I remember my father he was on the *Osprey*, cruising here and there, in Norway, the Baltic and the Mediterranean. As children we received postcards from all over the place. There are a number of them upstairs in an old ammunition box. Among these postcards is one to me from Nauplion in Greece. This was the port for Argos and Tiryns. Later, when I was in Greece, I had there one of the closest escapes in my life, and had a comrade killed beside me.

Information given previously about Bunty Whyte's death came from his older brother Tearlach with whom we were very friendly.

Here is another little story that came from Bob Campbell. There was a well known drunken rascal in Oban, and the bane of his life was a certain police sergeant. The sergeant had nicked him, and he had been sentenced to a spell in Barlinnie jail. The sergeant was taking him to Glasgow to serve his sentence, and being a good natured soul he had taken the prisoner out at Callander for a cup of tea. The prisoner ran away and the sergeant ran after him, took a heart attack and died immediately. Some three months after this, Bob Campbell was strolling down the street in Oban when he saw the rascal come out of a pub, and walk away very much the worse for drink, repeating to himself: 'There he is, he's away the sergeant, and I'm still here, and I'll live for some time yet, good for another couple of years, no I'll live longer than that. I'll live for ten years, no twenty years, no damn it, I'll never die.' According to Bob Campbell he did last a very long time. Bob Campbell trained with the Macraes, who were civil engineers in Oban. It may be that the Wick firm was connected to them.

At one time our relatives in Avernish were troubled by thieving from their peat stacks. Black Jess the weaver was blamed but they really did not know who it was. They would bore a hole in a peat, fill it with black powder, plug it, and leave it on the stack where it was likely to be taken. It would not do very much damage, simply blow the fire all over the room; but at that time many of the fires were built in the middle of the house, with a hole in the thatch directly above, so there was little danger. There was no record of anyone being caught; indeed they had maybe lifted the wrong peat themselves. When I was there as a child we were taken to see Black Jess at her weaving. She really was a repulsive creature; but she could not have been kinder to us, taking very great care to show us all parts of the process. She had the natural inbred courtesy and dignity of the Highlander. The loom was only about 4' wide. Blankets made on it were in two parts, stitched down the middle. We had blankets of that kind in the home for very many years.

Forty years or more later on my first revisit, the only place still in use was the Breaker's corrugated iron house. Everyone in Avernish had some kind of nickname. There was one called De Wit after a notorious Boer guerilla. The Breaker had been employed in the Wild West, taming horses. There was even one called the Bogie, and a real gentleman he was. At the time of my visit Jess's house was ruined, it was just a heap of stones. I dug down into the stones and found only the iron rod with the hook at the end which had been used to hold the moving part of the loom; that was all that remained. Outside the Breaker's byre there was still a large mound where the dung heap used to be with chickens running all over it. There were no chicks left; the only living things were wild birds. The little white rose flourished at the ruin of my relatives' home, the fuschia bushes were in bloom, and there was fruit on some of the apple trees.

On one of our early visits to Avernish we took a goat along to provide milk. It was quite an animal, largish with big horns, I would have been about nine at the time and it seemed quite big to me. We became very friendly, I would grab its horns and have a wrestling match every day, trying to push it down on its behind. One day I had been reading a book which mentioned cowbells in the Alps, and I thought that was an excellent idea. Making a bell was no problem; I obtained a small tin, knocked some holes in it, half-filled it with small stones, and secured some string to it. Then I approached the goat, it heard the rattle and was obviously a bit frightened but I managed to catch it by the horns and tie the bell round its neck.

Whenever it moved there was a rattle. The beast was terrified, I could see its legs move out like the corners of a pyramid and stiffen, its eyes grew bigger and bigger, then it made a standing jump about three feet in the air and ran. It went at such a speed that it broke the rope. After that we could not find the animal, it ran off towards the headland. Three days later Archie and Reggie were taking the boat to Balmacara when they found the goat, it was standing below the souterrain; what was left of the rope had got jammed round some rocks so that it couldn't move. They managed to get it into the boat knocking a hole in the planking as they did so, moving round Rhuscaravaig (the headland) and bringing it to Rhuscaravaig (the house). They had rescued it in time and obtained three times the usual daily amount of milk from it. After the war I was telling this story to some children, it must have been Archie's children, my mother was there at the time and she butted in saying, 'So that's what happened to the goat, I haven't heard that before.'

As a girl my mother sometimes visited her aunts and uncles in Avernish; she was introduced to the local people as 'Nighean Domhnal Mor Domnhal bhan,' that is, 'Fair Donald's Big Donald's girl'.

There was an interesting half-hour programme on TV today about Clan Gunn, which reminded me of a visit we had at New Year from a lad called Gunn, one of Iain's school friends. He got his eye on the model of the yacht *Britannia* and enquired about it. It was a present to Reggie on the day he was born from Lord Welby, since then I have passed it on to William. Reggie was named Reginald Welby MacLean, and being the eldest of the family was inclined to be a bit bossy, sometimes when he became over-powering, we would call him Reginald Lord Welby, this he did not like.

There was a shop in Auchtertyre in those days. I was walking from there to the house in Avernish, along the foot of the hill towards the steps. As I approached the cliff I could hear a very loud noise which sounded like regular shots. By the time I reached the foot of the cliff I could see two wild billy goats. Each was standing on his own little ledge. They would rise to the vertical in perfect unison and slam down on each other, hitting exactly in the centre of the forehead. The bangs went on for a long time and could be heard for miles, until at last either they were tired or their heads hurt too badly. That is the only time in my life I have seen such a performance.

It is now time to say something about our remote ancestors. So many of the lines go back to Bruce because he was so well known, that it is reasonable to start with him. His father was another Robert, a crusader, who died in 1304. Next was again a Robert who was married (1) to Isobel de Claire and (2) to Christiania, daughter of Sir William de Treby. Yet another Robert came next, 1230 is given as the date; he was married to another Isabel,

daughter of the Earl of Huntingdon, younger brother of King Malcolm IV
and William the Lionheart: this was the marriage that established Bruce's
claim to the throne of Scotland. Next was William, date 1200, whose father
yet again was Robert; his wife is not mentioned. Next was Robert (they
had a very limited list of names), who married Agnes, daughter of Fylk di
Pagenell. Now another name, next was Adam who arrived in England in
1051 (before the conquest) and who received his Scottish lands about that
time. The father of that Adam was Brusée, who married Emma, daughter
of Alan, Lord of Brittany, and who built the castle of Brus on the Cherbourg
Peninsula. It is now called Brix. This man had been called Ulf and he
changed his name to Robert Brusée when he became a Christian and was
the first Robert in the line. He was the son of Rognvald or Reginald, from
whom are descended the Norman kings of England, 1034. His father was
a Brussée who went to the court of Olaf in Norway, 1022. He was the son
of Sigurd the Second, who married Thora, only daughter of Hakon. He
married (2nd) Alice, daughter of Brian Biorn, King of Ireland. Sigurd's father
was Ludovic who married Somerled, Prince of the Isle of Man who was
also an ancestor of ours. Next was Thorfinn Hussackliffer whose father was
Eynor, the one-eyed Eynor, who was caricatured in a Hollywood film.
Next was another Rognvald, who owned the lands of North and South
Morei, and later the Orkneys and Shetlands as well. His father was Thebotaw
AD 720, and that is as far back as we can go. It is far enough.

Now what of the progenitors of the MacLeans? The father of Gillian na
Tuath was Rath who was married to Margaret, a sister of Somerled, her
father was Gillibride of Lorne and Morven. Before that there is a long list
of names, spelled differently from normal Gaelic spelling, until we come to
Old Dougal of Scone, who drowned in the river Spey. Then there are
more names listed until we arrive at Fergus, AD 764, and later in the list
Neil of the Nine Hostages, AD 375, King of Ireland. He was the progenitor
of the Neills, the MacNeils, the O'Neills, and so on. We could also trace
back to Conn of the Hundred Battles, progenitor of the MacDonalds, AD
125, and to Angus of the Tower of Tara, BC 263. There are many lists of
kings' names, and one list I have been using is contained in an old book
which I purchased for fifteen pence in Wick. It is called *O'Gorman's
Chronological Record* and was published 1860. It is based on the Jewish
Calendar. Many of the clan histories also contain lists, and among other
books with information are *The Early Chronicles relating to Scotland, MacDonald's History of Argyll, Scotland, the Early Kingdom*, and many others. The
lists agree fairly well as to the people named, the order in which the names
appear and dates frequently differ.

As a change from the endless genealogies it would be a good idea to have a contribution from the younger generation. On Christmas Day, Carol Jane, aged five, was entertaining her grannie and grandfather at home in Dundee, and for some reason she was not showing much interest in the Christmas fare, much of which she apparently did not like, not even the turkey. Eventually her dad said, 'I think you must be a vegetarian, Carol.' Carol replied immediately, she knew a thing or two, 'No, I'm not, I'm Scottish.'

Next day the twins, her country cousins aged 6½, were watching a film about Siberian tigers which Ailie did not like but Kirstina insisted on watching it. So Ailie Jane came down to see her grandad and uncle Iain. We had a very good time with her, then she said to Iain, 'Have there ever been tigers in Keiss?' Iain said, 'Oh no, I don't think so, perhaps a very long time ago, a very long time ago indeed,' and Ailie said, 'Would that be when Grandad was a wee boy?'

Ailie Jane's contribution was given with her approval. I'm afraid Carol's is a breach of copyright.

Now for a little bit more about the 'Monks'. There are I think still some seven or eight entries of the name in the Highland Telephone Directory, most in the Benbecula area, and there are a few McVarishes in the Mallaig, Fort William area. There were McVarishes on Boreray in 1692 when Martin Martin visited the island, it is recorded in the book. McVarish may reasonably be translated to Monk. I don't know when the Columban Monks first came to Boreray, but they were there centuries before the MacLeans; probably seven centuries before.

When we were young, we on different occasions received gifts of chickens, rabbits and the like, from different people. Often there were parcels from Uist containing rabbits, chickens and cockerels and I remember one particular occasion when eight rabbits came at the one time. Why there were so many at that particular time I cannot say, but I would think my Dad must have been at his old home with his gun. These rabbits were particularly well salted and peppered; very hot to the taste, but very good. One of my mother's specialities was rabbit soup which she browned with sugar. She had a large old soupspoon kept for the purpose, which she would fill with white sugar grains and hold over the fire. One had to be very careful, it could flame up very easily. It was held over the fire, lifted back, held over the fire again until it melted and turned an almost black colour. When this was added to the soup it turned a brown colour.

She also liked making meat pasties, hare paste, chicken paste, meat loaf, and many other things. She made very good use of everything she received.

My mother had a friend in Nostie, Annie MacKay by name; she was the Postmistress. She sent my mother a cockerel every Christmas for very many years. Sometimes a Mr Matheson, from Blackmount, sent us a haunch of venison. His boys were at school with us, and lodged near us in Oban. The father was gamekeeper at Blackmount.

One of Reggie's friends, George McGregor, was employed by the LMS railway in Oban. He lived for hunting, shooting and fishing. His mother had died and he was pretty well homeless. One time he was without accommodation and he stayed with us as a paying guest for about three months. While he was there I was mending a broken sash cord and he saw me working with a hammer which had a broken handle. He said, 'Is that the best hammer you have?' I said, 'Yes, it's the only hammer I have,' and he said, 'All right I'll get you a hammer.' Next day he came home with a beautiful hammer which I still have; it's now bashed a little, there are a few chips about the head, but it's still the best hammer I have. He left after three months. Some time later he came to see Reggie, and I was again working with the hammer. He said to Reggie, 'That one's doing fine, is it?'

'Yes, was there any trouble about it?'

'No,' said George, 'he came looking around the place quite a bit, and just before he went away he came in and said, "I lost a hammer here, any of you seen it?" Of course they all said they hadn't.' It turned out that these were the tradesmen who carried out a major reconstruction in the station. George had nicked a hammer and I had unwittingly received it.

I remember two stories that came from George. They used to have a great deal of fun in the parcel office. All sorts of things came through as parcels. They had a clerk who had some knowledge of chickens. One day they had hampers of live pullets awaiting delivery. The knowledgeable clerk drew a white line on the floor, took ten pullets one at a time and held the beaks on the line for a short time and then released them. The birds stayed transfixed, beaks touching the line, eyes open, and wings partly open. He then took other birds, placed the heads under their wings, swung them gently to and fro, and then was able to leave them, sleeping, at the edge of the counter. George asserted that a customer came in and there were ten birds transfixed on the floor and six sleeping on the counter, I have my doubts. There was an authenticated story about a collie that came with an address label tied to its collar. It was a sheepdog, probably quite valuable. They were playing with it when it took fright and ran. Then there was the spectacle of several clerks jumping the counter, and running through the station. One of them was shouting, 'Hi, catch that dog, it's a parcel!'

Well they never caught the dog. It was sighted two days later running about in Glen Sheilach, and that was the last the London, Midland, Scottish Railway Company saw of it.

Now I intend to go on to stories of my war service, starting with how I managed to get into the army and then carrying on, taking from my diary names of the places I visited and recording any stories I remember of each place. If in the mean time I remember any other stories of family interest I will record these as they are recalled.

My first attempt to join the army took place shortly after the war had started, in late September or early October 1939. I wrote to an address in Stirling in an attempt to obtain a commission. I was invited to call for interview and as I was entering the building I met two people coming out. One of them was saying, 'All I did was yabber on about the old school tie,' and he was given the commission he had requested. After waiting for some time I came before a certain Major Findlay. After checking my education record, I had the 'highers' as requested, and all else that was necessary, he said, 'Um, ah, did you have a public school education?' I'm afraid that got my back up, and I said, 'Yes,' and he then asked, 'Where?' and I said, 'Oban High School,' and it did me no good at all; I left without a commission.

The next attempt was a letter to the Royal Engineers asking if they had any places vacant; I have the letter covering that. Next was an attempt to join a Royal Engineers Company being raised in Argyll. It came to nothing as the Company was not formed for lack of sufficient numbers, I still have the reply. The fourth attempt was to The Border Counties Company which accepted me, and I became a soldier on the first of March 1940. The interview and medical took place again in Stirling and at it I met a lad called Jackson who later was one of my friends. My medical was just before Jackson's, and I was still in the waiting room when he came out. He said that the doctor had told him that we were 'cast in the same mould'. All our measurements were exactly the same: height, weight, width and all the rest of it. We left him behind in Egypt when we sailed for Greece, and he was killed about a year later. His father had been an Australian soldier, and his mother a nurse, in the previous war. His name is on the Kippen war memorial.

After the medical there was a swearing-in ceremony and we were then sent home to await embodiment. Next I visited the labour exchange in Oban and registered for anything the army cared to do to me.

There are picture postcards in my possession from as far back as 1905, the earlier ones having been sent to my father. It appears that he was friendly with a man in Norway – there are several postcards from him – and there is also one from Monaco, 1906 or 1907. I had thought that the signature was 'Ann' but it could be AMC. He was on the *Christine* at that time, a few years before the war. Most of the cards are addressed to the *Christine* at Rhu, Dumbarton. There are cards from Uist and other places, there is also one from the Chateau de Thorenc, and it is clear that the castle belonged to Lord Welby.

The first two or three days in the army made a great impression on me. On the way south we picked up Jackson and Ross at Stirling, then the majority of the company joined the train at Carstairs. Perhaps there were more at Oban but I do not remember any. The journey south was uneventful. We stopped at Preston and were invited into a free canteen provided by the generous citizens of the town. I thought of Prince Charlie's army going through in 1745. We also had a short stop at Wolverhampton and were very surprised at hordes of unkempt and undisciplined children swarming over the line; I had never seen anything like it, nor did I see its like again until some nine months later when I visited the back streets of Cairo.

There was a lad called Adam Currie in the company. He had been raised in the Queen Victoria School, Dunblane, which was at that time a school for army orphans. He spent his time on the journey south making up filthy puns from the station names as we passed through. I may say more about him later.

We spent a few hours in London waiting for our connection, saw Buckingham Palace, and visited a Lyons Corner House. Passing in the street we received a cheery smile and a wave from Anthony Eden. There were other parliamentarians with him but none of them took the trouble to look at us.

We entrained for Kent and eventually reached Chatham, reporting first of all to Kitchener Barracks, where we were very busy indeed for some hours. It had a very steeply sloping parade ground which we wore down a bit, and we were kitted out with boots, battledress (2 pairs), kitbag, large pack, small pack and all the rest of it. Then we were transferred to Brompton Barracks, the inside of which was in need of a great deal of repair.

We were allotted a barrack room, received our quota of blankets, then there was a scramble for bunks and mattresses. There were nine bunks, ten mattresses, and eleven men. First of all I went for the mattress, then made for the bunk and was too late. I did well enough; one lad claimed a bed and had no mattress, and he slept on the bed. Well, he lay on it all night, he could not possibly have slept. The beds were made of strap iron. They were made in two pieces and pulled out like a drawer. The part we lay on was in squares of 7' or 8' sides. The man without the mattress had a behind like tartan in the morning. He was called Dovis Russell and was killed in Greece later. I'll say more of him later. Between our room and the next was a stone wall about a foot thick with three large, semi-circular holes at the top. They were arched to save lintels and allowed circulation of air. There were different things flying through the holes intermittently all night, from one barrack to the other. Fortunately nothing hit me. Adam Currie in the next room was shouting out filthy stories all night, about old brown cows and other things. The night passed reasonably well and I got to know all my comrades.

I had been unemployed for almost a year after I left school, and I spent my time almost entirely in acquiring knowledge that might prove useful in later life. The reasons for being unemployed were many and various but there were three reasons in particular for my case: employment was indeed very scarce and Reggie had been unemployed for years. Also, I required by that time to use spectacles for distance vision. That fact effectively debarred me from a whole range of jobs. Some of these were jobs at sea, police, and armed forces at that time. Lastly, when I was in the third year, I was presented with a bursary application and told to sign it. For that I was bound to remain in school until the end of the sixth year, and was to receive five pounds per year for three years, and of course it was a condition that I had good marks in the forthcoming exam. I was thereby debarred from all jobs such as banks, legal offices or insurance: all these situations would be filled before I could leave school, trade apprenticeships at that time all starting at fourteen years old.

I worked right through the book on navigation, and acquired a fair knowledge of star-finding. At that time also I worked through many of Reggie's university books, being particularly interested in civil engineering. One of my father's books fascinated me. It was *The Ship Captain's Medical Guide*, a slim little booklet which must have been old even at that time. Later on in Austria I found the knowledge very useful. When men were on watch in the sailing ships, they would frequently go for long periods without passing water, and then sometimes found that they were no longer able to do so. The first instruction to the captain was, 'get two strong men to hold the patient down', then followed diagrams showing exactly where to make the incisions to let the water out, how to sterilize the knife in lysol, and so on.

After eleven months unemployment, through the good offices of my neighbour Alex McLaine, I was employed as apprentice by an architect and surveyor. Salary was 12 pounds for the first year, rising to 48 pounds in the fourth year. Soon I was supervizing my former classmates who were now journeymen tradesmen earning more than twenty times what I was getting. Not until I was in the army did I receive equal treatment to my mates, and I was out of the army before I could afford to ask a girl out.

In Oban there was in the early 1930s a minister called Donald Beaton. He was the acknowledged scholar of the Free Presbyterian Church. He trained the student ministers after they had completed their secular education. Usually there were one or two of them about but at one point there were three who went about together all dressed in black clothes. They were known rather irreverently by some as the three craws.

One day a number of us were playing shinty in the hollow to the north of where Tearlach Whyte's house now is. We had made goalposts with our jackets, and were playing strongly, all thoroughly absorbed in the game. There were two MacLeans (Free Presbyterians), two McInnises (Free Church), Mortons and some others (Church of Scotland), at least one Episcopalian, and Archie Gillespie who was a Catholic; a right ecumenical congregation. It was a very tough game with some very bad language, prolonged and very loud when somebody was hit on the shins. When we were busy a very thick mist came down on us, so thick that we couldn't see to the end of a very small pitch. Then a light wind got up and the mist quickly disappeared. Leaning over the fence looking down on us were the three students. I wonder what they thought of their congregation.

Shortly after that someone who had a watch shouted out the time and we decided to go home for lunch and began to pick up our jackets. My jacket was lowest and when I picked it up there was a very nice hacksaw lying underneath. I shouted to everyone but no one knew anything about it. It has served me well for over 50 years, and I don't know yet where it came from.

To the north-west of the playing patch is the hill known as Battleship Hill, and occasionally a wild shot would go off in that direction. Whoever went for it would take his shinty with him to help him find the ball. Before he returned he would hammer on a dead tree that stood there. An owl would fly out of a hole near the top, as regular as clockwork. The tree was in a poor state and probably blew down the next winter.

We had a very close acquaintance with the square at Chatham, so much so that in four days I wore through the heel and toe plates of my boots, and many others did the same. Then it was decided that we were going to Norway and we were sent home on embarkation leave. I had two days at home during which I cleared up the place as well as I could for my mother, got all the potatoes sorted out and cleared the garden. There was a revolver in the house and I asked my mother if she wanted to keep it. There was quite a supply of ammunition with it. She said, 'They'll die of old age before I'll use it,' so I took it outside, fired the ammunition into a tree, and buried the revolver. I had noticed there was no kick from it and no lift in the muzzle. I cut into the tree and found that the ammunition had barely penetrated the bark. I expect the remains of the revolver are still there.

It may have been while on that leave that I went for a walk with Thomson. There were many showers, and we sheltered from one under the bridge at Glencruitten. Two buses passed each packed with young children, each with a label round his or her neck. It is likely that they were going to Glencruitten House. Those I can still picture were about two years old.

We returned, this time to Margate, after the two days' leave and by that time it was too late to send us to Norway, that campaign was in its final stages. We spent about ten weeks in Margate, billeted in private houses, and receiving some training.

We had a bayonet instructor who had a peculiar twist in his face; he looked as if he had had a stroke, and had a permanent look of disgust. This suited him very well as he shouted out a hundred times a day, 'The motto of the bayonet is "blood and the lust to kill".' He was a very good instructor and likeable chap. We were equipped with Ross rifles (P14s), which were a bit larger, heavier, and longer than the standard Lee Enfield. The bayonets were much the same except they were not transferable between types. The handle of the Ross rifle bayonet had three scores on it to distinguish it in the dark. Our bayonet training lasted a few days and during that time we were re-equipped with Lee Enfields. These were much handier weapons, carrying eleven shots as against six in the Ross; sights were not quite so good but otherwise they were much better.

While at Margate we began to notice distant thunder, and there seemed to be a great deal of it, and one day an old chap said to me, 'The last time I heard that was in March 1918.' From then on the rumble became louder and continuous with occasionally much louder explosions; these would have been ammunition dumps or something of the kind, or perhaps demolitions.

We had a change in employment. We dug holes in from the cliff tops, well down into the chalk, and fitted posts to prevent gliders landing. We had training in action to be taken if we were caught by aircraft in the open. The nine men in every three files formed circles, threw themselves down with their heads in the centre, face down, with helmets on the backs of their heads – at least the heads received some protection. What I would call making the best of a bad job. Fortunately we never had to do this in an emergency. When the evacuation of Dunkirk was almost complete we were protecting the shore at Margate. There were two thirds of the company on guard at one time. Really we had too long a stretch to look after, and on that night – instead of four hours on, four hours off – I did eight hours on, four hours off. We stood guard at seven in the evening, orders were to fight to the last man, shoot to kill; there were troops behind us with tanks, but we would all be dead by the time we arrived. They were not joking and about 12 o'clock they arrived with the ammunition. I think that we were meant to throw stones at them. However, after the first night they had managed to get their act together, and the following night we had our bandoliers of ammunition, and the correct sequence of watches.

There were a large number of troops in Margate at that time, I now think it was about 2,200. We all ate in a very large dining-hall at Margate

Dreamland, in two sittings and I can't remember if it was 1,100 each sitting or 1,100 altogether. I was quite taken with the London Irish Rifles. They were a fine looking body of men.

There were several Scots companies in Margate at that time; in fact there were so many Scots that the man in charge of the dining-hall decided to give them a treat. We had a peculiar dish for breakfast, it was like a white, lumpy, milky pudding, very sweet and quite nice. I quite liked it but around 500 men stood up and complained. The corporal next to me stood up, a self-appointed spokesman, and the orderly officer asked what was wrong with it. 'It's just rubbish,' he said, 'what is it anyway?' At that the caterer was called over, was questioned, and said, 'It's porridge.' At that there was a howl from nearly 500 Scots at this. The man had evidently been trying to do his best, and I felt quite sorry for him. Next day we had 'real' porridge, and I think that they were sorry.

I visited a place called the Margate Grotto, an underground chamber decorated with seashells, and I have never been able to decide whether it is a Victorian folly, or genuinely prehistoric. On the Whit Sunday weekend Jackson and I walked to Canterbury to see the cathedral. I bought a book about the cathedral which I sent home. Next the pair of us enrolled in the Thanet School of Architecture. Unfortunately, two or three days later we were moved and received no instruction on architecture.

While at Canterbury we spent a night in a hotel in luxury I had not experienced since I was on the *Iolaire*. We started to walk back and two ladies, very pleasant people they were, picked us up and took us to Margate. They invited us to visit their home but we were never able to take them up on their offer. The general opinion in the company was that the Margate people had no time for the Scots, all I can say is that they treated me very well.

Now here is another snippet of family history. When my wife's grand-father, Matthew Yates, was presented to his new grandson he greeted him something like this: 'Well, son, welcome to the world, and I wonder what big, fat, lazy woman you will spend your life working for.' The baby was Matt Yates. The last I heard of him he was resident in Don Mills, Ontario. There's a photograph of his wife and twins somewhere in one of the albums. She was neither big nor fat; whether she was lazy or not I don't know, but with twins to look after I don't see how she could be.

We left Margate and the company was then divided among four aero-dromes in Suffolk. My section went to Martlesham Heath near Woodbridge. While there we managed to see Ipswich, Kings Lynn, Colchester and a few other places. I don't know how we managed it; we seemed to be on duty most of the time. On the way there we stopped at a station while another train was passing. Our train had barely stopped when the doors were pulled open and dozens of women, young and old, descended on us and thrust sandwiches into our hands with home-made cakes, and all sorts of home-made goodies. I had a sandwich in each hand and one under my arm when I heard a shout further along the platform: 'IT'S NOT THEM.' A very shamefaced lady came and said, 'Please may we have them back?' They were meant for the boys coming home from Dunkirk. How they could possibly confuse a bunch of well-polished recruits with the lads coming back from Dunkirk is hard to imagine. Most of the goods were returned but some of the men had eaten everything they could lay their hands on.

When we arrived at Martlesham we were billeted in the married quarters, they were empty of course, and this was a front line aerodrome. Hurricanes were taking off and landing all the time. We were on aerodrome guard and were on duty; about a quarter of us during the day, and everyone at dusk, middle of the night, and dawn, for an hour each time. It was quite a schedule. During the night, nightingales sang constantly. The farming folk were still in the area. The whole place was served by wells, there did not seem to be a public piped supply, although the aerodrome had a good supply. We were very impressed by the hurricanes and their pilots.

There was a tremendous explosion one night caused by the shooting down of a German Bomber at Felixstowe. The pilot was mortally wounded but he lasted for several hours, and spent his time haranguing everyone within earshot about the beating Hitler would give them.

We went from Martlesham to Gibraltar Barracks, Aldershot, and spent a fortnight there being fully equipped for overseas. There were rumours of going to France. If we were intended for there, France fell before we could be sent. We were equipped with, additionally, tropical kit. There were two pairs of everything: baggy trousers, longs, and baggy shorts, normal shorts, and all the usual paraphernalia. I was impressed with the gas masks, quite good but not proof against the latest gas Hitler had tested in Poland. In addition the gas mask specs I had been tested for in Margate were given to me late in 1945. By the time we sailed, the civilian masks were better than ours being proof against 'arthur' gas. Actually my first pair of gas mask specs were made for me in Switzerland on orders from the German army, in 1943.

We spent that time in Aldershot marching about, digging holes in Lavens Plain, filling them back up, and listening to singsongs. They practised regular army drill at Aldershot; small wonder the Yanks sneer at it, but it is much better than theirs.

The first two or three nights in Aldershot were spent in a coach house at Gibraltar Barracks. It was like an army museum with many coaches having regimental badges on the doors. Some slept in the coaches, some on the floor beside them. I saw there the first mosquitoes I had seen in my life; the place was alive with them. After that we moved to bell tents on Lavens plain.

From there we moved to Liverpool. There were several troop trains, and the whole operation was done in the proper army style. There was a Lt Colonel in charge of our train, which carried a very large number of men. We arrived in Liverpool on 23 June 1940.

We were in full marching order, which meant that on one's back there was a very large pack, fully loaded, and on the left side, over the bayonet, was the small 'battle' pack. Gas cape rolled up on top of the large pack, with gas mask strapped to the chest, and water bottle hanging on the right hip. In addition to all that were the rifle slung over the right shoulder, large kitbag under the left arm, and sea kitbag under the right arm. With all that we marched down a long straight road, one and a half miles long at least, to Gladstone Dock. It seemed that the whole population of Liverpool was there cheering us, flinging money to us, cigarettes, biscuits, almost anything one could think of. We had a tremendous send-off from the people generally, and the dockers were very good to us indeed.

Every now and then we would ask what ship we were to be on, and were told, 'We can't tell you that but it has four funnels.' The only four-funnel liner then afloat was the *Aquitania*.

Eventually we made it to the dock, and most of us were nearly on our knees by that time. Then the dockers took six days to prepare the ship for sea. We were told that we were the first convoy to leave the United Kingdom after the fall of France. It was quite a special convoy, able to travel very quickly, altogether there were three large liners and a cruiser. Before sailing we became accustomed to the ship and were well looked after by both crew and dock workers. The dockers did anything they could for us, buying things in the city, posting letters, etc. I had an unstamped letter and tried to pay a docker for the stamp, and he threw the money back at me. The letter, which contained all the money I had at the time, arrived home safely.

We sailed on 29 June, moved out, turned north past the Isle of Man, and an hour or so later began to start turning west into the Irish Sea, the North Channel. The *Queen Mary* emerged from the Firth of Clyde to sail with us. Also with us was the *Mauretania*. As we passed the Mull of Kintyre some of the lads had to restrain McPherson from jumping over the side and swimming. He kept saying, 'There's my home over there.' I don't know whether he was drunk at the time. This was Peter McPherson, from Campbeltown, not the McPherson who was later killed beside me at Nauplion.

It was a beautiful day and the sea began to lift a little as we passed Ireland. The *Queen Mary* was in the lead, next being the *Aquitania* and then the *Mauretania*. We had an aircraft and destroyer escort until we reached out into the Atlantic. We then had the cruiser far in front on the horizon. That was the pattern the whole way, right round Africa, and into Ceylon. To Capetown the cruiser was the *Cumberland*, then to Columbo we had the *Sydney* – unless my memory is telling me lies.

The Atlantic swell affected different people in different ways, and one man in particular who was a roadman from Ayr; quite a handsome lad he was, but as thick in the head as it was possible to be so they made him a sergeant. He came to me and said, 'What's wrong with me, Mac? I emptied my stomach there.' He was busy filling it up again, and he carried on like that for about three days, until either his stomach became used to the movement, or the swell moderated, and I don't think he knows yet what was wrong. He joined the regular army after the war, and he was still a sergeant in what is now Ghana the last news I had of him.

There was a tall, gangly roadman from the Stranraer area, a bit over six feet tall, thin as a rake, and with a real whisky face and a long red nose. His feet were much too big for the largest plimsolls available. This did not please him because the *Aquitania* was still being run like a liner, and soft shoes only were permissible. Jimmy was proceeding down the main marble staircase, in between the marble pillars, when an officer got his eye on him. He was a ship's officer, and a rather small man. He tapped Jimmy on the shoulder and said, 'Why are you wearing those boots?' Jimmy swung round, clenched his fist, and said, 'Wad ye say buits to me?' and the officer fled. Jimmy wore his tackety boots until we reached Egypt. About a year ago I met a man at Wick Airport who had been at school with Jimmy's son, and at that time Jimmy was still alive and well.

All our meals were served in the main dining-room, and we slept in the cabins, where extra bunks had been fitted. It was quite a good voyage. Our cabin was just below the waterline.

CHAPTER FOUR

My First Year in the Army

WORKING IN THE GALLEY on the *Aquitania* was a young Irish lad who claimed to be only twelve years old. He did not look any older. He was one of the many southern Irish who were on our side. The *Aquitania* survived the war and I hope he also survived.

Now for a correction: the owner of the Chateau de Thorenc was apparently Lord Rendell. Some more tales of family interest: in 1938 money was scarce and resources if anything scarcer. In fact about this time I passed a whole year without spending one penny piece on myself. One night I decided to go up on to the hill and see if I could get a roe deer. The only weapon available was the revolver. It was a bright moonlit night and as Donald insisted that he was not coming, I went alone to a part which I knew deer had a habit of visiting. I hid myself in a hole on the dark side of a little pass they used, sat down and waited. About fifteen minutes later I heard something coming panting up the hill so I cocked the revolver and waited. I was very careful; the shooter's manual says you should never fire at anything until you know exactly what it is. When it came closer I saw that it was Donald. He was rather stupid to come up when he had said that he was staying, but he was safe enough.

We were at this time becoming very expert at catching rabbits. We discovered that the best time to snare them was when hail showers were expected, and in the dark periods between each moon. Any other time it was sheer luck if we caught anything. One afternoon we went away about two miles into the hill and set a couple of snares for hares, where I had seen them running about. We then came back down. I left the snares till midnight and went back up. It was pitch dark, no moon, nothing but the stars. However, the stars gave a fair bit of light and I managed to go directly to the snares and pick them up.

On another occasion we were walking on the hill when a pheasant rose in front of us; I managed to hit it with a stone and took it home. Another time, near the ruins of the old chapel above Dunstaffnage, we came upon a stoat hanging on to the behind of a young rabbit, it was a fairly large rabbit and was squealing loudly. I relieved the stoat of the rabbit and it was not for running away. It stood on its hind legs and swore at us before it went away. The rabbit was very good – and so was the pheasant incidentally.

One morning I went out to examine a snare I had set at the back of the house. It was set at the fence; not a very good place, but I had seen rabbits there. Nigel's cat was sitting in the snare, caught round the stomach. I went away and came back with pliers, then cut the snare off the cat. It did not appear to be injured but it would not move, after I gave it a slight push it simply rolled over, meowed, and stayed there. I then thought that it must be very severely injured and I had to kill it as quickly as possible.

There was a large empty lemonade bottle lying beside the cat. I picked it up and hit the cat as hard as I was able on the back of the head. Instead of collapsing and dying the cat jumped about two feet into the air and ran, like the proverbial scalded cat. I saw it flash past the corner of the house and have not seen or heard of it since.

At one time I had carefully considered the options of snaring a roe deer but on three particular points I decided against it. First, it is a very cruel way to despatch a deer, second, the penalties if caught were severe, and third, I did not know the height to set the lower edge of the snare. In the early part of 1945 I discussed this with a French lad from a farm outside Nancy. He gave me the height and decided that he would have a go. If he ever caught anything I never heard of it. The correct height for the lower edge of the snare is decided (French style) as follows: place elbow on the ground, hold forearm vertical, clench fist, then set snare with edge lying along the top of the fist. Height for rabbits is set thus: clench fist, set it on ground, vertical with thumb uppermost, lay lower edge of snare along top of fist. Height for hares is decided thus: clench fist and set on ground as for rabbits, stretch thumb upwards as far as possible; set lower edge of snare along tip of thumb.

At that time French and Belgian prisoners could wander where they liked outside working hours, and in many cases this also applied to Russian, Polish, Ukrainian, and other slave workers. They could poach if they thought it worth the risk. From the beginning of 1945 to the end of the war food was very scarce indeed, even for the Austrians.

Of the small group of boys who were playing shinty in the mist, two later died on active service: Dugald Morton died of fever in West Africa, and George MacDonald died of TB in Bangor hospital. The TB was triggered by a football accident which took place in Gibraltar. MacDonald was a very likeable person and a good friend. He in turn had been very friendly with a lad called Galloway. About the time of that shinty game it was noticed that they were not seen together very much and someone said to George, 'What happened to your friend?'

George said, 'Oh, snag, he would let a friend down and it would not bother him.'

'Snag' could be Gaelic for 'sneak'. A lad who occasionally played with us in that place was Rory McCuish who died at Arnhem, when his parachute failed to open.

We played a great deal on that site and in the hollow below the road, much to the annoyance of the farmer Archie Struthers. He would move us on if he could catch up with us but we could see him coming about 200 yards away, and he seldom got near us. His son Bobby was quite good to us and would take part in the games for a minute or two. He wore 'Herd Laddie' boots; they were hobnailed, with heel and toe plates, and with a very pronounced lift in the toe. They seemed to be made for ascending 45 degree slopes. I used to wonder how he managed coming back down, and how long it took him to straighten out his toes at night. In fact had the toes been pointed the boots would have looked like something out of the Arabian Nights. One day we saw Bobby coming along the burn about 100 yards away. We thought we would get a good blether with him but George MacDonald saw him first and picked up the ball, put it under his arm and went. That was the game finished. We followed him and caught up with him at the main road, and said, 'We thought that you liked Bobby.'

He said, 'I do; but this is a new Tomlinson's T-ball, he's not going to kick it with those boots.'

A lonely little boy would come to play football and shinty with us occasionally. He stayed in a house overlooking the hollow, his name was Willie MacKenzie, and his father had married the widow who owned the house. The father owned a garage repair-shop in Airds Crescent, which later became Wilson's Garage. The boy was a few years younger than us and was known as Wee Willie; he was a general favourite. When all the playing had long finished, two or three years after the war, Willie's name hit the national headlines. He had married a girl from some part of America, who knifed him one night, her story being that he had come home drunk and attacked her. There was no way of disproving her story and I don't believe she was ever charged. I heard some women speaking on the street and saying, 'Poor Willie, it was all that tramp's fault.' However, Willie was just as dead as if it had been his fault, and was unable to tell his story.

Now for some explanation about facets of army enlistment. The British Army had always been a small professional army of volunteers and by contrast the Continental armies were huge. In the present century it has been necessary to expand the army at very short notice in a very short time. In the two World Wars this led to conscription and to exceptional difficulties in training men quickly. The available soldiers could not at the same time fight a war and train recruits. Many of those required for specialist units already had the specialist knowledge in their civilian jobs, and thus much training time was saved. Nevertheless, each man had to be trained to fight.

Bobby Struthers, mentioned above, had joined the local TA battery some time before the war. When he joined, it was a horse-drawn mountain battery, but shortly before the war it was re-equipped with two-pounder anti-tank guns. Shortly before the outbreak of war, Bobby left with his mates. Then after a month or two he was sent back home to work the farm. He protested bitterly but it did no good; he was needed to provide food, and he was good at that. After the armistice at Kalamata, when there was a silence that could be felt, I met, sitting at the roadside, a service corps lad whom I knew from one of the troopships. He said, 'That was rough, glad to get through it; but I'd go through that again a dozen times before I'd go back down the pits.' He had been in an accident in the pit and had been trapped underground for several hours. He then went straight to a recruiting office, told a few lies, and was accepted for the RASC.

Now for another tale about the Frenchmen; on the Sunday towards the end of February or beginning of March 1945, a party was in full swing in the room below our camp. This was the local French camp. There were probably about a dozen of them there. One of them who worked for the burgomaster in St Georgen was the centre of the party. When it was all over I went in and asked what the party was in aid of. There was a lovely smell of good cooking, and they were clearing the remains away. The carcass of a large bird was burning on the fire. They said, 'That's the burgomaster's dindon, pfou, peacock, just finished it.' I took a small feather as a keepsake and I have it yet.

About a mile west of us there was another British camp holding about ten men. Some of them were very intelligent lads. At that time they were constructing a small room immediately under their room. It was about six feet by three feet, and about four feet deep. They were very careful in the disposal of excavated soil, carpentry, etc. The place was to hold a calf which they had marked down for stealing, killing, and eating; they took such good care over the job that they were drastically slowed down. The room was just completed when we moved west. The calf escaped its fate.

Now more about the *Aquitania* – the general direction in which we were travelling was west south-west. We held to this direction for several days; sailing about 5 degrees to the west of the course for five minutes and then five degrees to the east. We zigzagged in this manner for the whole voyage, right to Colombo.

One of the first things I noticed on the way out was how the water changed to an intense deep blue colour on the edge of the continental shelf. This fascinated me and gave a new meaning to the expressions 'deep blue sea' and 'blue water sailor'. At this time I spent a great deal of the day at the stern watching the sailors practising with the two six-inch guns. I think these were the only guns on board. The Welsh Regiment seemed to spend all its time staging boxing matches on the bow foredeck. As we moved south we changed into tropical kit, shorts, shirts, topees, etc. and then our amusement was to stand near the stern and count the topees flying past. Any time I checked I reckoned that the army was losing at least one sunhat per minute. A bit further south we watched the flying fishes leaving, they were always flying away from the bow to port or starboard, going perhaps 100 or 150 yards and then going back into the sea.

After about a week or so we turned south-east again, and one morning when I went on deck, I saw to seaward a very large and extended convoy. There were ships from the southern horizon to the northern horizon. It was a very large convoy indeed and I think that it was almost the whole day before we saw the last of them. They were travelling much slower than us; we were doing about 26 knots.

The *Mauretania* was the slowest ship, we were next, and of course the *Queen Mary* could do well over 30 knots. Eventually we anchored in the river off Freetown. The river was very muddy and flowing very quickly so I assumed that it was the rainy season. We were met at sea by an escort of aircraft, and escorted in. There was a great fleet of bumboats, formed almost completely of small, low, dugout canoes. They descended on us, coming very quickly down the river. Most managed to grab a part of the ship on the first attempt; those who did not had to work very hard to get back.

They were all first-class swimmers and divers but it was noticeable that the older men were really outstanding, particularly at diving. They would dive for nothing less than a silver coin, and the older men seemed to have a sixth sense in that they could tell the difference immediately between a half-crown and a penny wrapped in silver paper; they paid no attention whatever to the latter. They had all sorts of produce for sale, throwing a weighted line up to the deck about 50 feet above, then sending up in little baskets, bananas, pineapples, coconuts and other items. Payment was then sent down in the same baskets. The ship's RSM did not approve of this trade. He started to shout and swear, and became livid when no one paid any attention. One of the lads had closed a deal and was hauling up the basket, unaware that the RSM was standing behind him. He leaned forward to pick up his large coconut, but the RSM beat him to it, threw it back down, and hit the sender on his curly head, who simply rubbed his head and said, 'You hit me on the head, Sir.' It could have killed him but he was not in the least put out.

I spent a very amusing morning watching this performance – following the RSM from one end of the deck to the other – and then went below for lunch when I discovered that I'd missed a parade. No one had said anything about it, but there was a notice in a place where there had been no notices before. So then I was hauled before the OC and sentenced to three days CB, quite a comical punishment considering that there was no way to leave 'barracks'. It was the best three days I spent on that ship. There was a platoon of redcaps from Aberdeen and we spent the time sitting on barrels down below and spinning yarns.

We were at Freetown for a day and a half. It is likely that we were there simply to pick up oil and water. I remember a tanker moored alongside; it was the *Ivy Leaf* of about 25,000 tons, a tiddler compared to today's tankers. Eventually we sailed out to about mid-Atlantic and then turned south. We had a great time in the southern part of the Atlantic until eventually we reached Cape Town. We attempted to go in there and I think we grounded; there was a great amount of mud being churned up by the propellors. We reversed out and then went round the Cape to Simonstown, which had deeper water and was the South African naval base. The *Queen Mary* was with us; the *Mauretania* stayed in Cape Town. From Simonstown we were given leave and went to Cape Town, I think on an electric railway.

In the station at Cape Town I met a gentleman called McKellar who came from Ardrishaig, his house was 'Iona, Muizenberg, Cape Province', He invited us to come and visit him the next day, but the next day we sailed. When I first saw Innellan it reminded me strongly of Muizenberg.

At this time I think I should tell what happened when I eventually left the *Aquitania*. While we were going down the gangplank the chief steward was looking at us leaving. He stopped me and gave me a very expensive cigar wrapped in cellophane. The two lads next behind me were also given cigars. We were told to smoke our cigars on Victory Day. When we eventually arrived at Corinth I still had the cigar and virtually nothing else. Some of the lads would have murdered for a smoke, so I gave it to a good friend, Jimmy Clark from Galloway, one of my own section. The cigar was covered in sand and dust from the desert but I had assumed that it would be all right under the cellophane. I was wrong, the sand had penetrated the apparently intact cellophane. Jimmy lit up and as soon as he sucked in, the cigar burst into flames, he blew it out and started again, and again it flamed up, he went on like this until he managed to control it better. It was all right when he sucked very gently, he finished it, holding it on a pin to prevent him burning his fingers.

We were well treated by the South Africans, black and white. There were no problems with either race. All the little white boys were looking for souvenirs, and the black kids were happy enough to be spoken to. When we left the next day we were in the lead for some reason; but the *Queen Mary* passed us and the *Mauritania* took up its position in the rear. It was blowing a gale when we rounded Cape Agulhas. This is the southern tip of Africa; the Cape of Good Hope is no more the extreme south of Africa than John O'Groats is the extreme north of the Scottish mainland. During this gale we clearly saw the bottom of the *Mauretania* several times. As the *Queen Mary* was passing us it seemed to be rising and falling gently; it was indeed a lovely ship. At that I looked away to the south-west and saw, about four or five miles away, a great creature that rose clear of the water, and fell back again with a great splash. For many years I wondered what it was until I saw on TV about twenty years ago, a whale breaching. Now I feel that I am very fortunate to have seen a whale.

As we stood on the bow of the *Aquitania* making for the Indian Ocean, Peter McPherson, John Carmichael, and others, were with us, when suddenly Carmichael threw out his hand and burst into song: *From Skerryvore to Singapore, From Mull to Mandalay, To travel and toil on alien soil to win the world for you.* He gave us the whole song: *FionPhort Ferry.*

Carmichael's impromptu concert reminded me of the time McPherson was watching his beloved home disappear over the stern, he too gave us a song. That song became known in the company as the *Campbeltown National Anthem*. It finished: 'And we will live in hope to meet in Campbelltoon once more.'

During our time together we heard that song many times, particularly when he was drunk.

It was mandatory on all troopships that life preservers be carried by all personnel at all times. I personally preferred, and always had, a Board of Trade lifebelt. This was essentially eight large corks in a canvas harness, it made a very useful little seat and could be used as such anywhere on the deck. Many people preferred the kapok-filled lifejacket, it was more comfortable and was less likely to break one's neck when jumping into the sea. There were strict warnings against jumping or falling overboard, it not being possible for any of the liners to stop and pick anyone up. There was much too great a risk of being torpedoed if they stopped.

Crossing the Indian Ocean we found various things to keep us amused. Jimmy, the roadman with the large feet, would seek me out before sunset and we would go to the stern to watch the sun. The setting sun fascinated him. It appeared to move down steadily until it sat on the horizon, hovered there for a short time, and then seemed to drop out of sight. Personally, I was watching the Southern Cross rising higher every night; but in the Indian Ocean we were heading in a northerly direction again, and the Southern Cross started to lower again. Apart from the ever-present flying fish, we frequently saw fins which we took to be from sharks, although we were never quite sure; there were many dolphins about. These things kept us going until we reached Ceylon (now Sri Lanka). We left the ship at Colombo, and the liners went round to the deep water port of Trincomalee in order to pick up Anzacs. Our lads were put ashore without pay and ordered to amuse themselves. Our officers were not to be troubled with such trifles as pay parades for the men.

There was a small amount of cash in my pocket but over 90 per cent of our mates had nothing. There was a fleet of buses drawn up at the pier manned by the Singhalese Salvation Army. They were fine people who took us on a conducted tour of several temples and other places of interest, things we could not possibly have seen otherwise, and they asked for nothing, some who had money gave them a donation. They then took us back into Colombo to do a bit of shopping before we went back to whatever vessel we had been allocated.

Shopping in Colombo was very interesting. In the bazaar I entered a shop and was questioned as usual, 'Are you English?'

'No, Scottish.'

'Ah, Wallace da Bruce.'

In that shop I bought a little book, which I still have – a Benn's Sixpenny Library book on Architecture – and I still have postcards I purchased there. The owners were the Khatab Brothers. There were some very doubtful characters in the company. One sneak in particular had his mates keep the shopkeeper busy while he stole whatever he fancied. In particular he had a beautiful ivory idol, four or five inches high and beautifully carved. That lad was captured along with the rest of us and I expect the little idol is now in Austria somewhere.

There was a lighthouse in the middle of the square in Colombo. Another interesting memory from Colombo was the ship coaling. There was a dirty little ship moored at the quay. It was fitted with long planks each about two feet wide, serving as gangplanks; they were fitted at the bow and the stern. There was a string of women, with hourglass figures, bouncing all over the place, running up one plank, and down the other. On the way up they had a kind of shallow brass bowl, full of coal, on their heads, this was emptied down a hatch, and they then left by the other plank and started the process over again. This was classic coaling, of the type in general use at the time of the First World War, and I think that we were watching the last of it. That ship was the SS *Ethiopia*.

We spent about a week on that ship. The company poet described it as, 'a floating garbage tank'. It was alive with little beasties which were known to us as 'Bombay canaries'; they were a type of cockroach, kipper coloured, about two inches long. They flew about all night, looking like little flying kippers, and chirping like birds. Our hammocks were slung above the deck, we slept there; before rising we would hear people shouting and water splashing, bucket after bucket of water being thrown down and chased along the deck by lascars with a broom in each hand, down the deck and out of the scuppers. We then rose, washed and dressed, rolled up the hammocks and hung them on the hooks. If one were lying on the hammock, and dropped a piece of biscuit, the beasties would remove it immediately.

On the third night on board, while I was on guard, Duncan McDonald spoke to me. He was wandering about in a kind of dream, with his staring eyes nearly popping out of his head. Later I discovered that he had been with the crew, and had been given some sort of drug, probably opium. Whatever it was it hit him very badly. After my spell I went back to my hammock and went to sleep. In the morning I found that McDonald had had an accident during the night. His hammock had been slung over the hold and in attempting to get into it he had fallen and broken his neck. He lay moaning next to one of his mates who was also on guard, and who did nothing to help. The medical officer was called in the morning and he failed to save him; he said that there might have been a chance had he been alerted sooner.

About two days later we reached Bombay. Because of the accident we were sent in first, and we were confined to the ship. Two or three of his closer mates went with the remains to a funeral service in Bombay Military cemetery. That was the company's first casualty.

It had taken us six weeks from Liverpool to Colombo and nearly another week to Bombay. The docks in Bombay were served by a very efficient system of hydraulically driven machines, gantries and derricks, completely silent. They were so silent that one had to be very careful not to be run down by them. There too I noted the red kites, who were very able indeed at fishing and other ways of obtaining food. I must have seen them before then in West and South Africa, but I don't remember them before Bombay. Also in this place there was one man, an old man with grey hair, who was an exceptionally good swimmer and diver. He had a very good catch of sixpences and shillings but most of the canoes held single men who were fishing with a circular net. The net was very carefully rolled up and cast so that it fell in a perfect circle. It must have been weighted at the rim; when it was pulled in by the attached rope the fish were inside. I found it rather difficult to understand how that net worked but it was very skilful fishing. There was a very large fleet of sailing fishing boats operating out of Bombay.

Here we transferred to a vessel called the *Khedive Ismail*. We were in Bombay about three days. We were allowed on the dock only once, and then sailed in a very large convoy, the largest convoy we had been in; there were two destroyers, at least two armed merchantmen, and aircraft escorts when near friendly coasts. The armed merchantmen were a sight to be seen, there were guns sticking out of them at all angles, they stayed with us to Port Tewfik in Egypt.

That was a notable voyage. It was very hot, being close to the Equator for a large part of the way, and the ship was not suited for that part of the world. One day they measured 190 degrees in the galley, the Indian crew members were being carried up from the galley every ten minutes or so. They would be laid out on the deck and given an injection of something to save their lives. It finished up that our people ran the ship, most of them from our company; we even had a lad acting signalman on the bridge. A number of the company went down with the heat; the worst affected in our group was Willie McNeill who very nearly expired when we were in the Red Sea. The heat was simply oppressive. When we were in the Red Sea, in mid-afternoons one ship after another would drop its ensign to half-mast. Then at sunset they would drop to the stern of the convoy and the weighted hammocks could be seen dropping into the water over the stern. Some time after arriving in Egypt, Peter McPherson received a letter from home to say that his cousin had died in passage through the Red Sea and had been buried at sea.

When in Colombo one of the Salvation Army lads stopped under a tree and handed us some of the fruit. It looked rather like a spiky chestnut; but it was a beautiful sweet fruit; I saw the same fruits at Kalamata but have never found out what they are. When we entered the Red Sea, through the Bab el Mandeb, what the sailors called the gates of hell, the Italians were quite close to us. The two destroyers went over to the African coast and dropped a number of depth charges. Large columns of water could be seen going straight up into the air. I was quite surprised how the water rose in an almost vertical-sided column. It was almost exactly the same thing later in Greece: when the bombs hit soft alluvial soil they would penetrate deeply and throw the soil vertically upwards. Whereas, if they landed on rock, shrapnel could travel horizontally for hundreds of yards. I don't know if any submarines were damaged or sunk by the depth charges.

The destroyers then returned to the front of the convoy, put out paravanes, and started to zigzag, crossing back and forth in front of the convoy. The cable to the paravanes was much longer than I had expected. This type of manoeuvre was continued until we were past the narrow part of the Red Sea.

The *Khedive Ismail* was altogether a remarkable vessel. It had a high turn of speed, which of course was not of much use in the convoy, but as you will hear it was very useful later. The convoy speed was about five to eight knots, there were a number of very slow vessels in it. The *Khedive Ismail* had a permanent and very severe list to port, which did not seem to affect its performance as a sea-going vessel. It was quite a good vessel and well appointed, made for the tourist trade I think. The *Ethiopia* had been used for tourists to Mecca more than likely. Our new ship was oil burning and altogether a cleaner ship. There were 'Bombay Canaries' in it but they were right down in the depths and we did not see them. I was on the boat party. There was a boat on each set of davits and another sitting inboard alongside it so it had twice the normal number of lifeboats, and also double the normal number of buoyant apparatus; but when all was said and done we were carrying 2,500 persons and had boats and buoyant apparatus for barely half that number. After that I looked around for anything to make a raft, and had worked out what to do if necessary and if we had the time. Fortunately the raft was not needed. The boat party was there to swing the boats out, see them filled with others, and then probably drown.

About that time McPherson remembered that he had been a Gaelic singer in his youth – he was about 24 – and he gave us a few concerts, singing several Gaelic songs. '*Mull of the Bens*' was his favourite, he sang it verse about, English and Gaelic; but he always finished with 'In Campbeltoon once more', until we were sick of it.

There had been a hold in the forward well-deck, and it was covered in from the deck above. An intermediate floor was formed below. There was a temporary stair about two feet wide down to the intermediate deck, and another down to the lower part of the hold. Our company was in the upper part, and a Scottish service corps company in the lower part. I checked on the first lifeboat drill we had. My hammock was just at the foot of the upper stair and I was on the deck in a few seconds. Then I started to time the other lads coming up. It was more than twenty minutes later when the last service corps boy reached the deck, and that had been a well-disciplined copy-book evacuation.

There had been a swimming pool on the stern well-deck, but the heat in the galley had been so great that they had knocked the floor out of it, and put a large canvas ventilator straight in to the galley. The ventilator would be about two feet in diameter, this greatly reduced the heat; but the watches worked in the galley were still restricted to twenty minutes each.

There were passages, port and starboard, to the stern of the vessel from our quarters. They were about five feet wide. On the sea sides of the passages were troughs formed of galvanized iron; these were half-filled with sea water to form latrines. There was a wooden cover on it with circular holes at regular intervals. Water was pumped in at one end and discharged at the other. It was so arranged that there was always a sufficient depth of water at the lower part. Many of the troops had diarrhoea, while others had constipation. With the movement of the ship there was always a wave flowing backwards and forwards. The latrine was very well patronized and everyone became very skilful in judging the wave and preventing behinds from getting too well washed. We would sit having our food and watch those on the latrine rising and falling like a wave that went for ever backwards and forwards.

The lascars would take their prayer mats out to the bow several times a day. At the beginning of the voyage they were looking towards the bow, but they gradually turned until in the Red Sea they looked to starboard; and by the time we reached Egypt they were pointed almost over the stern. They always looked towards Mecca.

Each ship had its own peculiar noises. For example, on the *Aquitania* one could hear the rudder chains rattling every two or three minutes, as the ship zigzagged and there was creaking and groaning even in fine weather; but in heavy weather there were thuds as the waves hit the bows, and a shudder along the whole ship, as it pitched, rolled and tossed all at the same time. In the other ships this had a very pronounced effect on the hammocks; as the ship hogged on the crest of a wave the centre of the hammock rose; as it sagged in the trough, the hammock centre sagged, and there were odd times when heavy men bounced on the tables beneath. This made sleeping fairly difficult, to say nothing of the effect of being flung from side to side in storms. At Reveille blankets were folded and rolled in the hammocks, in such a way that they passed inspection by the ship's officers. If, in their personal opinions, they did not look like Swiss rolls, the culprit was condemned to try again.

The heat was such that most of the time we wore nothing but shorts and plimsolls. When we sat at the tables, filling up with tea, the moment we drank sweat poured from us. One day, when sitting at the table with McPherson, doing just that, he suddenly said, 'When I get home I'll speak to those lazy b – s that I pay, and I'll say, "You complain about sweat. Why I've sweat more sitting on my a – s, drinking tea, than you sweat in a week".' We were instructed by MOs to drink salt water in order to replace the salt we had lost.

We had impromptu concerts on the well-deck in the bow, most of the performers being the men themselves. There was a row of nurses and one or two officers watching us from above. On one occasion a nurse, a very likeable girl, came down, and she really was a very good singer. She gave us a song and then a rendering of *There'll always be an England*. The next singer was one of our sergeants with *Hail Caledonia*. At the chorus, 500 Scots joined in with very dramatic effect. Then on a Sunday, services were held on the boat deck for anyone who wished to attend. Many of the Argyllshire lads went to them, along with others.

There were two real troopships in the convoy, that is ships built for the purpose, I think one was the *Dorsetshire*. The heat on the ship was so great that we finished all the drinking water and most of the water for the turbines as well. Then one morning, immediately after sunrise, we left the convoy and turned west. Travelling alone it really was a very fast ship. We entered Port Sudan and were there for most of the day. We picked up water and supplies and had caught up with the convoy by sunset.

In Port Sudan the effect of leaving the ship and going ashore was like stepping into an oven, and I would not like to be in the interior of the Sudan. However, it was a very interesting visit; the natives were not exactly as I had expected but they were easy to speak to. The most interesting place was the shore; it was like a big, beautiful aquarium. There were beautiful rocks, corals and above all lovely little fish: diamonds and triangles, some almost transparent, floating about in crystal clear water. I put my hand into the water and took a spray of coral, which at that time was very attractive, but is now broken and dusty. I keep it because it stayed with me everywhere I went.

When we left port and were beginning to pick up speed, a fast launch came after us; on board was the harbourmaster and one of the lads. He was put aboard and reprimanded immediately by the OC. He had, I believe, been with one of the Sudanese girls; he wasn't scared, but he was given seven days' close confinement for breaking the rules, and his name thereafter was famous throughout the company. From there to Suez there was not a great deal to remember. There were dolphins and alleged sharks which looked very small to me. It was cooler sightseeing on deck than staying below.

One night at sunset, as we neared the gulf of Suez, there was what appeared to be a brilliant fireworks display on the Arabian side, flashing and banging. I thought that it was ack-ack, but one of the ship's officers assured me that it was a normal thunderstorm for the area. It may well have been normal but I have never seen anything like it before or since. There were some impressive thunder storms in the desert but nothing to rival that.

We sailed up the Gulf of Suez to Port Tewfik, where we disembarked. Before leaving the ship a peculiar looking character arrived; he was like something out of a child's story book. He had a sword, a peculiar hat and a rat running about on his shoulders. After expecting a very interesting show the sergeant-major turned up and ordered him away. He looked daggers at the CSM, stayed long enough to curse him fluently and went. We did not see him again. When we disembarked, the CSM shouted out, 'All the drivers and lorry drivers fall in over here.' There were twenty or thirty of them. He then harangued them thus: 'First and only instruction; if you run over a wog you reverse over him and make sure he's dead, you'll cause the army less trouble that way.'

On the dockside were two very large piles of sacks, rather like miniature mountains; they were high conical heaps with an Egyptian soldier lying on top of one of them. He was supposed to be on guard, we thought he was having a nap. He had a martini rifle, and a canvas cover over his tarboosh which provided a skip to protect his eyes and a cloth skirt at the back to protect the back of his head and neck. He reminded me of pictures of the Foreign Legion. When we boarded the train we discovered that one of our number had stolen one of the sacks. It was filled with peanuts, and was very acceptable. It seemed to me that there was a large number of sneak thieves among the Borderers, and that perhaps centuries of sneaking away with English cattle had inbred a tradition of stealing. We left the train at Ismalia, and trucked south to Fayid Camp which was not far from the Great Bitter Lake. The whole voyage from Liverpool to Port Tewfik took nine weeks. The camp was set on a large flat area on the lake shore. There was a range of hills to the north, but it seemed to be flat desert to the south and west. The whole plain appeared to have been coverd with water at some time. There were portions of fossilized trees, and all the pebbles and rocks appeared to have been water worn. If any stone was broken open concentric rings could be found, usually with normal tree configuration, but sometimes more like ferns. I brought home samples of most of them but the best were lost in Greece. Nancy still has some of them.

One afternoon, when I had some free time, I walked to the hills and saw a number of fairly large lizards. Then while I was climbing up through a little gully, making for the top, I met three medical boys coming down with another man on a stretcher. They did not look very happy, and I wondered if they were on a punishment exercise. I spoke to them and received a very grudging reply. They were some miles from the nearest camp.

We did all kinds of work there; we built a bridge across the sweet water canal. Most of the remaining time was spent in training. When we had two or three hours off we would bathe in the Bitter Lake. One day in the water, McPherson was showing off, showing how well he could dive in three or four feet of water. He came up coughing and spluttering saying, 'My teef, my teef, I've lost my teef.' He kept diving and many others came to help, but the 'teef' were never found. We were in tents at this camp and the latrines were about half a mile away, behind a canvas screen. All work was done by contractors here; they collected all rubbish, and took it away.

Used tea was dried and sold for re-use. Contents of the toilets were sold for returning to the fields. There was a series of buckets, large buckets with hinged wooden lids on them, behind the screen. One day I was going to the latrines when I met McPherson coming back. He was a bit white and he said, 'Come on, Mac, come and see this.' We went to the screened area, lifted a lid, and he pointed into the bucket. There was a beautifully made piece of work at the bottom, at least fifteen inches long, tapered to each end, and approximately three inches diameter in the middle. Coming back to the tents he still looked shaken and he kept saying, 'I wonder who did that, who did that, what kind of a behind did that come out of?' That's a euphemism of what he said. Then he thought and blurted out, 'It must have been Bob Dargavel.' Bob was a First World War veteran, tall and heavy, with a very large beer gut. Indeed, he was a sight to see in his KD shorts. I don't remember him in Egypt apart from Peter McPherson speaking about him.

The sea voyages did different things to different people. Many were constipated, and it took some of these a week or two to settle down after leaving the last ship. The sand storms soon sorted them out; sand in one's gut has a very scouring effect.

We had two different nights in Ismalia which was about fifteen miles from the camp; we went on company transport. One night I bought a watch for 50 piastres, in the Union Jack club. Three or four nights later I was in again. There was a strict blackout at all times. I noticed a door open and saw that the place was a canteen, and went in for a cup of tea. Then I came out and continued along the pavement. I fell for no apparent reason, picked myself up, found that I had damaged my wrist and my new watch. The wrist healed in a few days. Two or three days later I was there in daylight and found that the footpath started at the right-hand end, rose along the face of the building to the doorway then carried on at that level to the left-hand end of the building, it then stopped abrubtly and fell three feet vertically to the general level of the surrounding ground.

Later that night I was making my way back towards the trucks, with no real idea where they were, when I heard a very drunken voice shouting out, 'In Campbeltoon once more'. I made my way to them and they were at the trucks. It really was a very dark night.

When we were building the little bridge over the sweet water canal, we were not permitted to touch the water; evidently it was full of bilharzia, which was a very bad fever caused by a tiny bug or snail. The fever was caused by eggs entering the intestine. At that time it was also known as Malta fever. The natives eventually realized that we were not permitted to touch the water and they had a strike. They said, 'If it's not good enough for them it's not good enough for us, there's death in the water.' A man with a long white gown came to try to settle the matter. I had a long talk with him and a fine, well-educated man he was. The labourers were given some extra pay and they completed their part of the work. We put our company's name on the bridge and I wonder if it is still there.

Many of our people had collected souvenirs on the way, and by the time we were leaving Fayid Camp many of them had realized that they could not carry their prizes. My last memory of Fayid was on a truck leaving to go to Ismalia to entrain from there for the Western Desert. Looking out of the back of the truck to where a tent had been, was a Nellie the elephant, a lonely black object about two feet high. It was up to its knees in sand, and the sandstorm was blowing about it. From Ismalia we went by train, via Ben Ha, Tanta, and Zagazig, on to the Western Desert. I have noted in my diary that we stopped at a place called Sidi Gaber; and I have no recollection of that place now. It must have been somewhere between Zagazig and Sidi Haneish, because we detrained there about midday.

We were stationed on the littoral plain, between the road and the sea. Our own Morris pick-up trucks took us down from the railway. They were 15cwt capacity, and very effective little machines. We were dumped at a site almost on the shore. The Rajput Sikhs were stationed near the road. Between them and the sea were two-pounder anti-tank batteries. West of the Sikhs were the Argylls, and I would assume that the Queens and Leicesters were there also – they were the 16th Infantry Brigade. There were batteries of 25-pounder guns, and some 60-pounders. They were all dug in and fairly well hidden

That part of North Africa is generally a plateau of about 1,000 feet high which finishes in an escarpment to the north. This escarpment reaches the sea at the Libyan frontier. There is a coastal plain not very high above sea level, right along the Egyptian coast, and this is where most of the action took place. At that time there was a railway line as far as Mersa Matruh only, which was about twenty miles west of us.

Some words about the fauna and flora would not be out of place. The most ubiquitous creature we noticed was the pied wagtail, it was to be seen everywhere and displayed no fear of man. When we were resting, fly covered, these birds would remove the flies from knees, hands, and even faces. Hoodie crows were plentiful, and there were a few robins about. There must have been red kites about although I don't remember them in the Western Desert. Flocks of geese would come in at very high altitude, mornings and evenings, and there was a current rumour that the Bofors gunners at Bagush landing field used them for target practice. Scorpions were very common, the green variety in particular; fortunately I was never stung. When we woke in the mornings the first thing to be done was to turn one's boots upside down, one at a time, and shake them thoroughly. Any animals emerging were hammered with the free boot. Black scorpions were greatly feared by the natives. If stung they would lie down, pull their gown over their heads, and wait to die.

They seemed to will themselves to die. There were ants of several sizes from just over an inch long to less than a quarter of an inch. There were, it seemed, millions of them. There were packs of wild dogs, lovely animals, rather like huskies, but light coloured with sandy streaks on them. They were perfectly camouflaged, and some of them became quite tame. Further west were gazelles; we saw a fair number after we started to push the Italians back. The Italians left behind a number of loose horses and donkeys. We were not troubled by mosquitoes in the desert although one of the lads went down with malaria, and another had sand-fly fever.

There was an abundance of large black fleas, and of course the scarab, and other beetles. The scarab was a magnificent insect, moving ponderously over the desert like a heavy tank. It appeared to be about 2′ long and over 1′ wide. Snakes were common, some of them poisonous. I don't remember seeing any desert rats (jerboas) although they were about. I think that they were more plentiful on the plain above the escarpment.

The flies were terrible; they looked like a common house fly, but they had a nose that could, and did, draw blood. They were exceedingly annoying. When we went to the cookhouse the drill was to get one's tea first in the smaller mess tin, cover this with the larger tin which was then filled with the main course – stew, bully beef, or whatever the cooks had for us – the canvas cover was then laid on top, and we went in to the tents to consume it. We would carefully lift a corner of the canvas and attempt to obtain a spoonful before the flies landed. With the best of precautions we swallowed at least two or three flies, until very soon we gave up and ignored them. Well, after all, the chameleons enjoyed the taste of them. If one drew even the smallest drop of blood by scraping a knee or cutting the back of the hand, a pyramid of flies, about an inch high, materialized on top of it. A drop of iodine discouraged them.

There were a few chameleons, very interesting little animals; one of the lads kept one on his shoulder as a pet. It spent the whole day catching and swallowing flies.

There was a sparse, low, ashen-coloured scrub, thinly covering large areas. The bushes were about three feet every way. There were larger open areas like where we camped, that looked just like more open parts of the desert, until on closer inspection one could see that it had been ploughed. There were little furrows about three inches deep, every foot or so. The desert farmers ploughed, planted the grain, and waited for rain. If it did not rain that year it would rain the next one, or the one after.

There were several large heaps of stones, perhaps as high as fifteen feet. These were the graves of sheiks and other famous men. One was a man called Haneish. Our lads were stopped from using them as road metal.

The landing field at Bagush was home to a few Wellingtons and Blenheims as well as a selection of other aircraft, some of them much older, but the Lysanders were of the same vintage. Probably the most important of the others were the Gladiators. There was one that looked like an older Wellington – the Bombay – and there was a large biplane called the Vickers Valencia. The Hurricanes and more Wellingtons were seen later.

On a level piece of ground a mile or two west of Bagush a dummy landing field was set out. One of the funeral mounds was dressed up with flags, rags and so on. I had no idea what it was supposed to be but the dummies were bombed more than once by the Italians. We had dummy buildings near us as well. We were constructing an underground headquarters which possibly was used in one of the later campaigns. We made a good job of it; very little showed on the surface, and it contained some very large deep rooms.

At this camp the latrines were quite close to us, in later camps and bivvies they were further away. No tent was more than a couple of hundred yards from them. Diarrhoea was very common and there were some very expressive names for it, but as soon as I felt it coming on I remembered medical instructions and took a liquid diet until the pains passed. It was not unusual to see a man leave a tent and walk smartly towards the 'bogs'. Then he would shudder and stop, and then start to run, but before he reached his goal, he would stop with a look of disgust on his face, then walk bandy-legged into the latrine.

The choice of a liquid diet was the correct action when we were with our own troops; we knew that we would have no trouble in making up lost strength as there was plenty of food. But later in Corinth, and more particularly in Salonica and Wolfsberg, I took the conscious decision that it was better to die of starvation than of dysentery. An added consideration was that food, far from helping one in a bout of dysentery, was not only lost but could do irreparable damage to the gut, it was better to save the food until it could do some good. The most dangerous time I had was the first few days at Wolfsberg.

When we arrived at Sidi Haneish each quarter-section was given a large tent, and told to dig it in as far as we liked, and then to camouflage it. We set about it with great gusto, and dug it in about six feet deep. The tents were twenty feet by fifteen feet; by about five and a half feet high to the eaves. They were lovely tents with double roofs. We had the tent erected and were camouflaging it when a sergeant arrived and said, 'Well, lads, you've made an excellent job of that one. It will do nicely for the sergeants.' We were thoroughly disgusted but there was nothing we could do about it. We took another tent and dug it in about three feet, and that tent did us all the time we were there. We thought that we had been very badly treated, until we discovered that another two quarter-sections had been hit the same way. The officers required two tents for themselves; one for eating in and one for sleeping. Surprisingly they did not ask for three. The effect was that one officer required the work of several men, at a time when an army 40 times our size was advancing on us and there were defences to be built.

About a mile away from us the Argylls' officers, warrant officers, NCOs and men were living without protection from the elements. They slept in little trenches the size of a man; the officers were no different. The Indian division slept in dugouts below ground, and I don't know what the others did. There were no Australians or Kiwis at that time. The general Australian method seemed to be to cut a circle on the ground, go down vertically two or three feet, then gradually widen out to a kind of bottle dungeon. Each man made his own.

When we reached further west we usually slept in well-appointed dugouts made by the Italians. We had to be careful as sometimes they left their calling cards; there were some rather diabolic booby traps.

The cooks, Archie Law and Jock McLarty, worked on wood-burning iron stoves in the open. Archie's speciality was doughballs, I don't know what they were made of but they were solid, and were known as Archie Law's bombs. A short time later Archie went sick and his long-suffering clients said he must have eaten some of his own bombs. After a spell in Abassia Barracks, he was sent to hospital in Cairo, where he eventually died.

Owing to the latitude of Egypt we had a reasonably accurate twelve-hour day and twelve-hour night cycle. The cooks rose about an hour before the others to light the fire and get breakfast ready for daylight at six o'clock. We were rudely awakened one night by bangs, clatters, aeroplanes flying around, and bombs bursting everywhere. There was silence for a while, then we heard an officer shouting at the top of his voice, 'Put out that fire.' It was nearly dawn but it was still quite dark. We went outside and there was a flare hanging in the sky above us. It was almost as bright as day for a long time, it must have been on a parachute and we felt naked; but we could hear the planes flying off across the Mediterranean. They did not return at that time. The fire was not put out and we had our breakfast. The officer returned to his hidey hole and we did not see him again for some time. We did not see much of them anyway. The next day there was a very large sick parade about three times the normal size. Some of the men on it we did not see again.

That was the first bombing that fell on us, and I kept a piece of shrapnel from one of the bombs for many years. It has now disappeared.

Extract from John O'Groat Journal
dated Tuesday, 24 November 1891.

A new steel screw steamer, ETHIOPIA, arrived in Wick on voyage from Calcutta with a cargo of linseed for the Aberdeen Line Company. The vessel belonged to Messrs Elder, Dempster and Company, Liverpool, and was on her maiden voyage. She was 297 feet long, 40 feet broad, 19 feet deep and carried over 3,170 tons of linseed. Her passage from Calcutta was made in 45 days.

Information researched by Douglas Cameron, Dunfermline

First
IOLAIRE, 999 tons, built 1902. Two 3″ guns. Hired as an Auxiliary Patrol Yacht 1/3/1915. Renamed AMALTHEA 11/1918 and returned to owners 1/1919. Hired as an accommodation ship 9/1939. Purchased 1/1943. Renamed PERSEPHONE 6/1945. Sold 1946. In WW2 her fleet number was FY.012.

Second
KHEDIVE ISMAIL. 12 February 1944, Japanese submarine I–27 *(Lt Fukumura)* sinks the *Khedive Ismail* (8,672 tons) with over 1,000 British troops on board; but is herself sunk in a destroyer counter-attack.

Quasaba 1940

Redbreasts and pied wagtails,
Black scorpions, wild dogs, green scorpions, and ants,
Camels, grey crows, and spindly grey-green plants,
Dark eyes behind the veils.

Refugees passing by,
Matilda tanks and Rolls-Royce armoured cars,
Lysanders, Gladiators, and chatty water jars,
Dust storms and dysentery.

Planes high above the place,
Italian bombs from twenty thousand feet;
Briton and Bedouin working in the heat,
Flies on knees, hands and face.

Blood soaking in the sand;
An Arab family ends in agony.
A side-show of the greater butchery,
Dead poor, on poor dead land.

We think of Highland homes.
Whistles blow, transport rolls, the line moves west,
And leaves them there in silence and at rest;
Graves where the scarab roams.

The First Echelon, NZEF, EGYPT, 1940

We were first when our country called us,
Gladly we answered the need.
Holding it light and a pleasure
To come with our utmost speed.

We asked not where we were wanted
Nor where they wished us to go,
The fact that there was a danger
Was all that we wanted to know.

The others so cool and cautious
Dallied and sought delay,
And while the camp life claimed us
They waited a distant day.

We toiled and sweated and studied
Alike in wind and rain,
Then off on leave to forget it
Then back to the camp again.

We asked no acclaim and worship,
These things we loathe and despise,
But yet we are only human
You passed us with scornful eyes.

But at last came the call we wanted:
We were bound for distant shores,
Then we were suddenly heroes
And subject to applause.

There was such a rush to join us,
The cry was 'follow the Flag'!
'Worthy, excellent, splendid,'
But, why was there such a lag?

They had waited and calculated,
Counting the loss and the gain,
And setting the balances even,
To be certain 'twas not in vain.

There were parties and games and evenings
And all of a great 'to do'
With homes and rooms to stay at,
And places to 'bill and coo'.

While out in the blazing desert,
Half of the world away,
Were the men who did the ground work,
And the men who paved the way.

The paper was full of the doings
Of the gallant Second and Third;
But of those in the dust and the desert
Scarce a whisper or voice was heard.

We read and our lips grew scornful
Of the fuss they were making of them,
And our thoughts were rather bitter,
The First, but forgotten men.

Then came a tale that stunned us,
A tale, a deliberate lie,
Of deserted wives and debts unpaid,
When we gave our last goodbye.

It is easy enough to slander,
Sitting at home in style,
But hard as Hell to bear it
On the banks of the distant Nile.

And though we are slow to anger
We may yet slower forget,
And though WE may be forgotten,
We have not forgotten yet.

The above written ode was first heard by me in the Western Desert, Egypt, late in 1940. It was recorded late in 1941, with the help of members of the First Echelon, 2nd NZEF at Bodendorf, Steiermark.

CHAPTER FIVE

Wavell's Campaign

HERE IS A LITTLE BIT MORE about the attacks on us in the Western Desert. The second time the Italians came over they were flying about over the place, backwards and forwards, for the greater part of the night. We had heard no bombs falling and assumed they perhaps were lost and had dropped nothing. But about midday the next day, two of the Argylls took an object to their officer, and handed it to him. It had been found in their area and looked rather like a thermos flask. When the officer turned it upside down it exploded, and killed, as we were told, one or two of them. There was a propellor in the top which wound out as the bomb fell, and this primed it. If it happened to remain upright in the sand it was fairly safe, but if it landed horizontally it was very dangerous, and even a slight tremor would set it off. Altogether, about 2,000 of them were found. The whole area was 'harrowed' by the two Bren-gun carriers with a long chain stretched between, and bombs were exploded at irregular intervals for about two days.

At the same time there were strong rumours that exploding tins of bully beef, and creamed rice, had been dropped – and even little bombs in the shape of fountain pens and jack knives – but I had no first-hand or even second-hand knowledge of this. These items, even if they had existed, would have been of little interest to us.

Along with Iain Mitchell I was picked to act as chain man to a chap who was taking levels for a water pipeline. This was to stretch from Fuka to Mersa Matruh, approximately fifteen miles in all. This job was all right except that the lad in charge, who was supposed to be an architect, didn't know what end of the instrument to look through, and he would not let us anywhere near it. He waffled away at it. We completed our section and the pipeline went through. Surprisingly it worked. There must have been a very powerful pump pushing it through. Soon afterwards the same lad was called out to set out a pillbox. One of the officers had given him a prismatic compass. I don't know why the officers were not there themselves, presumably they would have known how to use it, but our friend had no idea. It was so obvious that he did not know anything about it that, hoping to help, I said, 'Have you ever used one of these before?'

'No, but I don't anticipate any difficulty.' So that was it. The pillbox was built. Much of the reinforcement was only taking up space but it was a good strong job. Unfortunately the gunports were all looking in the wrong direction. Even more unfortunately several were built. They were useless for the purpose for which they had been built. Fortunately Wavell's attack was a success.

The officers at that time seemed to be spending most of their time dating nurses in Cairo and running trucks back and forwards; we saw very little of them. Our own sectional officer was the best of them. One of the other section officers came to see me and said that he had met a girl from Oban, I think he said that he had dated her; this was Bunty McNeill. I was on the point of telling him that she was too good for him, when I decided to say nothing.

Next we were sent to work at Quasaba, which was some miles further west. There was a large supply dump being run by the Ordnance Corps, and we were constructing a loop road to better service the place. While working there we saw one or two robins, the only ones that I remember in Africa. We had our usual supply of Egyptian labourers, as well as at least one company of Cypriot Auxiliaries The dump was protected by desert Bedouins with some very ancient firearms. I found these men to be very poor and very honest. One day, while I was employed elsewhere, there was an air attack. A bomb landed unusually close, on rock, and there were splinters flying in all directions. A splinter flew along the front of one of the Arabs which slit his abdomen open, and his insides fell out. Our medical orderly was on the scene in seconds. He threw the gut bck in and began to sew the lad up. He had a short distance to go when he was told, 'You can stop now; he's dead.' A whole family was wiped out.

I returned the next day, and at the place were four graves, two large and two small. It appeared that the bodies were simply laid on the ground, covered with stones to keep the dogs away, and neatly defined with larger stones round each one. There was an attack that day also, but back to their usual accuracy, the nearest bomb fell nearly two miles away.

The hot metal travelling over the desert was not all flying in the one direction. The British had, I think, three monitors; smallish, shallow draught vessels with two fifteen-inch guns each. We used to lie in bed and hear them hammering Sidi Barrani at night, about 60 miles away. We could feel the ground shaking as these very large shells landed.

The Rolls-Royce armoured cars carried out many raids, carrying the Long Range Desert Group very many miles into enemy territory to carry out raids. There were also high-speed raids carried out with light tanks. All in all the Italians were not allowed to rest. When we went out first the only fighter aircraft we had were the biplane Gladiators. The Hurricanes arrived probably two or three weeks before the push. The tanks we had at first were mostly cruisers and whippets. The whippets were very light, and the cruisers were not much heavier; we had nothing to compare with the larger Italian tanks. The Matildas arrived just in time, a few weeks before the push. I don't know how many there were but there were enough. We had Blenheim bombers from the beginning.

There was a peculiar incident while we were levelling for the pipeline. We were at Fuka, the eastern end, and could see clearly about two miles in every direction. The man with the level was about 100 yards away. A bullet passed between Mitchell and me, we both heard it quite clearly. But we heard no weapon, and could see no place where a rifleman could hide. We never found an explanation.

Our food was collected from a dump at El Daba, which was quite a bit further back down the line. A truck went there every day to collect a loaf of bread for each person. They were little square loaves weighing about twelve ounces. They were just loaded into a lorry and carelessly covered. They collected so much sand and dust that at least an inch had to be removed all round from each loaf. The bread was very good but the sand caused a great deal of scouring in the men. There were plenty of biscuits; any person could get as much as he wanted. About twelve years ago I was in the office speaking to Dan Tate, when he mentioned that he had been to the Western Desert. I asked him what he did, and he said, 'I was out in 1940, making bread at El Daba,' and I was able to tell him about some of the men who had eaten his bread.

When we started serious road-making and construction work, we received 50 American trucks; these were 30cwt Chevrolets, and they were pure rubbish for the work they were expected to do, and for where they were working. They were fast for as long as they were operative, and that in most cases was a very short time. The carburettors failed to work, and there were other faults. One of the Ardrishaig lads drove one of them; he was a likeable pleasant chap who looked much older than his declared age. He was in the habit of crossing the railway line to collect rocks for road metal from that part of the desert. He was in the act of crossing one day when the boys with him shouted a warning that the train was coming, so he went as he thought far enough and then stopped. It was not far enough and the train knocked the tail end of the truck off. The whole part that took the cargo was removed. It was replaced and secured with rope, and it operated like that for the remainder of the time we had it. There weren't many of them left by the time of the advance but the one repaired with rope stayed with us until we obtained Italian lorries. On the advance ten trucks towed another ten, that was all that was left of the Chevs. Of course we still had eight Ford, British-made trucks – four-wheel drive, 30cwt – which were very good. The captured Italian diesel trucks were excellent and served us very well; some of them went to Greece with us.

Willie Garmory, who had worked in the Creetown quarry, was delighted with his Italian truck. He was one of the fifteen or so who managed to get out of Greece. He eventually joined Donald's company. He, Donald, and several others were sitting in a dugout or bivvy, when he suddenly said to Donald, 'You speak like a boy MacLean who used to be in my company in Greece.' That incident took place in Italy, and I was told about it in one of Donald's letters while I was in Austria.

The Italian bombers had a very distinct throbbing sound when overhead; many of the lads said that they had diesel engines that caused the throbbing, but I think that the cause was the fact that they were three engined. I did not notice the same sound from the German three-engined bombers, but they were mostly troop carriers and we did not see so many of them.

We had several thousand local labourers and artisans working for us, they were dismissed by 75% of the soldiers under the general name of 'Wogs', and greatly despised by them but I found some very fine people among them. Some were well-educated and many very intelligent. For example I met an artisan, a carpenter, who was a coptic Christian and I learned from him. There was also a youth who had very good English, and he taught me a little about Arabic writing and other local matters of which I had been ignorant. He was an excellent worker who did not require supervision to keep him working. One day when I was not there, I was on guard duty, he fell foul of Jimmy the sergeant. He had his stern kicked and was consigned to the guard tent for a spell. Jimmy was one of those people who either couldn't or wouldn't understand. I don't know what Jimmy was trying to do, but what he did was to turn a good friend of the British into a bitter enemy, and this kind of thing happened frequently. When I reported to the guard tent after my four hours off, my Egyptian friend was sitting in the corner looking rather the worse for wear.

In charge of the discipline of these workers was a Syrian in British Army uniform. He carried a whip about ten feet long, and used this frequently, with reason and without. It was a disgusting practice, and enough to make a Highlander throw up.

Building the underground headquarters took quite some time – the large rooms were nearer the surface but the telephone exchange – or command headquarters, was deeper – but everything was complete in time for the push. The OC had been a county engineer somewhere. He was an awkward looking character, about six feet tall and very thin. His legs were vertical, then he leaned out to the right, and his head came back to the vertical again. Altogether he was a very peculiar-looking character. He wore a very large German automatic on his left side, one of those with the wooden holster which could be used as a rifle butt. Rab Chisholm maintained that he needed the weight to straighten him up; 'But it's a kind of an awkward draw,' he said. One day there was some trouble with the workers, and our chief decided to use this fearsome weapon; he blew a few holes in the sand, and work restarted.

Months later when we were in a camp near Alexandria, waiting to go to Greece, there was a little boy who used to come round the tents selling chocolate and other goods from a large basket. He had a smattering of ten languages, and a good command of English. He displayed the Arabic script writing as well, and it was then I found that it bore some resemblance to shorthand. I found out that three squiggles spelled out 'Mahmoud Mohammed Hassan', which was his name.

The lad mentioned above was another who could not do enough for us; he would shop for us in the village and charge very little for carrying the goods to our tents. His main line was selling different kinds of chocolate. The last time we saw that boy was in the station at El Amrya as we were leaving to go to Greece. He had come to see us off. He still had his large basket hanging on his arm. The train had just started to move when a sergeant jumped off, knocked the boy over, stole as much as he could carry, jumped back on to the train, and another enemy of Britain was manufactured in a matter of seconds. That boy was ten years old and making his own way in life. In spite of those I have mentioned we did have some excellent sergeants.

All the time we were at Sidi Haneish there were refugees passing going from west to east, in family groups of differing sizes, all moving down in front of the Italians. They would gradually appear on the western horizon, slowly approach, and slowly move away to the east. There were small families and large families; some had more than others, but none had more than enough. They are reckoned by some to be materially the poorest people on Earth.

Sometime in November a half-section moved up the line to well beyond Mersa Matruh. Jock Wemyss, with whom I was friendly, was with them. Before the war he had been interested in motor bikes, and had been friendly with Jimmy Guthrie, who had been a world-class motor cyclist. Wemyss had come off his bike and damaged his head, but was apparently all right. When he was up between the two front lines, it appears that the stress of attacks and night-time problems began to take effect. He would waken in the middle of the night and repeatedly kick the tent pole with his bare feet. They had taken a tent with them, it is difficult to see why. He was sent back down the line, and many of his mates said that this was his way of working his passage (army jargon for obtaining a discharge by cheating). He was hospitalized in Cairo for some time and then sent to hospital in Cape Town where he died. Obviously, the damage to his skull was greater than had been thought and he had been walking around with a well-damaged skull for two years.

Mersa Matruh means Matruh Bay – the army called it Matruh Fortress – and it had a fortified perimeter.

One night the lads in our tent manaaged to get a truck to visit the canteen at Matruh. The whole place was completely blacked out, and it was almost completely ruined; the only intact building was the mosque, which was believed to have a charmed life. The Italians came over when we were there and we went outside. There was a cut off at the blackout so no light escaped. Just as we reached the outside a bomb burst a little way off. It landed on rock, and the flash could be seen going out almost horizontally. Fortunately nothing hit us, we were very fortunate indeed with that one. It was the first time I had a very close view of a bomb going off, and the darkness of the night made it even more dramatic. The truck driver refused to stay, and we had to leave the place in any case. We did manage to have a cup of coffee, and then went back to Sidi Haneish.

There were reckoned to be some Roman remains in the Matruh area, if so, I was unfortunate because I saw none. There were also stories of a Roman army which left Matruh, walked into the desert and was not seen again. Some of the Arabs had this story.

Once or twice I spoke to men of the Cameron Highlanders, and it was quite apparent that they were the sharp end of the 4th, Indian division. They had lost several men in the desert; but their biggest losses were in Abyssinia. One place where they lost a large number is still known as Cameron Ridge. There would have been two English Regiments with them to form an Infantry Brigade. Their names escape me at the moment.

Now a little story about the dump at Quasaba: we had a public school type sergeant who came from the Edinburgh or Haddington areas. He was quite a reasonable chap in many ways, except that he thought that he had a right to rule the world. Otherwise he was a fine lad. There was a little English lad who was always with him. We were at the dump one day and the two mentioned wandered away through the dump; about ten minutes later they came back at the gun point of a Bedouin. They had had a little altercation with the Bedouin and finished by telling him that his gun was rotten; however they were afraid to try it and were marched up to the RAOC officer. They were asked what was wrong, and said that they didn't know what the man was playing at. The Bedouin was then questioned in Arabic and he said, 'Wahid askari klifty, wahid sergeant klifty' – 'One soldier thief, one sergeant thief'. After some more Arabic, the officer said, 'You've been stealing something,' and they denied it. The Arab then showed the officer which pockets to search, and the goods were recovered. It was something of which we had plenty; there was no need whatever to steal. Later I came to the conclusion that they had been looking for chocolate emergency rations, and had settled for what they could find. Nothing much came of that affair. The sergeant was killed in the desert war a few years later.

There were about 6,000 of our troops in the Western Desert area when we arrived there. The numbers gradually built up until about the end of November, when the Australians arrived, then there were about 30,000 – The Army of the Nile – 'Wavell's 30,000'. The Italians had in Libya and Egypt over 250,000 (and they had about the same in East Africa) to face our 30,000 although we were being reinforced all the time. When we reached Sollum, a troopship was discharging a number of white skinned and white kneed soldiers, and a very smart looking lot they were as they marched ashore. I expect they had come through the Canal; at least they were unlikely to have risked coming through the Mediterranean.

About the beginning of December things began to hot up. The attacks of the monitors became a nightly occurrence, and often we could see our planes going over – Blenheims mostly. The Bombay went out to sea with an escort of ten Gladiators, and the Hurricanes were more frequently seen. I don't know how many there were, but they had enough.

The painters of our company received instructions to make signs for attaching to the fronts of the Matilda tanks, written in Arabic and Italian. 'Surrender and be saved.' Then on 8 December, Wavell issued an order of the day. Effectively, he said that we were superior to the enemy in everything except numbers, and that it was more dangerous to sit still and wait for him. He was going to 'have a go', but we had to be prepared for being knocked back and going the other way, and trying to hold them on the Canal. The next day we started off.

The sunsets at Mersa Matruh were beautiful; not quite so good as Oban, but very good indeed. We travelled through the town in daylight and had a very good look at it. We even stopped for a few minutes.

All the time in Egypt our letters home were sent in 'green envelopes', uncensored on condition that the sender signed on his honour that the envelope contained nothing detrimental to the war effort or to one's own unit. Just before the push it was said that there were not enough green envelopes and we were each issued with an envelope that would definitely be censored. Then I had the idea that at least I might be able to do something about the pill boxes, and some other items of lesser importance. So I decided to say some nasty things about some people in the company, enough to get me an interview with some one in authority, perhaps even a courtmartial. Unfortunately, the censors were our own officers and the letter was sent off unaltered, cheating me completely.

The next stop west from Matruh was a place called Gerawla. There was nothing there but one tree; there may have been houses or huts on the shore which was some distance from the road. The history of the advance is very well known, and one soldier sees only a small part of the action, so what I record is the war as I saw it. At that time the general strategy was unknown to me.

The next stop, for a few minutes only, was at Charing Cross. Here was a signpost pointing to the south-west saying Siwa. This was at the junction of what looked like footpaths; but were really camel tracks. They were only about two feet wide and they would disappear with sand blowing over them, and reappear further on. It was said that there was a tarmac road further in which went as far as the frontier. It did not matter very much, as by this time the Italians were in Sidi Barrani, and their own 'victory road to Suez' was in an advanced stage of construction. This road ran at that time from Libya to Barrani. The road to Barrani from Matruh had been well scarified by our troops, and ensured a very rough ride for anyone using it.

Another little scheme employed by the British when retreating in the desert was to salt the wells rather than poison them. They would then wait until natural processes had made them safe but not palatable. They had been thoroughly salted so almost everywhere we went we lived on very salt tea and had no worries about the effects of losing too much salt in sweat; in any case it was now winter and the climate was similar to summer in Great Britain.

By this time the frontal attack on Sidi Barrani had gone through; the Argylls, Queens, Leicesters, Camerons and others had lost their mates and were now much further ahead. The only troops at Barrani were a unit of very young Poles, young lads far from home, in a foreign army and uniform.

At that time there were a number of Lysanders to be seen. These were modern planes, high-winged monoplanes, roll winged. They could be flown very slowly without stalling. They had a fixed undercarriage with four machine-guns in the spats, and could carry some bombs under the wings. They had been designed as army co-operation aircraft, and made excellent 'spotters'.

At this time also I was given a little poem. The lad who let me made a copy said it had been given to him by a dying Argyll. Here it is:

The Argylls at Sidi Barrani.

They will always remember the tenth of December,
The morning broke cold and clear,
As the Highlanders rose from their deep repose,
To be shelled from the front, flanks and rear.

Like true Highland sons they advanced on the guns,
That were scattered around on the heights,
The shells from their flanks took toll from their ranks,
But the Highlanders' goal was in sight.

In every fixed line they left more behind,
Some of them well beyond aid,
And the Scotsmen saw red as their comrades fell dead,
It was then that the charge was made.

Each laddie knew well as they charged through Hell
The position, they had to obtain it.
With true Scottish pride, they took it in stride,
As they advanced with rifle and bayonet.

Now the Dagoes should know, for they were the foe,
With a Scotsman you canna 'ca canny',
For on that fateful day the Argylls held the sway,
When they captured the heights of Barrani.

We stopped at a place called Hagasan, where there was a water point, and this may well have been the place where the lonely tree was.

The next stop was at a place called Bug Bug, in a hollow of the coastal plain. There was a saltmarsh here, a fairly extensive one, with a shallow salt lake. In the marsh was a line of whippet tanks which had been bogged down and then caught by the Italian artillery. I think that there were nine tanks, burned out, the crews mostly wiped out.

The first night we were there we slept in the open but the next night we were organized, and had managed to find reasonably safe Italian dugouts, although some of the drivers had constructed their own by digging holes in the ground and placing the waterproof cover of their trucks over them. The Italian dugouts had all sorts of things in them, from booby traps to vermin and a selection of very dirty postcards. We were there for about a fortnight, keeping roads in passable condition, using crushers, rollers, and so on which the Italians had left behind.

The 'Victory road to Suez' mentioned above was being built in what I took to be the Roman method. Dressed cubes of stone, about one foot six inches every edge, were laid on levelled ground, the surfacing being apparently applied directly afterwards. The road was not completely finished but the major part, the dressed blocks, was all in place.

Above Sollum was the original Halfaya (Hellfire) Pass but it was not the easiest way to the top, the Italians having built a new road called the escarpment road. However, the 'Hellfire Pass' was reckoned to be safer, and both roads were under attack from the long-range gun in Bardia. This gun was known as 'Bardia Bill' and was not an exceedingly heavy weapon. It was fired at regular intervals of about two minutes, I think, but in any case those repairing the road could time it precisely, and it was reasonably accurate. They would hit the road in one pass or the other, and immediately our lads would move in, fill the hole, and move away before the next shell arrived.

There were many thousands of prisoners beginning to come down the road, about 40 or 50 thousand at that time. At the end of the push the figure of 180,000 was published.

There were very large groups of prisoners coming down the road in the charge of very few of our soldiers. There would be thousands in each group. They were in no condition to cause trouble; either they came in and had food and water, or they went into the desert and died.

'Fixed lines' mentioned in the poem above, were previously arranged fixed lines of fire for automatic weapons, enabling the defenders to lay down withering fire on any possible attack, even in the dark. It was perhaps more expensive in ammunition, but was very dangerous indeed to the attacking force.

At this time Peter McPherson was in the same dugout as me. I had completed my spell and was lazing in the dug-out when he came in for a short break. He then set out to lorry stones to the escarpment road. He arrived back in a very short time; I think his truck must have sprouted wings. I said, 'What's wrong?' He said, 'I'm not going back up there again. I was standing up there with a load of stones to put in the holes, when there was a bang and a quarry opened in the hill, so I took off.' He was back at work next day.

There was a company of Palestinians about half a mile away from us, but working in the same area. Some had been stationed in the Hellfire Pass area, and all the sergeants and their sycophants were based in the one tent. They had lined the tent with a wall of folded blankets from the Quartermaster's store, right up to the eaves. Bardia Bill dropped a shell right in the centre, and knocked out about a dozen of them. Almost the whole company took off down the road. They picked one up in a boat at Alex the next day, and others were found at various points on the way there. I was in our company headquarters, when their RSM entered and asked for a copy of 'King's Rules and Regulations', to see what he could legally do to them, and he was in a very bloodthirsty mood.

One day a walrus came over. This was not a large whiskered sea mammal but a type of amphibious aircraft that was carried on many of the large warships; it circled once or twice and then landed. We all ran towards it immediately, when four crew came out of it and waved us back. Apparently they had set it on fire. It burned very fiercely for a short time, then there was an explosion and we were able to approach and examine it. There had been two bombs under each wing; one pair had exploded and the others were still intact, and were still there when we left that place. The bullets exploding in the fierce fire travelled only a short distance, they were more like poor fireworks. The four officers in naval uniform looked very out of place wandering about the desert. They had come from the cruiser *Southampton*, which had been sunk after a fierce engagement with Stukas. The Stukas had been shot down in very large numbers.

Whilst I was working at a crusher one day, preparing material for filling holes, I dropped a stone on my left instep, and was in considerable pain for some time. It was about a year before it stopped hurting but it never slowed me up. I had assumed that I had chipped the bone but did nothing because our medics had more than enough to do wih real wounds.

The crusher was situated on a slightly elevated piece of ground to the south of the main road, and from there we could see the whole plain to the sea; it had obviously been a very large Italian base. The first day we were there the second-line troops were entering every dug-out checking everything. We could see them all moving slowly forward in groups of eight.

There was a very great deal of interesting material in these dug-outs and dumps. There were thousands of grenades lying about, but they weren't really very dangerous. No doubt, they could have killed but it would have been a very unfortunate man who was killed with one of these; they were blast grenades made of very thin metal. Many of the lads played about with these grenades; one lad would throw them at bottles some distance away, and while the grenades exploded the bottles did not break.

There was a great deal of different sorts of food. There was an abundance of tinned tuna, very tasty, very like salmon, but canned in olive oil. There were a few tins of sardines, and tins of canned meat — mutton, which was good enough but we preferred our own bully beef — and much more. There were some very large cheeses, rather like Cheddar, that were very well appreciated. Each cheese was about three feet high by about two feet in diameter; the skin was almost two inches thick, and we cut them up with saws. We found butter and bread and for a short time we dined very well on sandwiches made of white bread and butter, filled with slices of cheese almost half an inch thick, washed down with very good tea made with Italian mineral water.

Each Italian soldier carried a tiny glass with him, not much larger than a thimble, for the equivalent of our rum ration. This was a red wine, in huge barrels which could barely be carried on one of our lorries; they were about six feet diameter at the ends. Some of our lads got into a barrel with an axe and drank it like water. At least one soldier died, he was not in our company, but we had one man paralysed, and he was still paralysed in hospital four months later when we left for Greece. It was very powerful stuff and must have been at least 120 per cent proof. There were thousands of field dressings, coloured white; I don't know what they used as a germicide, but I found them quite good. I took a supply and used them for minor cuts and grazes. There was everything that an army might require, the quantity of gear was unbelievable.

There were very large heaps of rifles, about 30 feet high, and perhaps 100 feet through the middle. There were lovely little automatics, berettas, which we could take if we liked. They were for the use of the blackshirt divisions who were distributed among the ordinary soldiers, one to every two men to keep them from running away; that was a story current among our troops. It is said that many of these weapons ended up in the hands of criminals in Cairo.

There were peculiar little flat tanks, about six feet square and three feet high, entered from a hatch in the top, very fast like a Bren-gun carrier. They were fitted with a machine-gun firing forward, which had only a four degrees movement, which meant that the tank movement had to be used to sight the gun. I don't know what the little tanks were intended for but they did little good in the desert.

There are two points I had forgotten about our time in Sidi Haneish. We worked all the hours of daylight, we were up before dawn, had breakfast and left. We returned just before dark, had our meal, and went to our tents, talked for a while then went to sleep. The days dragged and the weeks flew past, there was no Saturday or Sunday: we did not know what day of the week it was, or what day of the month, unless someone came in with a newspaper.

A padre made the habit of going up and down the Western Desert road every day. He was a very tall man in an open Baby Austin, and had a side hat sitting on his head. He looked exactly like Noddy, and I think that he must have been the model for that character.

There were things happening all the time, and it seems to be the most unlikely things that I remember and pass on. One day we were heading back down the line in McPherson's lorry, when I noticed the Vickers Valencia coming along behind us. The lorry was travelling at its maximum speed at the time, 150km per hour. McPherson made the habit of keeping his foot down. We were at our destination, an hour down the road, and the thing still had not passed us. It was indeed a very slow aeroplane.

There were more prisoners inside the barbed wire every morning than were left there at night, not surprising.

I took a small Italian rifle, the best one that I could find, dismantled it and put it into my kit bag, and it was still there when I lost the bag in Greece.

There was a group of graves at the foot of Hellfire Pass, they had been there since July with a monument above them. There was an inscription which said simply 'Men of the Leicestershire Regiment'.

One night we were moving up in bright moonlight; this was a rather dangerous thing to do, the chances of an accident being fairly high. We saw a lorry coming towards us on the road and we drew in. I looked into it as it passed and to me it seemed to be full of kit bags. It was a big, long lorry. I mentioned the kitbags to Reg Tarling, a lad from Gloucester, who was standing beside me, and he said in a sepulchral voice, 'These were not kitbags, these were dead.' I don't know whether they were dead or not but the general opinion was that Tarling was right. I am not yet convinced as usually casualties in action were buried where they fell.

One unit had a greater than normal influence on the fighting at that time; this was the Cheshire machine gunners who were a very steady bunch of regular troops. They were distributed where they were required, and they really did make a difference.

About this time the 6th Australian Division, came up, went through, and set up round the perimeter of Bardia, preparing for the attack; with that we packed up and went up the escarpment road to Fort Capuzzo, which was on the Libyan plateau about two miles from the head of the escarpment road.

We set up camp in front of the fort, but found that the ground was too hard to dig in at the top of the rock, so the tents were erected at distances not less than half a mile from the next tent. The Company HQ tent was exactly at the centre. At night we were supposed to dig in but found that to do this would have taken all night. So instead we arranged our kit to give us individual sleeping places, where we were protected from everything except a direct hit.

Anywhere in that area I could draw a square with sides of a yard, and find within it at least two or three pieces of shrapnel. I did not examine the fort, it was a likely place for mines and booby traps. A few days after we set up here, a section was working as usual on the escarpment road filling in shell holes. They had a break at lunchtime and one of them wandered off, entered a minefield, and was blown up: he was twenty years old. A number of twenty year old lads had been sent out as reinforcements for units requiring them. Six of these were posted to our company, and the lad mentioned had been one of these. It has always been a matter of regret for me that while I can remember his name, I cannot remember his face; at least his mother would have rememberd his face. His body was found, with hands, feet, and face looking to the sky, utterly shattered. The whole company was at the funeral service. I don't know where he was buried at that time, but by now he will be at El Alamein.

Then one morning the Australians rose and stormed Bardia. The mornings were quite chilly and they were in battle dress, with greatcoats and leather jerkins. We had stopped wearing the KD shorts and shirts some time before. The leather jerkins were the first I had seen, and evidently the first the Italians had seen. The Aussies lost some men but not as many as they had expected, and most of those hit had been hit in the head or legs. It was discovered that many of the Italians thought that they were wearing armour. Bardia was cleared in a very short time and some 60,000 prisoners were taken. One dump of lorries contained 708 vehicles, that was the number of our company and easily remembered.

We were now some distance away from the dump at Bug Bug and were back on salt water tea, bully beef and biscuits. This diet kept us healthy but it was by no means palatable. The brass hats then decided to take water from the nearest place, which was 40 miles away, and for the remaining time there we were very happy with our rations

Around this time the Scottish residents of Cairo had a fund for the soldiers, which was known as the 'Come-and-get-it Fund'. One of the lads was asked while on leave in Cairo, how he had enjoyed the eggs. It transpired that a delivery had been made to the company and the officers had scoffed the lot. The Cairo folk were not at all pleased. At this time also it was discovered that the containers for the rum ration were empty. The Quartermaster's group were blamed but many refused to believe that all the officers were guiltless, and occasionally we would hear shouts of, 'Who stole the rum? Who stole the eggs?' When we were on leave in Cairo four or five of us visited St Andrew's Church and were made very welcome.

Near the middle of the camp a lovely little Italian tent had been erected. It had a domed top, and looked like a ladies' pavilion from the days of chivalry. This thing intrigued me, and although it was officer area and forbidden, when the coast was clear I took a peek, and there was a bath for the officers. It was discovered that they weren't happy about bathing in salt water and had large quantities of fresh water taken in by lorry for their ablutions. There was a war going on within earshot and I was very annoyed for a long time.

Here too I noted another very selfish action. The company postman was a man called George who had some pre-war connection to one of the officers. He appeared to be either too tired or too scared to walk between the tents. I happened to be in the office about some other item when I noticed some mail almost covered by sand lying round the edges of the tent. We seemed to be receiving very much less mail than usual. A quick kick around disclosed a great deal of mail; evidently he simply was not troubling to do his job. His excuse was that the mail had been for lads who had died or were in hospital and it was an obvious lie. The letters were still there when we struck camp and moved forward. How much was lost it is impossible to say.

While lying awake at night we could hear the Second Armoured Division as it moved forward and passed us about a mile away. It took two or three days to pass and there was very little of the road in good condition after it.

They met the Germans later and, out-gunned and under-armoured, many of them were destroyed. On two nights at least we had some heavy air action above us. There were Bofors guns on the edge of the escarpment to provide protection for Sollum harbour. There were also searchlights and Vickers machine-guns. We could hear planes coming in at night, and they were very persistent. I would lift the wall of the tent and watch the show. The searchlights would come on first, and pick up one or two planes. The Bofors would start and we could see the 'flaming onions' apparently floating up slowly towards the planes, which by now were diving down the beam with their machine-guns firing. The searchlights would switch off and the Vickers would start firing. The planes then apparently swooped upwards again and the whole cycle was repeated, again and again. After one particularly severe attack, at dawn the next day Willie Garmory took four Luftwaffe officers into custody. These were the only prisoners ever taken by the company. We knew then what we were up against; it was rather different to what we had been told. But at that time we still did not think that there were German troops in Africa.

The Australians had a very mixed population. There was a lad called Mendoza in the force attacking Bardia: he was called 'Spag,' short for spaghetti. His brother had gone to see his grandfather in Italy a year before the war and had not returned. During the attack on Bardia, Spag heard a shout from the Italian positions; this proved to be his brother shouting to him. The brother changed sides immediately and they fought side by side through that push, went to Greece together, and were captured together at Kalamata.

One night, when the working party returned to the tent, one of them was singing, 'Your tiny hand is frozen'. He carried on for some time, repeating what he knew of the song over and over again. He was known as 'Red' Callender, to distinguish him from other Callenders in the company. At last one of the others could stand it no longer and shouted, 'Shut up, he's just another mother's son.' Callander stopped and said, 'I'll take a glove out and put it on him tomorrow.' There were Italian dead all over the place, one never knew where they would turn up next. There was one particular deep sand drift at the side of the road, and after a sandstorm there would be a hand sticking out of it. After the next storm it would be covered again. The lad who complained about the discrepancy was Willie Garmory, mentioned above.

Sometimes a peculiar-looking Wellington would fly in from the desert and dip down over the escarpment above Sollum. It had a large ring about two feet wide and twenty feet diameter to the outside circumference, fitted to the nose, under the wings and to the fuselage. I could not understand what it was used for but much later I found out that it was for raising magnetic mines to the surface. It was quite an attractive looking plane. It appeared that the Jerries had been sowing mines at night, and diverting the opposition by attacking the defences of the escarpment.

There was quite adequate barbed fence and entanglement, running southwards along the frontier to Jarabub. There was a bit of a squiggle at the northern end, but for the greater part of its route it was on a straight line running exactly north and south, approximately 150 miles. It is likely that there were accompanying minefields. Jarabub was an oasis on the Italian side, and was the holy place of the Senussi. There was another oasis on the Egyptian side. This was Siwa, which was a very famous place; a great many of the dates sold in Egypt came from Siwa.

Since we had arrived in Sidi Haneish the company were being sent on leave in small groups. My turn came at Christmas 1940. We travelled down the line in McPherson's lorry from Capuzzo to the railhead at Matruh. Those I remember on the trip were Peter McPherson (Campbeltown), Ian Gillies (Islay), and Tom Pomphrey (Lochgilphead). These are all that I can remember at the moment; but there were at least nine or ten of us. We saw a very good sunset at Matruh, before boarding the train in the dark and going from there direct to Cairo. On the train we did not sleep very much – we had travelled overnight – but I remember going up and down the passage between the seats, and accidentally stepping on a chap who was sleeping in the passage; he was a wounded Indian artilleryman. We talked for the best part of the night, and I learned a great deal about Anglo-Indians, he could see trouble coming in India. He appeared to be a first-class chap, in spite of the fact that I don't think that I ever saw his face.

We may have stayed at Abassia Barracks, or at one of the smaller hotels; I do not really remember this fact clearly. We handed our rifles in to the armoury at Abassia, which was in the care of a Cameron Highlander, who was a very likeable gentleman indeed. In later years I often wondered if he survived the war, or if he had been killed in one of his battalion's many engagements. We had five days in Cairo spent in various ways. Most of my group wanted to spend most of their time in nightclubs, drinking and watching belly-dancers. One or two would have liked to spend all their time in the red-light district. One particular evening was spent with McPherson and Gillies in a nightclub. McPherson annoyed Gillies greatly because he spent most of his time rubbing the belly dancers' bellies with his fly switch, and he was rather more than half seas over. Gillies decided that we had to take him out before we were all removed. Before this, they had had a discussion regarding the whisky they were drinking. It came out of a bottle labelled 'White Horse'. Gillies said, 'That stuff never saw Islay; White Horse is twice as strong as that.' We manhandled McPherson out bodily, and then Gillies sat down on the pavement. It might not have been as strong as Islay's favourite drink, but it was too strong for the Islayman.

The next day I decided that I had had more than enough of this kind of performance and, right reason or not, I was going to see the pyramids and a few other places. Ian Gillies came with me and at the end of the day he came to me and thanked me for the best day he had in Egypt. We went to the cinema every night, and became very well acquainted with the Egyptian national anthem. The pictures themselves I don't remember very much about, although I remember a very young Ginger Rogers, and some of the more famous British actors.

We decided to go for a walk one day and again McPherson made a nuisance of himself. He started to talk with a crowd of natives – what he said I don't know, but he stirred them up very well – and they came after us, and things looked black for a time. There were three of us, weaponless and virtually lost. We backed slowly away keeping our faces to the mob. That part of Cairo had no planning whatever; the buildings were at all angles and distances. They looked as if they had been lifted in a giant aeroplane and dropped anywhere. We backed in between two buildings at an acute angle to each other. There was a slit at the end about a foot and a half to two feet wide which we went through, and we surprisingly came out into a large square. A man came out of a building, shouted at the mob, which quietened and dispersed. The man then invited us into the building which was a school. He gave us a great time showing us how he worked the school, and greatly improved my education, while we helped his pupils a little. He then took us into the building next door where a few men were making fire extinguishers by hand, and making a good job of them. Then we returned to our base.

The trams were single-storey vehicles, which were often connected, two or three together, like trains. The other method of transport was by means of a type of horse-drawn cab, which was known as a 'garry', the correct spelling of which I do not know. The cafés were excellent, clean and well nigh perfect; many of them were run by Greeks. My favourite meal was chicken, egg and chips. Helpings were ample, and were served with tea, white bread, and butter. The basic price in modern money was six pence. We never at any time paid more than ten pence for the complete meal with extras, but having said that I must point out that I was not a boozer.

Street traders were everywhere, and it was sometimes difficult to walk the pavements because of their importuning. Turkish-delight sellers were the most common. The boxes were about six inches by five inches, and they had all been opened and expertly resealed. About three-quarters of the contents were removed, and the remainder jammed into the box in an 'H' or a 'T' shape so that they did not rattle. After being cheated once I always accepted every box handed to me, gave it a vigorous shake and handed it back. This annoyed the traders intensely. Even a quarter-full, the sweets were at our prices quite good value, but I could not accept that they had been inside the box, and believed they were attempting to cheat me. Occasionally I found a box which had not been tampered with.

On the trip to the Pyramids, Tom Pomphrey and Alex Cormack were there when we arrived They climbed the outside while we went inside, but first we went round the Sphinx, which was still noseless as Napoleon had left it. The rock temple of the Pyramids had been excavated out of solid rock. It was cut out of the rock below the surrounding surface level, and was open to the sky. The white alabaster floor was damaged, and there is a little piece among my souvenirs. (With reference to the nose of the Sphinx I read in a book, when I was a child, that Napoleon had shot the nose off. Since then in another book, I read that Turkish artillery was responsible. Napoleon's general did fight a battle in the area.)

On the east side of the Great Pyramid was a large depression in the ground. It had been dug out in the shape of a boat, and the dragomen (guides) said that this was the boat of Osiris. In a TV programme it stated that a boat was obtained from there after the war. It was dismantled, but has been reassembled and is now in Cairo Museum. It is complete and quite a large ship.

We then entered the Pyramid (the great one) and I think that I remember both chambers, but I remember our exit better. The passage would be about two feet wide, and perhaps four feet high, so that we were crouching the whole way down, and slipping and sliding on our tacketty boots. I went first and was tired with the crouching, but managed very well. The only light was the opening away in the distance, and this I could see the whole way down. However, Gillies was not so lucky. I almost filled the passage and he travelled the whole way down in the dark. He was cursing and clattering and swearing the whole way down. He emerged glowering and said, 'It's nothing but a big heap of stones; Carmichael would put it through the crusher in a week.' That was quite a summing-up. He had bought a fly-swat just before we visited the Pyramids, with all the usual souvenirs, badges and all, and he had left them all in the passage. No one could persuade him to back for them.

The passage into the Pyramid was very steep; I would say at least 30 degrees.

There was a high-class and very pleasant Egyptian family about the Pyramids when we were there – a father, two teenage sons, and a teenage daughter. The daughter could have passed for a twin of Carine McCulloch.

If I remember anythng else of interest about Cairo I will note it later. Five days went past very quickly, and we went back to the barracks. The Cameron Highlander had cleaned and polished out rifles, they looked beautiful, and he gave us a lecture about how to look after them. He said, 'This company of yours is a disgrace to the British Army. Your rifles were not so bad, I could see through them, but that pair of twins from Fife had rifles I couldn't see through for sand and spiders.' He was evidently thoroughly disgusted with the company generally. I could have made a friend of that man, he was a great character.

McPherson persuaded me to accompany him to a race meeting, and he did enjoy himself, studying the form of the horses as they cantered past, laying bets and becoming very excited. I have mentioned this because that is the only horse-race meeting I have attended in my life.

To my surprise, Cairo had an excellent zoo, and we spent a very good day there. The animal which I remember was the polar bear, walking backwards and forwards the whole day, attempting to escape the heat. That was our last outing in Cairo. We moved west next day. Not much happened on the way back, we stopped at Zag-a-zig and as usual I went out to the platform at the end of the carriage. I was munching on an army biscuit and half a square inch fell to the ground. Immediately a group of children dived on it and started to fight over it. I knew then what it meant to be a poor child in Egypt. The next stop was Tanta, where again I was on the little platform, when I was approached by a lad in his twenties with the usual basket of edibles over his arm. We agreed a purchase for which I paid him and immediately he turned to jump off, but he was not quick enough. I held him with my left hand, grabbed a very good handful of goods with my right, then pushed him off with my left. The train was moving by this time and, when I checked, I had several times the value of what I had paid.

I had a good look at Alamein in the moonlight as we went through. All we knew of the place was that there was always a donkey standing in the station square. It was there as usual. We went back the way we had come and eventualy arrived at Capuzzo.

The company were preparing to move and we then moved up to Gambut. About this time I was in a dugout with two or three other lads, one of whom had a radio. Churchill was speaking. He said that he had decided to send 60,000 of his best troops to Greece, and that we had to honour our word to the Greek people. He did not know how things would turn out but one thing was certain, the Germans would not have the same superiority in aircraft that they had in France. He never spoke more truly; the air superiority in Greece was several times greater.

Gambut was called an oasis by the British troops; but it was not really an oasis. It was a place where surplus water was collected and stored in great rock cisterns, instead of flowing into the sea. A considerable amount of rain does fall on the desert; but the sand and rocks do not retain the moisture and most of it is in the sea in a few days. There was also an Italian roadhouse at this place. We stayed a few nights there and then moved on to the Tobruk perimeter, where we stayed for a longer period. The cisterns at Gambut were about twenty feet cubed. There was a flight of stone steps in each one in order that, as the water was gradually used up, it could still be easily reached.

We were in tents again at the Tobruk perimeter. There were units of the Australian Sixth Infantry Division round about us, and they had a canteen. Our lads patronized this canteen, which stocked a South African drink called 'Lion Lager', and a very fierce lion was shown on the bottle. I don't know what was in this brew but the lion bit them and 90 per cent were 'roaring fou'.

There was a boat beached on the shore about a mile away, and there were a number of gazelles about; we saw a pair almost every evening, perhaps it was the same pair each time. There were the usual wild dogs, flying beetles, ants and such like things. One evening John Primrose and I went for a short walk. We had a bit of trouble in crossing the steep-sided *wadi* beside the camp, and on the far side we found a hole about a foot diameter, with several wires entering it. We then found a larger hole we could have entered but decided against it. There was more than enough danger withot looking for more. We were just leaving that place when two planes came over fairly high up, and at the time I thought that they were British, mainly because we had never seen any other kind in the daytime. They fired two or three bursts as they passed over. Now I think that they must have been German. Something hit me on the stomach, I felt it clearly, it was quite a solid blow but we found nothing, and we decided that it was either a spent bullet or a scarab flying faster than normal. It had done no damage.

When we reached the tents the drinkers were returning. The tents could be entered from either end, but we found it better to keep one end open only. We had the landward side laced up. One of the Galloway lads was at home, very well oiled, and singing *Bonnie Gallowa*. Someone came to the back door and had a problem in trying to enter. The singer who had been disturbed was shouting 'keep out', probably thinking that it was a foreigner from the borders, and raising the tent mallet to 'crown' him. The intruding head suddenly popped in almost at ground level. It was one of the most amusing things I have seen in my life. He happened to be one of our tent mates and he was left with his head undamaged.

Not much else of interest happened there to us. The war was moving further away from us – the fighting was at Augilla by that time, which was 2–300 miles away, and the Italian prisoners were still coming down the road. To relieve his boredom Gordon McPherson shot one of the dogs. He was attempting to find out the greatest distance at which he could hit. The sergeant-major was horrified and Gordon nearly got himself a court martial.

We then started to move back; we set off in single trucks and were to meet in Mersa Matruh. I was in Johnny Primrose's truck and he was away ahead of the rest, he just kept going, and we were some hours in Matruh before the remainder turned up shouting and bawling, 'Where the h★★★ have you been?'

'We've been to Matruh as you ordered, Sir.' They had spent half the day looking for us over cliffs and everywhere except where we should have been, but they were very far from happy. However, we boarded the train and finished at Beni Yussif camp just outside Cairo. It was about two miles south of the Pyramids. We were in that camp only a few days, and were not allowed outside it, and eventually we left it at 2 a.m. in great secrecy, one morning.

Before we left there we were invited to apply for commissions. I didn't try but about half a dozen left for the course. I believe that they all obtained commissions, and about half of them were killed later in the desert.

We went then by the Egyptian railway system, by the usual route for the Western Desert, and detrained at El Amrya which was about twelve miles west of Alexandria. There was a mustering camp there, which was very well filled. The largest contingent was Australian.

While I was at Capuzzo I was permitted to make a copy of a poem composed and read out by a lad named Bisset. He has, I believe, added to it and polished it up a bit but the Capuzzo version is the only one I have heard. It is given below.

The Trail of 708

You've read of the trail of '98
But I've a more wonderful tale to relate
For I'll tell of the trail of 708,
General Construction Company.

The company was to be Borderers all,
But back on the Highlands they had to fall,
For volunteers to answer the call
For a General Construction Company.

They rounded up scores of council men
And some of the old sweats joined again,
From crowded city and lonely glen,
To this General Construction Company.

There were men who'd been beadles in country kirks,
Drapers and bakers and butchers and clerks,
Tradesmen and navvies from public works
In this General Construction Company.

They trained at Chatham and Margate too,
Drilled till the sweat poured from the broo,
And wondered what all this had to do
With a General Construction Company.

Then among aerodromes they were scattered
And, though with barbed wire torn and tattered,
They felt they were doing the work that mattered
For a General Construction Company.

But they all united at Aldershot
Where they dug and trenched the moors a lot
And mourned the hardness of their lot
In this General Construction Company.

Then marooned for a week at Liverpool
Waiting until the transport was full
They lost all their money in a housey school.
Poor General Construction Company.

So they drank and gambled the time away
Till the ship dropped anchor in Table Bay
Where two of the sergeants slipped away
From the General Construction Company.

Each day as they stood at their lifeboat station
The ship seemed to have a new destination
Which rumours enjoyed a great circulation
In this General Construction Company.

'Twas leave without pay in Colombo's fair city
But some officers on the boys took pity
And subbed some rupees from their private kitty
To the General Construction Company.

A week in a floating garbage tank,
Living in quarters dark and dank,
Proved very unpleasant for every rank
In the General Construction Company.

Then they cruised about in the Indian Ocean
And where they were bound they hadn't a notion,
But who kept the ship's galley in motion?
The General Construction Company.

They stopped for a day at Port Sudan
Where one of the saps was an also ran
And the OC gave him seven days in the can
In this General Construction Company.

The Company went for a rest to Fayid
Where a start on construction work was made
And the founds for a concrete bridge were laid
By the General Construction Company.

Then by the shores of the Mediterranean
They were digging in the passages subterranean
And scores went down in the hospital train again
From this General Construction Company.

From El Daba up to Mersa Matruh
The CRE found them work to do
With crushers compressors and mixers too
Oh! pity the General Construction Company.

Who saw the water convoy through,
Driving like demons across the 'blue'?
None but the gallant twenty-two
Of the General Construction Company.

To Bug Bug they travelled one cold night,
Frozen stiff in the pale moonlight.
In convoy a weird and wonderful sight,
The General Construction Company.

There one of the officers, fond of a prank
Encircled the camp in an Eyetie tank
Enjoying his fun in spite of his rank
In the General Construction Company.

Now the Bardia road they are tarring and patching,
A host of fresh rumours quickly hatching.
Where will the brass hats be despatching?
The General Construction Company.

Now that I've brought you up to date
There's really no more I can relate
Of the wondrous trail of 708
General Construction Company.

But

Here's a toast to 708
When free beer's going they're never late.
When half of the bunch went down with the sh★ts
The rest went hunting for Eyetie buits.

'Crown Copyright Reserved'

The Light of Courage

He grew and trained in the gathering storm,
Poland was in his heart and in his mind.
For twenty years his country had been free,
Then the panzers rolled and the jackboots marched.

Their families murdered in the open fields,
Their cities shattered in mass bombing raids,
Their helpless refugees shot down like dogs,
Four thousand officers in one great grave.

And still they fought – biplanes and horse soldiers -
Till they were swamped beneath unfeeling hordes
That flooded in from east and from the west.

But some escaped to carry on the fight,
Large groups and small they filtered through the trap.
Through Greece and Egypt; by France and Sweden;
Through Turkey and the Middle East they came,
To stand (in arms) by our sides – our first friends -
In those dark days when friends were few and far.

I saw them first in Egypt's western waste,
Some infantry in British uniforms;
Next, exiled slaves, with proud unbroken hearts,
And the quiet light of courage in their eyes;
In wartime Europe's fields and factories.
Then, at the close, a few sharp boys and girls;
Living remnants of that teenage army,
Betrayed and battered down in fire and blood;
Abandoned allies, erased in Warsaw.

What of the man who later was my friend?

Peter reached Morocco, joined the Legion,
And, when France fell, came to the RAF.
With us he served until the days of peace.

Then came the long, heartbreaking, fruitless search
For his young sister, taken from her home
Like a draught animal; disposable;

Because, 'The wheels must roll for victory.'
It may be that I met her – at Marburg,
One of the group at Murau, or perhaps
Little Marie at St George – that lonely,
Childlike, pregnant girl with the bright young face,

And the soft, sad eyes, underneath her snood;
Looking on a harsh, lovely hostile land;
As the young men from far-off homes marched past
In patched, and threadbare khaki uniforms.

With nothing else to give we smiled to her,
Perhaps we helped a little. Who can tell?

A cold, harsh world it was indeed. Much worse
It would have been, had not those mountaineers,
Kind-hearted people of the Styrian Alps,
Valued and kept their own humanity.

They say, 'Forget. It could not happen here,
People are kinder now; the lesson learned.'
But the hopeless shrug of youthful shoulders,
And the bold, hurt face of the tinker's child,
Bring cold cruelties flashing back to me;
Proud re-views of pain and hate and courage.
They build up bitterness for tomorrow.

Rebuilding Britain; business of life,
Marriage and family, were his whole world;
But as time passed, the veterans, the few
Who knew and understood how much he gave,
Grew less in number. Kindred minds were scarce,
And scarcer yet were understanding friends.

Then came retirement, a new kind of life,
And home to Warsaw. A few happy months,
Till his old illness struck him down again,
And stilled the mind which held far more than minds
Of fifty fearing, staid, self-centred men.

Who remembers now? Poland stirs once more.
The thunder mutters in the East; and now
In Warsaw, Peter's spirit lives again,
Though his body lies beside his parents.

CHAPTER SIX

The Greek Campaign

B EFORE THE COMPANY LEFT BENI YUSSIF, Peter McPherson was sent to have a new set of teeth fitted, and I did not see him again for ten years. His brother, Gordon, went with us to Greece and was captured along with us at Kalamata.

The toilets at El Amrya had been designed by someone who must have been a genius at hygiene. He had brought in a well-boring company, and had holes bored, at least fifty feet deep and a measured distance apart, about two feet apart in this instance. He then had a purpose-made box placed, open side down, over the holes. Circular holes were then cut in the top at correct centres, finished and fitted with hinged lids. The whole apparatus was enclosed in a canvas screen, and was a very neat job. Every now and then he had large cones fitted over the holes at specific times. The cones were made of fine gauze and fitted the holes exactly. Invited by the smell the flies arrived in their millions, crawled under the wooden box and flew up into the cone where the light was. As more and more flies entered those first in could no longer move and when the cone was full it was removed, held over a fire or stove and the flies knocked out. It was a very effective apparatus.

It was said that the Aussies would sit next to one another and lay bets on how long it would be before the sound of the deposit hitting rock bottom could be heard. Any person who served with the diggers would know that this is a very believable story.

We were in that place approximately two weeks. One night Hugh Carmichael from Tobermory said that he had met a lad from Oban in the canteen who would wait to see me there. I went down immediately and found no one, indeed I never found out who it was. The Australian transport was parked in a group, a rectangle. I counted 40 vehicles each way, 1,600 in all. They evidently did not anticipate air attack. Some weeks later one of the British Armoured Divisions parked in the same manner in north Greece, and the place was known to the troops thereafter as 'Death Valley' when the Luftwaffe had attacked. The place may have been Trikkala.

At El Amrya we did have time for some extra training and a game of cricket. There was a football match with the local lads who all played in bare feet. Some of these boys were excellent players.

Now for a little bit more about chocolate. Egyptian chocolate was very tasty, and was made in one of the Royal factories. The Palestinian chocolate was also very good, but it was much harder, apparently made for warmer climates.

El Amrya must have been on the western fringe of the delta; I saw no grass but there were a number of date palms, so water must have been available.

We left there by train, went straight to the docks at Alex, boarded the *Cameronia*, and were three days on it. Very little of note happened on the passage, the crew were very good, and there was a majority of Scotsmen in it. There was a large section of the French navy anchored in Alexandria. They were fine-looking ships, some of them being very large capital ships, the names of the individual ships I have forgotten, and unfortunately I had to destroy my notes at Kalamata. When these ships were closely studied it could be seen that they had all been temporarily disabled. Aeroplanes and flying boats sitting on the decks were without rudders, and it appeared that the ships lacked rudders and propellers

Only two troopships went to Greece at that time, the other being a Dutch ship called the *Pennland*, which was sunk by German bombers in the evacuation later. I can remember nothing of any escort we may have had.

A week or so before we sailed, an advance party went to Greece under the command of Captain Keir. They landed at a place called Volos which is to the north of Eubia. The trucks were landed at the same time, and the party was waiting for us at Athens when we arrived. Two days before we arrived, the Luftwaffe mounted a massive raid on the harbour at Piraeus. A munitions ship called the *Clan Fraser* was blown up, and the harbour was practically destroyed, at least for a time. Personally I think that Keir never got over that raid; he was in a bit of a state when the remainder of the company arrived

This may be a good time to revert to the desert war. You may remember that Wavell had said that his rather cheeky attack might not succeed, and that we might have to move eastwards, so I decided that it would be well to think out what actions to take should I be cut off from the main force. In that hypothetical case I had decided to go up the left bank of the Nile, and if I survived would hopefully eventually reach British controlled territory. There was very little information about the territory, and I had no map. At Bug Bug I found a very good map in an Italian dugout. It was a British map with overprints in Italian. I studied it carefully as an exercise to help me with my geography, and eventually lost it in Greece.

Now some more about Egyptians and the nomadic way of life. Drinking water was kept in unglazed jars known to us as chatties (I believe this word comes from India, and I don't know what the Arabic word is). This jar had a long narrow neck, when filled the water soaked through and the whole bottom surface became damp without actually leaking, this formed a classic evaporation refrigerator and kept the water very cool. When baking bread the oven was formed by means of cutting an excavation, preferably in soft rock, with a small opening which could be closed with a large stone. A fire was built in the cavern and left until it burned out. The ashes were removed and the unbaked bread inserted. The opening was then closed with a suitable stone. When opened some hours later the bread would be perfectly cooked.

We arrived off the coast of Greece on 13 April 1941. At that time we were not sure where we were but there was nowhere else more likely. There was a city with a temple on the hill, and a Kiwi beside was scanning it with binoculars. I asked him if he was able to count the number of columns on the front of it. He checked it once or twice and then said that there were eight. The Parthenon being the only surviving temple with eight columns on the face, I was able to tell him that it was Athens. It was some time before we went ashore. We were anchored for several hours in a great bay, and at several points along the shore were ships burning. I counted three ships still smoking, each of them about three miles distant. We were informed later that one of the ships had 200 Hurricanes on board; so much for Churchill's promise about air power. He did his best I suppose.

The delay in going ashore was caused, of course, by the massive damage to the harbour. A fleet of little boats, caiques, came out to ferry us ashore. It did not seem much of a way for an invading army to disembark, but that is how it was. I don't know how we managed to get the goods ashore. All we had with us was our own immediate equipment. From the port we went to a place called Hymettus. Our camp was in a valley beside an old Greek Orthodox church. The first day we were there I saw a squadron of Greek cavalry passing, silhouetted against the skyline; a very dramatic, anachronistic sight.

Here is another little story out of date order. When we left Fayid to go to the western desert we entrained at Ismalia. The train had started and was moving slowly along the platform, I was hanging out of the window and one of the boys from Dumfries was with me. There was a KOSB standing on the platform looking forward, and as went alongside him the lad beside me said, 'Hello, Shug.' 'Shug' started and made a dive for the train, but was by this time a little way behind us. He sprinted and tried to scramble into the train, and with great difficulty the two of us managed to pull him in. We had a long talk about life at home before he got off at the next station.

Now back to the war in Greece, and I will start with a yarn about one of the corporals. He was a man 40 or 50 years old, and I am not sure if he had served in the Great War. He was very fat and bloated, so much so that the quartermaster had had a difficult time kitting him out, especially with a greatcoat; and that described the coat exactly. His gut was so large that a standard coat reached nearly to his ankles, and he was known as the 'bell tent'. We were given an afternoon leave in Athens at a time when there happened to be an air raid in progress; there were Junkers 88s bombing all over the place We happened on a large crowd of people outside a cinema, with our corporal standing in the middle of the road trying to shoo them inside like a flock of sheep, when more than likely they had been sent out of the building for their own safety.

There was another anecdote about our friend. He had been on leave in Abassia Barracks in Cairo, shortly after a long spell on hard tack and salt-water tea. He had been to the cookhouse and had been given the first appetizing meal he had seen for a long time. He had filled his canteen in the approved manner – big one on top of the smaller one, and canvas cover on the big one to keep out flies – so he felt safe to cross the parade ground to his hut. He had reckoned without the red kites – they were generally known as sh-t hawks – and they were everywhere. He was almost at the hut when a kite swooped in over his shoulder and stole most of his food; the remainder spread over the ground. He was standing in the barrack square shouting, 'Come back, come back, you clifty b-d.'

There is very little else that I can remember about that corporal. I expect that he survived the war but I cannot be sure. I saw little else in Athens; there was no hope of visiting the Parthenon or any other building on the Acropolis. We had time only to walk back to camp, it being several miles back to Hymettus. It was beginning to get dark when we met some Greeks. Communication was very difficult: they were trying to find out where we were from, and kept saying what sounded like 'Inglisi' and I kept repeating 'Scottish'. Suddenly it dawned on one girl and she said, 'Scotia, Scotia,' and we were made very welcome, being invited into houses but we were unable to stay.

Now another anecdote out of its correct time and place. The Lion Lager was mentioned earlier, and it reminded me of a rather nasty little Englishman, who was well enough liked but was always looking for trouble, and was always 'agin the government'. He had done everything from CB to Field Punishment, and was always sneering at someone, usually the Borderers for the way they spoke. He came from Manchester so it was a case of the pot calling the kettle black. He was in a very intoxicated condition when he arrived back at his tent at the time of the great booze-up. The tents were pitched on rock, and angle irons had been used to secure the guy ropes instead of the usual stakes. He tripped on one of these and split his face on the next one. The boys in the tent, all Scots by the way, patched him up and put him in his bed, he being in a drunken stupor. In the middle of the night some of them heard him waking up and saying to himself, 'I've been in a bit of a mix-up, lost one or two teeth too. I wonder what I said to these Scots b-s, I better be quiet or I'll lose some more.'

When the port installations had been destroyed at the time of the *Clan Fraser* blowing up, the ship had among its cargo a consignment of new Turkish pound notes. These could be picked up anywhere, and I had one for a souvenir for many years, unfortunately it is now lost.

We left Athens to go north by train, and it was a very scenic journey indeed. In particular I remember entering a tunnel and emerging to glimpse a sunlit valley far below, then back into another tunnel, longer this time, then out again then slowly turning from north right round to the south, then stopping at Lamia station. We waited at this station for some time and I had a long talk with a Greek officer. He was despondent about the way the war was going, very pessimistic indeed. We thought that he could have been a bit more hopeful, but we found out that he knew more about it than we did.

We then noticed a few Greek soldiers moving back along the road. It did not occur to us at the time, but obviously they had run away.

When our transport arrived we went from the station down into the gut of Thermopylae, to a place where there was a hot spring. This was the kind of thing that gave the place its name, Thermopylae meaning hot springs. There was a stone wall about two feet high enclosing a hot steaming little pond, which was being fed by underground springs. It was full of hot sulphurous water, and behind this was a very large cave which the officers had commandeered, and in which they hid all the time that we were there. We were there about a fortnight. When we had arrived at Lamia we could see people out in the fields. We noticed a man crouching behind a bush, then another behind another bush; indeed, almost every bush had its man or its woman. Obviously there was an air raid in progress, although we could see no sign of it.

Some seventeen years ago I gave Nancy information for an essay; she made a very good job of it and it is factually accurate, so I can do no better than give it here. Here it is:

About 22 April 1941 a Scottish Company of Engineers was bivouacked on the Plain of Thermopylae. They looked out across the plain to the modern town of Lamia. In the middle distance was the river and the bowstring girder bridge with the charges already set. To the left was the vast mountain range where another invader had carried out a flanking movement 2,500 years before. To the right lay the sea, to the rear slept Leonidas and his 300 heroes. Each day they had travelled out to construct defences, some went to the high pass to the left where the roadway zig-zagged slowly and painfully to the top. Some prepared a reservoir which was to be blown up, some manned Lewis guns to help the Royal Artillery with their solitary Bofors gun, but the greatest number was digging a large tank trap at right angles to the river. This last group contained my friends and me.

The day started with an attack by the Luftwaffe and from then until sundown the attacks were almost continuous. A whistle would blow, often after the planes had arrived, and the khaki-clad fiigures would scatter into the growing crops on each side of the road. The whole attack was dominated by different kinds of noise: the comforting double reports of the Bofors gun which went Bang Bang – Bang Bang – Bang Bang; screamers on the Stukas and the bombs; short rattles of machine-gun fire from the Junkers 88s and the Dorniers; more definite cracks from the cannon shells, and in the background the steady chatter of our antiquated Lewis guns. I would count the falling bombs and try to tally this with the number of explosions; there always seemed to be one or two duds and the numbers never tallied. The whistle of the bomb would grow higher in pitch as it approached, and after it had passed its nearest point it gradually lowered in pitch. I could feel my eyes dilating as it approached and I tried to flatten myself closer to the ground. A locust was busy feeding within inches of my nose, and I studied it carefully while at the same time thinking of many disjointed events in my life: a summer's day in the Highlands of Scotland, the comrade I had left in Bombay, Italian prisoners in Africa, and refugees in the desert; and the note of the bomb still grew higher. It did not change, and I felt rather than heard the explosion. There was a sudden lack of noise, the whistle blew, and back we went to our tank trap. From the fields the character of Goering's darlings and their yellow-nosed machines was described in English, Greek, Maori, Broad Scots and even Gaelic. A dozen Stukas approached Lamia from over the hills to the north, formed a circle, and then peeled off successively into vertical dives. Columns of debris rose from the town until it appeared to be covered with clouds of dust and again there was a short spell of silence.

As daylight was beginning to fade the last of the refugees had reached us. One of our mates arrived in a small truck and took us aboard. As we started away three Messerschmidts came in low from the sea to the right. They shuddered as they opened fire and thin lines of tracer fire shot towards the group of refugees who had scattered into the fields. A toddler, not more than three years old, was hit and left screaming on the roadway, he lay on his stomach with his head back and his feet in the air like the rocker of a rocking horse. His mother appeared, lifted him up, shook her fist at the planes, and scuttled back into the field. Throughout the whole incident our truck, a legitimate target, was not molested.

Soon we were back at our HQ. There was a distant roar as the dam was shattered, and a sharper crack as the bridge settled into the river. By this time it was raining heavily and steadily. A pitiful fence had been erected between the cliff and the sea; two strands of barbed wire were strung between widely separated posts, sagging so much that it would be easy to step over them. I said to the captain, 'What is that meant to be, Sir?' and he said, 'That is the last line of defence in Greece.' Fortunately for my peace of mind I thought that he was joking.

The water now covered the road to a depth of about three inches, and the marshes on the coast were almost impassable. I stood on guard at the edge of the road with my rifle slung upside down to keep the rain out of it; water ran from my helmet over the gas cape and on to the ground. A figure appeared out of the gathering darkness; a girl about twenty years old, tall with long black hair, and barefoot. Her skirt was ripped diagonally from her left thigh to her right knee. She walked with her head high, through the rain towards the pass. She looked at me as I raised my hand in salute, saying 'good evening' in my best Greek. Half-clad, soaking, beaten, poverty stricken but unconquered and courageous, she seemed to typify her country as she strode southwards to pass the monument to the Spartan dead.

Very lights rose out of Lamia, signalling the arrival of the Germans. We were paraded in front of our OC and told, 'It is now every man for himself; get down that road as quickly as you can.'

It seemed that the Germans had forced the pass over the hill on our left. Some yards down the road a 25 ton tank pulled up and we scrambled onto it. For several hours we were carried southward until at last we met little groups of New Zealand Infantry, Maoris and whites, moving north on each side of the road. Shortly afterwards we reached Atlanti. The advance party said, 'This place is hotter than Hell.' We crawled under some bushes and went to sleep.

That is the end of the essay.

Now I will offer some additions and explanations. One of my friends was working on the high pass and at the time of this anecdote was digging a personal slit trench; each man was responsible for his own. It was almost complete when there was an attack. He crouched down in it and a bomb landed beside it. This closed the trench and blew him out of it. He was physically unhurt, at least he appeared to be, but he shook for about a month afterwards.

When the little boy was hit, the peculiar way he was lying was evidence that he was dying (this I found out later), and it would have done no good to go back to help. But at the time I said to the driver of the truck, who was the person in charge, 'Aren't we going back to try to help?' He said, 'You go back if you want to, but if you go you will go by yourself, and we won't be here when you get back. I'm getting to Hell out of here!' After hesitating I went with them, being disgusted with them and with myself. Had I gone I could have been charged with desertion, and those on the truck would not have told the truth. My conscience troubled me for a long time, but it may be that the driver saved my life.

On the second day in that area I met Johnny Primrose as I entered the Bivvy at dusk. He said to me, 'Keir's away.' I paid little attention, it made no difference to me but later it was quite clear that he had 'scarpered,' had taken a truck with him to Athens, and had attempted to get away from Greece. Those in charge at the port sent him back, and he took a load of rations with him when he returned. He was very fortunate; in another time and place he would have been shot. Perhaps there were so many trying it that they couldn't afford the bullets. The next time I saw him he told me that he had gone for rations. It was noticeable that he did not go near the other officers from then on. He did go down the road and search a bit while the others were in the cave, and found a spring of good drinking water. We had good tea from then on; until then the tea had been made from the hot spring.

Recently I found out that at least one man was shot for doing exactly what Keir had done; but then he was a 'squaddie'. I myself had been bathing in the hot spring on more than one occasion, I wasn't the only one who did that, and they made our tea out of it. After every bath there was a scum of salt water soap covering the spring. After that time it was noticeable that every time there was an attack Johnny Primrose would appear at my side as though I had some special protection. A day or so later I noticed Keir at the same caper, there was one on each side of me, and I did not object to the extra protection.

The British Army biscuits were of several kinds, some were very tasty like cream crackers. Others, for example the Co-operative make, were very hard indeed, and under two inches square. At the tanktrap I had been eating one of these before the planes attacked and I dropped it into the trap, which was beginning to fill with water. When we returned after the attack the biscuit had swollen to four inches square and a half inch thick, and that in a very short time.

Just before the Very light went up in Lamia I was standing fairly near the cave entrance when I met John McArthur and had a long talk with him. He said, 'What do you think of this?' and I said, 'I'm not very happy with it, but I'm OK.' He said, 'Well, nobody's very keen on it, but anyway I'll see you in Alex,' and I think that was the last thing he said to me. On the way out, near the crossroads to Yanina, I think it was, he came off his bike and broke his leg. He was on the King's yacht – the *Hellas* – when it was sunk by Stukas in Piraeus, I'll come to that later.

Early in our stay outside Lamia, an engineer corporal and eight sappers walked into the bivvy. We were lying under trees and bushes; there were no tents or anything else to give away our position. The corporal said that a good bit further north their officer had commandeered the truck and left them. From there they had to walk and were very fortunate to get as far as they did. They were attached to us until as far as Kalamata.

The 60-pounder artillery, which has a shell 5.9 inches diameter, was based on the high pass, and was firing right across the plain of Lamia to the hills on the far side, on the approaching Germans, With all the other noises we did not hear either the gun or the shell, indeed all my information about the gun came from company members working in the high pass. We could see the Bofors guns and Italian Breda gun, which was slightly smaller than the Bofors firing against the aircraft. A year or two later an artillery man, Alex Barlow from Glasgow, told me that the Breda was much better than the Bofors. The main weight of the defence was in the high pass.

With regard to the Italian Artillery, we found a gun in the desert with a bore about three inches, and wheels not more than a foot, in diameter. It must have been a pack battery. The Italian artillery was rated as very good by all who had contact with it.

The Junkers 88s reminded us of Blenheims. For about ten minutes after we arrived in Greece we mistook them for Blenheims; after that we dived into a ditch whenever we saw any planes. In appearance the Messerschmidts were rather like Hurricanes. They had a large number of Heinkels, which were large slowish planes with a large number of machine-guns; the machine-guns troubled us much more than the bombs. Their rear gunners got some of our boys. The Dornier (Flying Pencil) was a long, thin, deadly, beautiful plane. A very effective plane was their spotter. This was the ubiquitous Storch which was a high-winged monoplane, it could fly at a very slow speed.

The transport plane was the three-engined Junkers, 55. The Stuka-Junkers 87 was the dive bomber, the main attack bomber. It was a low-winged monoplane, with the distinctive cranked wing, single engine, and fixed undercarriage. In Greece it was armed with a large number of smallish anti-personnel bombs.

The different weapons all had distinctive sounds, sounds which are not easy to represent in words. Machine-guns of the bombers went prubt-prubt, our old Lewis guns went tut-tut-tut-tut-tut; every bullet could be counted separately. I believe the Bren had a faster rate of fire, but we did not have any of these.

After we had been asleep for about an hour and a half the dawn arrived and with it the Luftwaffe to waken us, and Johnny Primrose arrived with a 14 lb tin of carrots. For years after that I couldn't look a carrot in the eye. I was never keen on raw carrots but I took some to keep him happy, after all he had gone to the trouble of stealing them. He managed to finish a quarter of them.

The company was under bushes all around us, and the cookhouse was set up under a group of trees about a quarter of a mile away. The road was about half a mile away at the foot of a gentle slope. There were fighters up and down the road all the time; nearly all Messerschmidts, but definitely all short range machines. There were no bombers. The RASC lads had a terrible time, they couldn't leave the roadside.

We had the whole day under continuous attack, and did not make it to the cookhouse until dusk. We could hear a whistle at the road, then machine-guns would open up and the Messerschmidts would come in. I don't know if any lads were killed but for the amount of stuff they dropped and threw at us there were very few casualties. We went down to the road just after dusk, and the RASC brought up what transport they had. We filled the trucks 50 men to each, and there was not enough room for the whole company. Half of my section were left behind, this was the Argyll, Dumfries and Galloway section. There were fifteen men left there, and I remember particularly waving to Hugh Carmichael. By a twist of fate these men were the only members of the company to reach Egypt. They arrived at Argos a day later than we did and caught the vessels that were supposed to go to Kalamata that day.

We travelled down through the night, it was very dark with minimum lights on the lorries, until we came to a crossroads which I had thought was the road to Yanina. Now I think it was simply the road to the high pass. There was what looked like a river of light coming down the two roads; a few miles further on it looked like a huge letter 'Y'. It was about there that McArthur broke his leg. It was impossible to sleep at night. On the plain of Thermoplyae we were too wet and cold, and there were bull frogs shouting all night in the marsh, and many other noises of the night which I was unable to identify. After the armistice I worked out that I had no sleep for a fortnight, but it was a long time ago and the details are blurred. Certainly from Atlanti until the armistice I had no sleep at all. We were under continuous attack all day, and standing up in a bumpy lorry all night. When dawn arrived I would spend some time watching the faces of the men in the truck following. What struck me particularly was the tense look on the faces of the men, particularly the look-outs and the lads on the Bren guns. There was a Bren gun on each truck. I noted that I saw much more of the white of their eyes because they were looking upwards all the time, and scanning the skies with binoculars.

There was one attack in a little village, a place with many olive trees. As usual Keir arrived on one side, and Johnny Primrose on the other. We were in a little lane with dry stone walls, and were reasonably safe. We were there a short time and then it was up and away again. The next place I remember was a fairly extensive town. We stopped for a short time in a square. The town would be Thebes. A lady spoke to us for about five minutes; she had a few words of English. What she said was that she had two sons in Albania. She hoped that they were well and that we too would be all right. Everywhere we went the Greeks were very good to us. Their sign language was rather different to what we were used to. When waving goodbye they appeared to be beckoning to us, and they would shake their heads to signify 'yes'.

The next place south must have been the plain of Marathon, with the ground falling gently from the road to the sea. There were the usual groves of olive trees. The ground rose more steeply further from the sea. We had an attack and ran up the slope and into a grove of olive trees. I stood behind a tree which was only about four inches through, keeping the tree between me and the planes. After the main attack a Messerschmidt came in with guns blazing: one wheel only was down, and I could hear the whing-g-g whing-g-g of the cannon shells passing my head, and it troubled me not at all. One could take so much and then just laughed at it.

After a sort time we left there, not having received any casualties, and went to a Bivvy in wooded country outside Athens. The place was known as Daphne number one, we then went a short way further to Daphne number two, but at Daphne one was a large group of Aussies. Their cook was an excellent chap, who had kept working through all the attacks and had a huge boiler full of excellent stew ready for us. Everyone was so tense that very few people were able to take very much. The cook was understandably very much annoyed saying, 'It's damn good skilley and nobody is taking it.'

We were in and around Daphne for the rest of the day. The officer crew were noted making a large bonfire and being inquisitive. I went to have a look, and there, half burned, was my book which they had agreed to carry for me. This was *Mechanics for Engineers*, by Ewart S. Andrews, which I had purchased in Cape Town for about two weeks' pay, and had by that time worked three quarters through. I could have done with it later on. All the drawing boards, company gear, and company records were destroyed at the same time.

Some Greek women came to speak to us, hoping that we would reach our homes safely, when we were interrupted by a little rat of a man, who stripped off in front of them. I was never so ashamed of my company as I was at that time. Some of the things that had happened in Egypt were bad enough, but this treatment of friendly allies was disgusting.

However, we left there at dusk and moved out to the west and later on a long slow bend to the south. It was a black, dark night, and we kept moving until we came to a level crossing where we were stopped. It appeared that there was a very steep slope or a cliff falling away to the left, and only the railway between us and a steep cliff rising at the far edge of the line. There were large numbers of dead and dying horses and mules on the line. They were being cleared away to let us through. Archie Stewart, who was in one of the other wagons, said that he had seen some men as well but I saw only horses and mules, lying, kicking and moaning. These were the 'Remounts', a regiment that had been raised in Palestine to help the Greeks; there were lots of Greys, Hussars, Black Watch, any soldier who was available, but they preferred men from cavalry regiments. They had served in Greece and Albania, but I don't think that many of them got away from Megara.

We went south from there and over the bridge into the Pelloponese: daylight was breaking by the time we crossed the bridge. I don't remember seeing Corinth at that time because it is at the far end of the Isthmus. A very short time after crossing we were attacked again, and again Keir and Johnny Primrose arrived as if by magic, although they had been on different trucks. We ran up a hill this time – we were short of cover on the rocky hillside – and this time the bombs caused more than usual apprehension. They were exploding on the surface, with shrapnel and pieces of rock flying for very long distances.

When that attack was over we went south through a beautiful valley with a fortress on a hill at the end. This was Argos, where we turned in left to Naplion, and bivouacked under the hill fortress of Tiryns. On a plain before we turned left were about twenty Hurricanes, and we thought, 'We are all right now.' There were also about sixteen or twenty Bofors guns; we thought, 'We are quite safe now.' It turned out that the Hurricanes had no engines; it had been possible to land the planes but not the engines. There was no air cover whatever; we saw nothing in the air over Greece except German planes, and the odd Sunderland patrolling the shore.

Now, thinking back to the exit from Thermoplyae, a young lad about twenty or twenty-one had been on the high pass. During or after an attack he had run away and thrown his rifle away to make running easier. Just as we were leaving the Plain of Thermopylae, after the 'every man for himself' order the CSM gave him another rifle. Three or four yards down the road he threw that away as well. He finished up at Kalamata. I saw him once after the armistice, and he was wearing a Highland Balmoral.

There was a sergeant, a good one, and we thought the world of him. He had just missed the fighting in the First World War, and had been in the army of occupation in Turkey; he was good, he was pleasant, and a first-class drill sergeant. He too was in the high pass; if the lorry he was in was attacked he would jump out and run for miles. It mattered not if the lorry was doing ten or sixty miles per hour, he would exit no matter what. He would then hare away over the countryside giving other people problems in getting him back.

We bivvied among the olive groves. The Argolid plain and the port of Nauplia were close to us on the south-west. Argos was to the west and Tiryns to the north-west. Tiryns was closest, and was in fact so situated that it was difficult for us to see. We arrived early in the forenoon, and dropped down in any hole or corner we could find. At this place a couple of lads came in who hadn't turned up when we left Athens; I think that they had been looking for female company. They reported that they had been on the King of Greece's yacht, the *Hellas*, when it had been sunk at Piraeus, and that two of the company had been killed. The dead were McArthur and Russell, the lad I met in the barrack room on my first day in the army.

The *Hellas* had been a very fast, timber-built yacht. It had been carrying a number of wounded, and some other soldiers. 580 AT Company lost approximately 50 per cent of their strength. When this company was boarding the vessel, there was an attractive young Jewish girl cracking jokes with them, and the men were delighted to have some pleasant fellow travellers. Minutes later their survivors were marching off down the same gangway, and the girl was lying on the deck with both legs blown off screaming her life away. The story about the girl I heard several times from a lad called Hibbert. The number of men lost in the company I heard when the officers called the roll at Corinth; but it did include men who were in hospital and who had temporarily disappeared. I spoke to a survivor recently and he reckoned that the final tally of dead in their company woud be about 60; perhaps 30 per cent of their strength at the time.

We heard about McArthur just as Jerry was arriving for his usual attacks and this time there was a deafening amount of anti-aircraft fire. I thought that it was naval pom-poms, until I remembered the Bofors guns. But Jerry pressed home his attacks and we were bombarded with everything from machine-guns to bombs and leaflets. I never succeeded in obtaining one of these leaflets. We had the same treatment that we had on the plain of Thermoplyae. One bomb came down and the note did not get lower until we heard a rush of air and a lad a few yards from me was killed. He was a First World War veteran from Inverness, by name Duncan McPherson. He had been trained as a Vickers machine-gunner, and had served in France. He died instantly and that was the only good thing about the whole affair. We had attacks all the hours of daylight. The planes came in again at dusk, and hit a ship in the harbour. It turned out that the ship was the *Ulster*

Prince, a relatively new ship that used to visit Oban every ten days or thereabouts, and was the vessel we should have boarded.

So we did not sail from that port and as we moved out the whole sky was lit up by the burning *Ulster Prince*; there were flames several hundred feet high coming out of it. It must have been full of fuel. It lit up the whole area and must have helped the drivers. All our own transport had been destroyed during the day. One sergeant drained all the oil and water from the engine of his truck, started the engine then weighed down the accelerator and went away for an hour and the thing was still roaring away when he returned, then he took his rifle and emptied the magazine into it, and still the engine ran. I was not there to see how he finally disposed of it. Then as we were moving out to go further south a Sunderland arrived and took off again with the brass hats and nurses aboard – at least I hope the nurses were evacuated; certainly the generals looked after their own safety.

McPherson was a very likeable chap, and I don't think he had really settled down after the First World War. Many First World War veterans fell in the Second World War. My dead friend had been a very good and steady comrade. During many of these attacks we were among trees, and after the bombing and machine-gunning had finished one could always see a few leaves drifting down to earth.

After the war, Tommy Ross from Stirling came to see me. He was one of the lads who had been left at Atlanti, and he told me that he had sailed from Nauplia the night after we had left. There was a transport available but it could not take all the waiting men. He said it was like something out of the pictures. They were paraded and marched slowly forward, and at one point a hand descended between his file and the one behind him, and a voice said, 'This lot on the boat, the rest need to go further south.' They went straight to Alex.

Another little story came from the same time and place. A company of Service Corps were in the area, and a small detachment were sleeping peacefully in some sort of building when their officer came running in and shouted, 'They're here, they're here, I don't know where they are but they're here. Follow me, men.' He then turned and ran out with the men following, pulling on equipment as they ran – straight into a full company of German Infantry. They were all captured, two days before us.

We saw a fair bit of Arcadia on the way south. I remember it as a beautiful highland country, with very distinctive red soil; with high, tiny fields and fruit trees.

The sailors from the *Ulster Prince* were with us as far as Wolfsberg, perhaps as far as Zeltweg, then they were sent to Marlag. While I remember, we were at Nauplia on 25 April; the Aussies and Kiwis were celebrating Anzac Day. There was a fine Australian lad with me for a number of years, called Lionel Bigmore, from Victoria somewhere. He had a very bad back indeed. He would be fine for two or three months, and then he would collapse in agony. His spine had been damaged when he was in the Nauplia area, when the Germans had cut off the peninsula. They were being more or less hammered into the ground but they had quite a few German prisoners. On one occasion, when the Stukas came in to attack, he was shepherding the prisoners to a place of safety; he had them all in slit trenches, and was turning to go into his own trench when he tripped and fell backwards into it, and that was how he damaged his spine. The Germans had him X-rayed and disclosed a gap in his spine. Len, as he was called, was not with us when the war ended, and I don't remember when we parted company. His party story was about events at the time he was captured. When it was obvious that there was no hope and no way out, his officer surrendered his small force but one man said, 'I'm not having this, I'm getting out.' He took all his clothes off, left them in a heap, and began to swim. The nearest land was well out past the horizon, perhaps Turkey. The last they saw of that lad was his head far away on the horizon. His mates watched until it disappeared.

We travelled southwards through the night, it was very dark so there were no attacks, and at daybreak we came on one of these mountain barriers that are to be found in different parts of Greece, with the road zigzagging to the top. We had passed through a plain with orchards and all kinds of trees in it, before we began to climb. It took quite a long time to reach the top; all the turning back and forth, and sharp turns in a steep road, made for a slow journey. From the top the view was magnificent, like that from an aeroplane, a panoramic view of a whole countryside bathed in sunlight, it looked lovely.

I had been hoping to see Sparta but was not sure exactly where it was, and I now think that we must have passed through it in the dark. We crossed the highest point and rolled down to a point some distance outside Kalamata, and bivouacked for the night. We were on standby for boarding a troopship. During the night there were sounds of sirens and much coming and going in the harbour, then we were told to go to sleep, we were not needed that day. The next day we began to move down to Kalamata along a gentle slope about twelve miles from the pass, until we reached to within two miles from the town. The attacks had started again; we could hear bombs falling on the town, and some more were falling near us. There was a large ditch about six feet deep beside us. All the trucks were tipped into the ditch, and we began to walk.

There was an officer stationed at the edge of the town guiding the individual soldiers as they arrived – for example, 708 go that way, 580 this way – and we were directed to an orchard with fruit trees like those we had sampled in Ceylon. By this time it was dusk, and the Greek farmer came out of his house to greet us. He spoke to me and invited me to eat any of the fruit I liked. He laid his hat down and was showing some of us which were the best fruits, as I stepped back out of his way, I stepped on the crown of his hat. I was very apologetic, but he would not have it; he knocked the bump out of the hat, filled it with his fruit and handed it to me.

Before reaching that orchard we had been ordered to go through the town in ones and twos. I was a one, and had an awful feeling that I was sitting up in the air and looking at myself, bombs exploding all over the place, my head full of Gaelic songs, old psalm tunes, and all sorts of things; but very well aware of everything that was going on.

None of the bombs dropped very close to me at that time but I noticed that in the town there had been one or two big ones. There was a crater at a crossroads that had ripped up the road the whole way from edge to edge; this in contrast to the anti-personnel bomb craters which were only about six feet across. Bombing started again when we were in the town and I nipped into a cellar; an old lady who was sitting there screamed and ran out. She was sitting at the end of a large barrel, a large one like those I had seen in the desert, about six feet diameter at the end. I sat there until the raid was over. I then went out and went to the dispersal area.

Reverting now to the sergeant who destroyed his own truck at Argos: as well as the methods already described, he removed the rotor arms, and other essential pieces, attacked the engine with a sledge hammer, and attempted to slash the tyres. British Army tyres are very difficult to disable.

Kalamata Hill looks rather like the rock of Gibraltar. We were sent up there to hide during the day, and I went with a lieutenant, the one who had spoken about Bunty McNeil in the desert. He was a likeable, intelligent character and, as you will see, was quite good at looking after himself; but, as far as I am aware, he did not do this at the expense of others.

We were ordered to be back down in the dispersal area by half past seven, and we spent all day in a rocky glen high up on the hill. I was under a rock and looking at soldiers coming down a cliff at the far side. They were dropping over, coming down a little, and hiding among the rocks. They looked very like Yugoslavs, and that is what I thought they were. None of them seemed to be carrying any arms, but some of the lads with me were absolutely sure that they were Germans. Their uniforms did have some resemblance to German parachutists' uniforms which I saw at Corinth later.

So I did not know what they were, but they did not disturb me; in any case, it is unlikely that they could see me. It was beginning to get dark and we were still waiting for the officer to come and collect us, so eventually I went up to him and asked him the time; I didn't have a watch that worked. He told me that it was half past seven. I said, 'I thought that we were supposed to be down there by half past seven.'

He said, 'Yes.'

'Aren't you going down?'

'No, I think I'll wait a wee while.'

'OK, I'm away.' So I went away and I met one of the lads from the Company. There were seven Scotts in the Company; JO Scott was the one I met, and we started down the road together. We were on a country road about seven feet wide running along one of the higher contours. We were passing a little cottage, and at the same time a shell came up from the town and exploded a short distance away. It did not worry us very much, but a Yugoslav officer burst out through the door, shouting 'Germano, Germano'. He was carrying a baby in his arms, had a lady hanging on to his coat tails, and he started to run round in little circles in the road, shouting all the time. This gave me such a surprise that I jumped into a ditch on top of a prickly pear: this makes a very uncomfortable seat so I was out of it and away almost immediately. I never saw that officer again. From the amount of insignia on his shoulders he must have been a brass hat. I find it difficult to imagine a more horrible predicament – a wife and baby to look after in the middle of a battle.

We moved quickly down into the muster area and found the greater part of our company. Explosions were more frequent and there was a great deal of automatic small-arms fire. It was a very dark night, made worse by our cover of trees. We were paraded and ordered to fix bay-onets. The darkness was such that the bayonet could not be seen if held edge-on against the sky; it was just visible if held side-on. A machine-gun opened up fairly close to us, and masses of tracer bullets came through the trees. Every one seemed to be coming straight at me. They swung away, left or right, up or down as they got really close. It continued for what seemed a very long time, but it must have been only a few minutes. The bullets sounded like birds chirping. We were drawn up in review order, the whole company in a single, long, thin line, under command of Second Lieutenant Waddell. Since then I have often thought, 'What were the other five officers doing?' Then down to our right a huge uproar broke out; the noise was deafening; there was shouting, continuous explosions, automatic fire, screaming and squealing, all at the same time. Above it all was one particularly horrible high-pitched, long drawn out squeal, which is still with me. After some twenty minutes of action everything became quiet.

Our thin khaki line advanced with the officer approximately at the centre but a few yards in front. As we reached a side road at right angles to the shore there was a great hubbub; there was shouting and running feet and scrambling noises. There was a disorderly mob coming down the road shouting, 'This is the Australian 6th Division: make way, we're coming through, we've done our job,' and much more in the same vein. So we let the rabble go running down to the shore, and we crossed the road and carried on with our job. The lieutenant reached a wall, jumped over it and landed straight down a well which happened to be on the other side. Those nearest pulled him out and he was not badly hurt. It was like a comic opera. The lieutenant would pause and decide to change direction: he would whisper, 'We'll go this way, turn to the right, pass the word along,' and a whisper, which could be heard 100 yards away, would travel up and down the line; as they turned they would bump into each other. It is a miracle that no one got stuck with a rogue bayonet.

Eventually we came out on the main road at the seaside, and turned down onto the shore; this would be about half past twelve at night. The ships should have been there long before that. Up on the hill there were people sniping and lights signalling. Our side started to reply with machine-guns and shot out all the lights. This quietened them and we could see boats signalling out in the bay and eventually they came in to the beach. They would not go near the harbour. I thought that they were destroyers, and the latest information I have been given gives weight to this; certainly the *Gloucester* had not been there as I had been told.

It was a very steeply sloping beach, and a destroyer came in almost to the shore. They put down a boat, rowed in, took a load of men aboard, rowed back to the destroyer, while we marched down. I was standing with my feet in the water. I saw the boat reach the destroyer, saw the men go aboard, saw the boat hauled aboard, and the destroyer turned around and glided away. The other five ships did likewise. The our OC called us back up on the beach and said, 'The Brigadier has asked for an armistice at six o'clock tomorrow morning. The navy has gone and will not be back; this means that you are now prisoners of war.' That was the last of some notable speeches we had from our commander.

Then I moved back to near the place where the lieutenant fell down the well. I disabled the rifle and threw bits of it down the well. The bayonet caused a problem: I was unable to break it, but I did manage to bend the top three inches, at right angles to the rest of the blade. The bolt was too difficult to break, as we were meant to do but I did remove the top, and bent the firing pin right back, so it was useless. I threw each cartridge in a different direction, and then sat down to take stock of the position. There were all sorts of stories about the general débâcle, some of which I can remember. There was one in particular about the commander of another company of RE. His men had no time for him because of his actions during the whole retreat. He used to hide his insignia when planes were attacking; he would fall to the ground with his hands on his shoulders. It seems he thought the Messerschmidts coming through at 300 or 400 miles per hour would notice that he was a lieutenant-colonel and come back to shoot him. At his part of the beach the boat had been loaded with wounded men. He approached a lad at the stern and said, 'If you don't mind, I would like to go on this particular boat; you can take the next one.' The lad had no choice, he agreed and became a prisoner of war. When the officer reached Egypt, for his initiative in escaping from Kalamata, was promoted to CRE. That was the story as his men told it to me, I did not see it myself. Our part of the beach was quiet; you could have heard a pin drop; the discipline was first class.

Later, when we were in Austria, the senior NCO in the charge of the first working camp was the CPO from the *Gloucester*. He had several ratings with him one of whom was a redbearded chap who claimed to have served at Jutland, and who also claimed to have been at the evacuation at Kalamata. I asked him, 'Why did you leave 10,000 men on the beach, when the ships could have taken another 8,000? Did the Navy lads not object?'

'Oh, there was panic on the beach.'

'No, there was panic in the Navy,' and that was my view for many years. It is possible that the 'Jutland' rating had been on one of the vessels sunk, and had then transferred to the *Gloucester*. In recent years I had time to think more about it and thought of the mob of Australians, and that there may have been panic at a part of the beach of which I knew nothing. Owen Davies said that at Crete the Australians rushed the boats. Several books have been written with information which tends to show that the army commander on the spot and the local commander of the evacuation naval vessels should share the blame. There was an imaginary Italian Naval Force expected, among other tales.

Peculiar things happened in the morning. There was Yugoslav money all over the beach, and many Yugoslavs were captured along with us. I remember these men at Corinth but not later. It was said that the Yugoslav army treasure chest was opened on the beach and the money left to blow away. I saw the money, I know nothing of the chest. One of the Jewish lads was sitting beside the road in tears, and when asked what the trouble was he said, 'You don't know, but they'll take us all up into the hills and shoot us. I'm a Jew, I know.' There was a Jewish unit with us, and we had met them on the way up to Lamia. We found them to be intelligent, likeable lads. We said, 'They're civilized people,' but he obviously knew more than we did.

Many people were short of clothing and one lad in particular was hunting for a pair of boots. He found one then nosed around for the other. He found it and was about to put his foot in when he noticed that there was already a foot in it. Numbers of casualties are notoriously difficult to estimate, especially in battle conditions, and frequently final estimates are lower than the first estimate. The figures we were given were that the enemy had lost about 200 dead and we had lost about 40 dead. The British used one tracer to every four bullets in their machine-guns; perhaps the Germans used the same proportion, but in any case there was much more danger flying about than could be seen.

The next day we watched the Germans burying their dead. They dug a large square hole with a bulldozer, about 4 feet deep and perhaps 25 yards along the sides, into which the dead were unceremoniously dumped. The bodies had stiffened in all sorts of weird shapes and positions. I don't know where our dead were buried at that time but I think that they were collected after the war and reburied in the military cemetery in Athens.

The Germans had captured the port in the afternoon and our attack was to clear it out, and it was very well cleared. Some of the Greeks said the Jerries were still running well outside the town after the attack, and it was a long time before they stopped. I had kept a very full diary of my time in the army up until then and I tore it into little pieces at Kalamata. Later, in Austria, when we were more settled, I noted the names of all the places I had visited. I still have that note and that has been used as the basis for this book. I have recorded everything of interest, from each place, that I am able to recall. I was much impressed by the poverty of the people in South Greece: many of the fields, particularly in the hills, were very small, little larger than the average living-room. They could be tilled by hand only. The people were first class.

The official excuse, given to us at Kalamata for the naval scuttle, was that the ships required three hours of darkness to clear the coast, and to be reasonably safe from bombers, and that safety of the ships was more important than safety of the men. No doubt there was an element of truth in that view.

There was a tall dark Fijian called Tom with the Maori battalion. He had a more than average effect on the Jerries who would run for miles when they saw him. Some of the service corps lads who were in the same sector told me about him. They went down with the bayonet along with the rest of them but he was always in front. Speaking to some of the Jerries later, these lads were asked, 'What were you doing with the great big nigger?'

I walked along to the eastern end of the beach just before daylight. At dawn, while waiting for Jerry to arrive, I met a service corps lad coming down with his rifle and bayonet, rubbing the sleep out of his eyes. I don't know where he had been but he said to me, 'What are we doing now?'

I said, 'There's nothing we can do, the whole force has surrendered. There's been an armistice.'

'Are we not going to have a go at him?'

I glanced at his rifle, and it was jammed; he could not even get the bolt out. I was in a hurry to get back to my mates at the time. Thinking about it later it was obvious that the rifle was at the half cock. We threw the bayonet into the sea, took the magazine off and sent it after the bayonet, broke the rifle and that went the same way.

There was a great deal of bitterness and resentment, particularly amongst lads who had lost good friends in the counter-attack which had cleared the beach and the town: it seemed that their lives had been thrown away for nothing. The Germans were very surprised at the large number of men they had taken. They were particularly surprised, knowing that the ships could easily have taken 1,500 men each. We knew that they had gone away with only 1,500 in all. I heard of one or two suicides, and various other bizarre affairs. One of the lads was next to me at Corinth when we were incarcerated there. He lay down on the concrete floor, pulled his coat over his head and just lay there. About three days later he was carted away to the camp hospital, and I heard no more of him. He may have been what we called 'bomb happy', or suffering from what was known as shell-shock.

About an hour after the announcement of the armistice, Archie Stewart came up to me, and said he thought of trying along the shore to the south to see if he could find a small boat to take off in. What he needed was someone to navigate. This I could have done had I known where we were, where we were going, and had a map; but we really had nothing. In fact, Archie himself had told me when we left Nauplion that we were going as far south as it was possible to go. All I wanted to do was sleep, so I was against the idea, and no one went. In addition anything that could float had been well shot up.

There was an eerie silence after the armistice, it felt as if all sound had been switched off. The mind was clear; one could think of anything and everything; the brain seemed to be working overtime. At daylight Jerry arrived and treated us with respect, I saw no abuse of any kind. We were marched through the town to a field at the far end. As we were passing a shop I nipped in and bought half a dozen eggs (I had not eaten for a long time). As we marched I cracked the shells one after another, and swallowed the contents, and that was all I had for three days after.

We were in this rather large field for some time: it was ringed with machine-guns and there was a large 6″ bore cannon pointing over it at one end. It is difficult to see the purpose of the gun, maybe it was psychological warfare. It was at the lower end of this field that the communal grave of the German dead was situated; of the ceremony we had a grandstand view, as we lay about in the field and managed to snatch a little sleep. Lack of sleep had a devastating effect on me, and I expect my mates felt much the same. In addition we had not had the opportunity to feed very well since we left the bivouac outside Lamia.

We marched down into the town and along to the station. The railway was a very narrow-gauge one, popularly known as the toy railway. There an officer stood up in front of us and shouted, 'All dis tousand man must get on dis train. Here ve haf no bret, in Tripolis ve haf bret in plenty. Any man who leafs de train vill pe geshott.' Never mind, his English was better than my German. Before that, at the end of the line, a child had handed some food to one of us, and some one took a shot in her direction. It was a child of school age; it may have been a warning shot, the child was not hurt. If I remember anything else from a very full two or three days, I will bring it in later.

The train left the station and began the climb over the mountain barrier. It took a slightly different route to the road. We were halfway up this very steep incline when the train stopped. The reason given to us later was that the last wagon was full of Australians, and somehow they had managed to unhook it, and of course it began to run back down the hill. Again I don't know if the story is true, and what happened to the men if it is; but we stopped for a quarter of an hour and then restarted.

Before we left the hot spring outside Lamia a small group of our soldiers went through the pass. They had a large letter 'P' on their sleeves, and also, I think, an elephant. These were the legendary 'Phantoms'.

Rendezvous

'I'll see you in Alex,' Johnnie said,
'We'll have chicken and chips, fresh butter, and bread,
With gallons of char, at ten ackers a head;
And I'll sleep for a week – in a nice clean bed,
When we have leave in Alex.'

John slept in Athens, Bill did as well,
(John's still nineteen, and they sleep there still).
Then a bomb met Mac by Tiryns hill,
While our troopship flamed and leaflets fell.
They had no leave in Alex.

We stood in the sea at Kalamata bay,
When near empty ships backed, then glided away,
To outrange the planes before dawn of day,
To live and fight in another affray.

So – none of us saw Alex.

NE SECTION/M~

Regimental Pay Office,
Radcliffe,
Manchester.

Mr *R. MacLean*   23 - 6 - 1941.

Laurel Lodge Oban Argyll

Dear ~~Sir/~~ Madam,

Re: *1930294 Spr Mac LEAN G.* Royal Engineers.

With reference to notification recently sent you, that
your son has been reported missing, in addition to expressing
my deep regret, it is my duty to advise you of your position
regarding allowances due and payable to you.

The present rate of   14/- per week will be continued for a
period of 17 weeks following that in which you were first notified
your son was reported missing, i.e. until   5-10-41

If any news of your son is received by you, I shall be
pleased if you will notify this Office immediately.

I am, Madam,
Your obedient Servant,

Ident.
for Regimental Paymaster, R.E.

From a very sympathetic government.

O.F.230.

N.E. Section/M. 1

Mrs. C. MacLean

Dear Sir/Madam,

No. 1930294 Spr MacLEAN G. Royal Engineers.

It is understood that you have now been notified that the above-named soldier who was previously reported "Missing" has now been posted as a Prisoner of War.

You will doubtless wish to know without delay your position in the matter of allowances payable to you.

In consequence of the soldier being posted as a Prisoner of War your allowance will not cease on 5-10-41 as was previously notified but will continue in issue at the rate of 14/-, which was in issue before being posted Missing.

I am, Sir/Madam,
Your obedient servant,

Lieutenant,
for Regimental Paymaster, R.E.

Army Pay Office,
Radcliffe,
Manchester.
4 / 8 /41.

If a soldier was 'missing' any voluntary allowance was also missing. They were a logical mob, these fireside strategists. If the soldier was killed the allowance died also.

CHAPTER SEVEN

First Year as a POW

Captured along with us at Kalamata was a canteen worker from the Salvation Army who ran a canteen for the Aussies. He was the only person resembling a padre we had for a very long time. Several doctors had stayed behind, when some of them at least could have got away. One of these was a Dr Munro from Dumfries, who gave me some help later. We had great respect for these people. About a year ago there was a major earthquake shock at Kalamata, which was world news for two or three days.

We travelled northwards, or generally in a northwards direction, for several hours and I may have passed quite close to Sparta, but not knowing the geography of the place I missed seeing many places I woud have liked to see. I knew about Sparta from my primary school days; there was a chapter in one of my school books about it and about Leonidas and Thermopylae. While in the Thermopylae area I found no one else who knew the history of the place.

We stopped for about an hour in the station at Tripolis. The platform was packed with young Greek soldiers going home. Two very young ones were studying me carefully while I was leaning out of the window. Then they came over to me and handed me a large lump of soft white cheese. I shared it out with the other five persons who sat at the same table, and noticed later that some of these people received food and shared with no one. That was the last thing I shared with anyone until I had a mate that I could trust.

It was getting dark by the time we reached the outskirts of Corinth. We stopped somewhere and left the train, and were put into a stable for the night. We lay down and slept there on top of all the manure, and we were covered with fleas in the morning. We then carried on to Corinth and were taken into the prisoner of war camp – an old Greek barracks. There were one or two events of note. For example, we had left a lad behind in Athens: he had been with some women and then found that he had VD which he very likely had caught in Egypt (perhaps I should say that it had caught him). The Germans were delighted to offer him accommodation, and he had been in the camp for some time. He felt very sorry for himself, thinking that he might pass the remainder of the war with no mates. When we were marching into the cage the first thing we noticed was this character dancing like a Dervish, delighted that he had his own Company back again.

This is a description of the camp as I remember it, and it should be made clear that we were there during May and the first half of June 1941. It was approximately square, about 400 yards each way, surrounded by a barbed-wire fence, through which flowed either 5,000 or 10,000 volts. The fence consisted of two perimeters about 10 feet high and 6 feet apart; between them was an adequate barbed-wire entanglement. This I studied carefully along with a Kiwi. He summed it up thus: 'Well, we can forget about that: a cat couldn't get through it, never mind the electricity.' However, it was possible in some places for a person outside to reach the outstretched hand of someone inside, and I remember doing some bartering with a small Greek man for some fish. This was about four weeks later.

There were the usual guards with machine-guns, and I think a few elevated sentry boxes, although the whole perimeter could be covered from the higher building in the centre. The gate faced northwards looking over the town of Corinth. There was a landing field in this direction also. Above us and to the west was the wonderful bronze-age fortress of Acrocorinth. There was a small command building at the centre, which I think had been used as a hospital: the German commanders were in a larger block which housed the German soldiery. There were other buildings which I think had been harness rooms. I was in one of those. We lay on the concrete floor, and I think there were three or four of these 'harness rooms'. There was a small building about 15 feet by 20 feet at the western end of the site – I'll come back to that one.

Most of the men slept outside in foxholes. There were many nationalities represented in the camp. The largest contingent of our boys were Australian (there might have been 6,000 of them; I'm guessing of course), Kiwis (about 1,000), about 3,000 from the British Isles, and about 1,000 odds and sods, such as Indians, Cypriots, Jews, Palestinians, Maoris and at least one Fijian. Also there were a large number of Yugoslavs, and a fair number of Albanians. There were many Italians, at the beginning – these were the 'Wolves of Tuscany' and a stamping, posturing lot they were. At that time also there was a large number of young German parachutists.

At first the Italians were allowed out every day; but they gave the civilian population, and especially the young girls, such a hard time, that the Germans rounded them up and packed them back in again. There was an independent unit of Medical Corps – the Friends Ambulance Unit – they were Quakers. I think there were 125 of them originally, but they lost some of their men. That was one unit that certainly earned our respect, and did not always receive it.

The Germans had an obvious dislike for the Italians, and when there was trouble between them and our boys, the Germans took our part, even to the extent of shooting into the bulk of the Italians. The officer fired several times but I saw no one being hit.

There were three rows of slit trenches at the highest part of the site, zigzag trenches about three feet deep. Obviously they had been used for the defence of the barracks against air attack, and most of the buildings had signs of having been shot up, but I saw no bomb holes; they must have been filled in. There were a number of wells at the lowest part of the site. When we arrived there the wells were in good order and the water very good.

For the first three days we had nothing at all to eat, then they started to issue two biscuits per man per day. These were identical to cream crackers; the British army pack contained sixteen of these, and they gradually worked up, over a period of ten days, to eight biscuits per man per day. Along with these we had half a saucer of cooked rice per day and this also was gradually increased to a full saucer. Occasionally we received some olive oil, and very occasionally a cabbage stew made with purple cabbage. It was known as 'purple death' because by this time many of the men had dysentery and this stew seemed to increase the damage and infect more men.

In a comparatively short time the signs of malnutrition began to show. Almost exactly two weeks after the surrender our own officers paraded us and said, 'The first man died today.' The wells began to stink and very soon one could smell them 100 yards away. Everyone was affected by lice; this was the first time that I had had them, and the reason was that I was now sleeping in my clothes, because if I had taken them off I would have lost them. It became more and more common to see a man who had been sitting in the hot sun, spring up and immediately fall down again. We would all feel ourselves grow weaker, and all were noticeably gaunt looking. I spent most of my time on my back to conserve energy.

Fuel also was a problem, and the little building in the western corner suffered. A pair of Aussies assessed its possibilities. Soon the inner lining had disappeared, then the outer lining went, and it was left with four corner posts and a heavy tiled roof. Then the Aussies removed two posts at opposite corners. A Sikh then had a go, he stood inside the outline of the building and removed another corner post, and found himself lying on the ground under the wreck of the roof.

By the end of the third week, three quarters of the men had dysentery. Other signs of malnutrition were skin diseases such as dermatitis, boils and carbuncles in the worst case, together with styes and swollen ankles. There were many nests of very large ants, with different kinds of smaller ants. We would sit in the sun and put our shirts on the anthill hoping to get rid of the lice, the ants always left some to carry on with the good work. I think that the ants were very good farmers.

I had been to a good school and knew something about the working of the human body, and I remembered our English teacher telling us about Fletcherism, and to take '30 chews to every bite', so in order to get full value of any food I had, and also to guard against dysentery, I took 60 chews to every bite. This I found very difficult indeed for a starving man but I had no dysentery all the time I was in Corinth. The solids (what there were of them) were passed once every two days, and I was fortunate indeed compared with the majority. Some of the men would swell up and last a very short time after that. Awake, and indeed dreaming, food and hunger dominated our thoughts. If one awoke during the night there was always someone speaking in his sleep. Someone shouted for his Mum, and many other things were said. The regular soldiers said that this was not peculiar to prisoner of war camps, and such noises could be heard in any barrack room.

As I said, there were three rows of slit trenches at the high end of the camp: these were used as latrines, and of course those worst affected were there longest, and were seldom away from the trenches. It was my habit to patronize the highest line of trenches, for various reasons, modesty among others. The others had their backs to me, and of course those worst affected would go to the nearest trench, and frequently even that was too far away. In front of me there was always someone in trouble. One particular time there were three lads immediately in front of me, who had arrived just after me. They were in KD shorts and shirts. They squatted down, and quickly the diarrhoea poured out of them. This was followed by part of their insides; the gut of the left hand one projected about eight inches, the next one about two inches, and the third perhaps six inches. I particularly remember the end of the gut rising and falling as they strained. Whether the respective guts returned to their correct places I don't know, but I began to think, 'When is this going to happen to me?' It was not a pleasant thought but there and then I put it out of my mind and carried on as before. It was a common enough experience; many men would talk of their insides dropping.

Now one or two points about food; rice varied with cooked lentils, again the quantities were minimal. Occasionally, we received a single Greek Army biscuit instead of eight British Army cream crackers. This was the original 'hard tack', about five inches diameter, and three quarters of an inch thick. It was an impossibility to bite it, one had to gnaw away round and round the edge, and it would last nearly all day.

Although life was dominated by the thought of food and trying to keep oneself alive, there were other things. I spoke one day to two other chaps; they were thoughtful characters and, like me, had noticed that as the body grew weaker the mind grew very much sharper and clearer.

The Australians were particularly good at entertaining themselves and others, and there were several concerts. They excelled in very dirty suggestive songs. The Maoris gave us their war dance, the *haka*, and some beautiful songs, particularly the lovely *Maori's Farewell to New Zealand*. We had Gaelic songs from different people; Alan McKechnie, from Islay, is the one I recall.

There were also German troop movements to take our attention, and we noticed that the parachutists were becoming very active; to us they looked like schoolboys. One day 100 Junkers three-engined transports took off for Crete, I can remember only about seven returning, and some of these were well shot up. One came in with a whole wing and not much more than a quarter of the other.

A small Italian naval ship had come into the Gulf. The next day the Italians held a large parade in the camp, stamping and marching backwards and forwards with large standards (Gonfalons). These were unlike any other army flag that I had seen although I had read of them in the book, *Rienzi, the Last of the Tribunes*, by Lytton or Kingsley. The standard was held along the top and not on a vertical edge, as is more usual. As they were performing, an Australian spat on the sacred standard (at least, the Australians were blamed for the ensuing riot.) The Australians were backing off, with the Italians screaming, shouting, and throwing rocks. There was a moving cloud of stones, sticks, cans and much more hanging above the contestants.

In a very short time the German guard came along and faced the Italians, who refused to move until the Germans had fired once or twice, then they went away. The next day the Italians were away, and I presume that the majority went by sea. How the remainder travelled I do not know.

The Germans had established a barter area down at the main gate. Bartering with civilians was permitted at times on the whim of the German Commander. At other times there would be a blast from a machine-gun and everyone had to disperse quickly. Not having much to barter I did not visit the place. One of the British troops was being chased by a guard, having obtained something illegal, and he led the guard to an area where there were a very large number of foxholes, and instead of shooting, the guard went after him. The prisoner knew his way about but the guard kept breaking through the crust and falling into the foxholes. At last the guard gave up, having had enough amusement for the time being.

The only bartering I did was on the western side. There was a little man standing outside the wire. I managed to communicate in sign language and he had some very small fish for sale. I offered a broken watch, having explained that it did not work and he gave me about a dozen little fish. Right away I put the first one into my mouth and he was most disturbed, he indicated that he wanted them back, and I handed them through the wire. He then carefully scraped salt and scales off them and returned them. He then stood for a minute while I ate them, heads, tails, fins and all.

Now I intend to record my opinion of my fellow inmates, and would stress that these are personal opinions, and many, perhaps a majority, of my friends would have seen them very differently. First the Friends Ambulance Unit: they were generally quiet and kept very much to themselves, and seemed to be able to trust each other. They appeared to be happy to work anywhere if they were able to help people and do their work. So I assume that, as I was told, they went to the eastern front eventually. The Indians, and particularly the Rajput Sikhs, were fine people; quiet, gentlemanly and courageous. The Albanians seemed to be happy people, always joking. The Yugoslavs were much the same but the characteristics were not so marked. The Jews were intelligent, likeable lads, very pleasant to speak to. The Australians were very happy to mob, but individually I found them very good indeed. The Kiwis were excellent, and that included the Maoris, who were more volatile. I got on very well with the Cypriots; there were some very likeable people amongst them. The Greeks outside the wire were first-class people, as good as any to be found anywhere. They were not averse to dodging machine-guns in order to throw things over the wire.

The Red Cross representatives arrived and immediately caused improvements in our lifestyle. There was at least one Swede, and they may all have been Swedes; there were three men. As a result of their visit we had good water from outside the camp every day, and the rations slightly improved; not enough to repair the damage that had been done, or even to prevent further damage, but nearly to subsistence level. Every day a small water tanker was sent out to the lower Peirene spring in Corinth, where it was filled and returned to the camp, and always one or two went with it and filled up water bottles for their mates and themselves. One day I was standing minding my own business, when a guard came up to me and signed that I was to go with him, he was an older chap. We went down with the water wagon into Corinth to a spot where there was a stream of water gushing out of a low vertical face of rock. It was emerging with some force through a hole of about four inches diameter, from a point about two feet six inches above the ground. It looked like a very ancient place and I took it to be the lower Peirene spring; the upper Peirene spring being in Acrocorinth. Beside the spring was a row of cottages, rather like Highland cottages, and, after we had filled the tank and water bottles, an old lady came out of one of the cottages and thrust a large piece of bread and three hard boiled eggs into my hands, turned round and scuttled back, while the guard made a show of looking the other way. That guard was a gentleman. You should know that contact with civilians was forbidden and another guard might well have shot her. I still wonder if she had enough food left for herself. They were very poor people.

I played my first game of cards in this camp, and did not like it very much. It seemed to be a rather stupid game being completely dependent on chance. However, I did enjoy the games of draughts and rather surprised my mates. After thrashing one of them at it, he came to me shortly after and said, 'Hey, Mac, where did you learn the pub games?'

About this time, and probably urged by the Red Cross, Jerry decided to have us deloused. We took all our clothes off, and were left with only boots, towel, and identity discs. Our clothes were bundled, labelled, and left. We then marched through the town of Corinth, dressed in our towels, kilt fashion, until we came to a beach on the gulf. It was a steep, longish beach, which was covered with these shellfish that look rather like the spine of an animal, with rows of sharp spikes along it. At the top of the beach was a big grinning Jerry with a knapsack type spray container. We were marched in front of him and liberally sprayed, back and front and particularly on the private parts, and then sent down the beach to have a wash. After I was finished (and it was a painful experience), I was able to watch my mates perform – they would carefully pick their way for two or three paces, then suddenly they would shout and sprint to the water: they didn't give two hoots for the spikes. We never found out what was in the spray, but it felt like nitric acid. After we had dried ourselves we were marched back to the camp, wearing wet kilts this time. By the time we reached the camp our towels were dry, our clothes had been deloused and all returned in good order, then life went on as before. The delousing was very effective.

One day a Blenheim flew over the airport and the camp; it was being fired on all the way, but none of the shells exploded near it. Probably they were checking on the airfield while the attack on Crete was proceeding.

Another day, Heinrich Himmler came strutting in to have a look round and pat himself on the back. I was sitting outside in the sun with my back to the hut, and I stayed that way all the time he was about. His motorcade came in to the command building, and he was strutting about and speaking to the guards of honour, and all the rest of it. It started to rain and I went into the hut, and did not see him leave. Some time after the war I bought a second hand book called the *Bull of Minos*, and I see from it that he was back in Nauplia in 1942, and stayed in the Hotel.

One morning about the middle of June, we were marched off with all our gear, carrying it to the far end of the Isthmus, which was a distance of several miles, and in our weakened condition it felt much more. There was a steepish hill on the way. There were vineyards sloping upwards to the south, and every few yards there were women and young girls at the side of the road handing out packets of currants, one to each prisoner as he passed. They were very good to us, and I am sure that the great part of the crop must have been given away. Not so very long after this there was a virtual famine in Greece. When we reaced the far end of the canal the bridge had been blown; that's another story, and I had better give it now.

There was an engagement at the bridge between the Fourth Hussars and German tanks, and of course our tanks were heavily outgunned, but as one of the lads told me their particular commander insisted on going into battle with his head stuck out of the turret – looking for a VC? He had his head shot off which lost the tank, and helped to lose the engagement. Another man told me that the command wire to the explosives at the bridge had been destroyed by a bomb or a shell, and the charges failed to blow. One man fired his rifle at the detonator, by very good fortune hit it, and the bridge was destroyed. It had been replaced by a pontoon bridge when we arrived at the end of the canal. There was a steep access road on each side of the canal and we were quite tired by the time we had climbed up on the far side.

We did not have far to go to reach the train. It must have been somewhere around Megara. We were taken by train to Athens, and I think that we just sat there in a siding for a while, and then went north to Gravia, which was on the high road, the high pass round Thermopylae. It was at the end of a series of tunnels and bridges that we had blown on the retreat. There was great destruction for many miles.

From this point on, all my pals, those who had worked on the high pass, kept saying, 'How are we going to manage this in the state we are in now?' We were paraded outside the station and were told by a German oficer, 'All you prisoners must climb over this pass to Lamia. You must march till you drop; there will be no transport, even for the wounded; any person who drops out will be shot.' We were then walked past a tap at the station to get drinking water for the march; it was a mere trickle. Most of the lads had dishes that they could fill and add to their water bottles later; but all I had was the water bottle, and I was holding up the march. A little Gefreiter, Obergefreiter, or something, he may have been an officer, I neither knew nor cared, was going stark, raving mad. He kept waving his little automatic in my face and getting very annoyed. I don't know what he was trying to say, but I kept saying 'nix'. That was the only 'German' word I knew, and I did not care much what happened. He was livid and it seemed as if he was going to explode. Then he gave up and pushed me away, and I left with about a quarter of a pint of water, and a hatred for the pompous little man with the pistol. My anger kept me going over the hill.

After being warned so much about the difficulty of the hill, shortage of water, and knowing a bit about mountains, I expected a really rough climb: because I had expected it to be tough it did not worry me at all. First of all we met a Greek shepherd coming down with a sheepskin cloak over his shoulders, he was on a donkey. Then, with the blown-up series of bridges on our left, we started on the steeper part and came to a place where there was a bit of a gully. Of course the bridge had been blown, and Jerry had blasted a road through the rock at the back of it, blasting all the rocks and the cliff away to allow a level road through on a much sharper bend. There was a wayside chapel beside the original bridge; this was a picture of the Virgin and Child in a glass case. The glass had blown off and everything was shattered. I noticed this on the way past, and I expect that it was repaired many years ago.

Then we met a company of very young German troops coming down. There was a Glasgow lad by the name of Purdie with me and he was not impressed. He say, 'Huh, German Army. If that's it I could eat them all myself.' Round the next bend we met a company of veterans, and they were a fine-looking set of toughs. The Purdie said, 'I've changed my mind about the German Army.' Up a bit more and round the corner we met a German officer on a lovely horse. He was organizing the removal of some guns. They were their own guns, I don't think that they had captured any of ours at that point, and I remembered my mate saying, 'We're all right now, it's downhill from here,' and me still looking for the big hill they had been speaking about. It was a warm sunny day and we continued through the pass, which was a straight, gentle, incline downwards but at the far end there was a steep highway going down the face of the hill. Like all the mountains in Greece the road would go 2–300 yards along the face at the maximum allowable gradient; then turned right back on itself, and reversed again and again to the foot of the hill.

There was a young Austrian Alpine Trooper with us – Gebirgsjäger, they called them – mostly by signs he took me and three or four others, straight down the hill, cutting off all the zigzags. It was very good of him. I don't know how many men came down with us, but I was right up with him and there were three of four others with us at the foot while most of them had not reached halfway down. Then we marched to the river (where we had blown the bridge on the other road). We stopped there for a while and the first thing I did was fill my waterbottle, and have a good drink.

I was quite happy to sit down and have a rest, and I had been sitting there for a while when a chap came up to me and said, 'Have you been drinking from the river?'

I said, 'Yes.'

'Oh well, there's nothing we can do about it now; there's a dead Jerry up there.'

I said, 'That's good, at least we got one of them.'

Chaos

At Corinth, when our time began -
Ten thousand in the pen –
Enough food for one healthy man
Was shared out among ten.

Meeting place of many races,
Hope in extremity,
Wary eyes in tense, drawn faces;
Vermin and lethargy.

King Peter's boys (with rings to sell)
Meet Cypriot Pioneers,
Some fighting sons of Israel,
And King Zog's mountaineers.

Quiet, gentlemanly Punjab Sikhs,
And men from far Fiji,
Superb, unselfish, reckless Greeks,
Staking their lives for me.

Australian jokers raising smiles
Among the big, black ants,
Sweet, sad songs from the Western Isles,
Then haunting Maori chants.

Visions of Bronze Age infantry
Manning the mighty Dun.
Three thousand years of history,
Black in the setting sun.

The humbled Wolves of Tuscany –
Ill tempered in defeat,
Watch paratroops from Germany
Fly off to die on Crete.

Slit trenches full of dysentery
Drain to the only wells,

The revolting drinking water,
And all-pervading smells.

Men rising in the noonday heat
And falling down once more.
Big sharp seashells and bleeding feet,
Delousing on the shore.

Herr Himmler, far off from the front,
Comes in to gloat and lie,
While some swell up, and all grow gaunt,
And some lie down to die.

At Corinth, when we marched again,
Another round to start,
Enough hate for ten healthy men
Was lodged in every heart.

We then marched on to Lamia, and I don't remember much about that; two Black Watch lads were about 100 yards ahead of me, and going very well. A few years ago when at last I was able to contact Rab Chisholm, he mentioned in his first letter how well I had performed on the march. At the time I noticed nothing special.

It was a very long straight road to Lamia along the plain of Thermoplyae. Either at Lamia station or at one of the small halts about that area, there was quite an entertaining incident. The guards were in the front and rear carriages, and we were in a long stretch in between. At the place mentioned there were two small sheds and a space of about ten feet between them. A young Greek civilian was in this space, hidden from the guards. He was throwing packets of cigarettes to the boys and many of them missed, to fall on the platform. He would then dash out, pick them up and hand them in as Jerry was taking pot shots at him. Fortunately he was not hit; it may be that they did not intend to hit him. The performance lasted about ten minutes.

That was the kind of incident to be seen daily. The Greeks were generous, reckless and very good to us. We had a forced stop at Larissa. We had a short walk down to a pontoon bridge (of course the original bridge had been blown up) and a walk up the other side to a different train. I kept a good lookout for Mount Olympus and am reasonably certain that I saw it. However, there is an anecdote about Larissa – Bob Judd who was in the same camp as me for some years was captured here – he was in an NZ anti-tank two-pounder battery which had knocked out a couple of German tanks, before being captured. One of his mates was shot through the head and blinded, but he insisted on walking with them to Salonika. I don't know what happened to that lad but I have a feeling that he recovered.

Eventually we came to a large plain which I took to be the Plain of Thessaly, and this it turned out to be. After a long time we came to a city which I assumed must be Salonika, we detrained and marched through an ancient arch into the city. There was a name on the arch and I could not at first make Salonika out of it. My memory called up the mathematical Greek letters and the first letter was theta. Then I succeeded in reading it as I passed under the arch. It was Thessaloniki. The arch proved to be the arch of Galerian. We then marched through the town and up the hill. All the time children were running out of passages, giving food to some lucky ones – and getting sniped at for their pains. This went on for about twenty minutes: they were little children from four to seven years old, and I don't think that the Germans were really trying to hit them, but they were firing. I was in Salonika on my birthday; I caught dysentery that day. However, a few days later I did get a birthday present; the Germans attacked Russia. The guards were very nervous, they were scanning the skies to the north all day, as if they expected the Russians to come over at any minutes.

The first camp was again a Greek barracks. It was surrounded by a high wall I think; at least I could see no openings in it except the big gate. I don't remember any wire there. We had a meal shortly after we arrived and it was the only reasonable meal we had in Salonika.

We were in Salonika about a fortnight altogether. The food was no less than we had at Corinth, but by this time we were very weak and more men died there, some of them I am told from my own company; either they died there or shortly afterwards.

As we entered the gate of the first camp we were directed by Australians to three very large cooking pots full of excellent stew: the whole operation was organized by the Aussies, who had done an excellent job. The meat had been carefully cut up so that no one was without a reasonable sized piece of meat. This was dark meat with tubes running through it: I thought that it was horse but some of my mates insisted that it was donkey; whatever it was it had died in a good cause.

After a few hours there we were moved up the hill to Salonika Number Two. This too had been a barracks, and it was built next to the British Military Cemetery from the First World War. There was a small stretch of wire at the entrance. Before leaving Oban, as I was leaving for the train, I met Duncan Macrae the draper, and he said to me that if I ever reached Salonika he would like me to find his brother's grave and tell him what it looked like. Here I was within a few yards of the grave and there was no way I could get permission to look for it. When I reached home eventually he was rather annoyed; he seemed to think that it was my fault that I was unable to get out to see it. For a man who had served in the First World War he should have known better.

Healthwise I was at a very low ebb in Salonika. Several incidents took place there; the most notable was the reaction of the Germans to their attack on Russia. Many times the Greeks came to the gates, and the German sergeant major in charge of the camp had no objection to them handing in food. One or two people did quite well from this but one chap was handed two two-kilogram loaves – dark brown loaves, very good food – and he was so hungry that he sat down and ate both of them. Within a few hours he was dead.

One day we received a new set of guards, and the first morning three Greek girls were coming up to the wire when a guard stopped them 100 yards away from the wire. He was quite abusive to the girls, and eventually one of them spat in his eye. Within seconds they were being knocked to the ground with the rifle butt, dragged along the ground by their long, black, hair, face down or face up made no difference, they were kicked in the groin and stomach; they were thoroughly savaged. We did not find out what happened to them afterwards; but it was the most disgusting thing we saw. No one who saw that could possible forget it.

Now what else happened at Salonika. There was dysentery, and the now ever-present feeling of growing weaker. Salonika was in a malaria area and we received one pill of quinine daily; but it was some pill. Spherical, and at least half an inch in diameter, and probably more, it was very difficult indeed to swallow. Many of the lads refused to take it; but I did not want to risk malaria on top of all else, so I took mine. When the dysentery really took hold of me I had to rise in the middle of the night. There were toilets, eastern types, really a hole in the floor, but far better than Corinth. This was because we were all in barracks. In these barracks I met the first bedbugs that I had seen in my life. There was not much to look forward to; even with persistent over-chewing of everything I ate, and all other precautions, the dysentery refused to go away. But there were many people much worse off. I had dysentery all the time I spent there. We left after about a fortnight.

It was at this time that I took the decision that If I was to cure the dysentery, I would require to take no solid food and see how things went. I took tea and water only. Very soon after beginning this regime we were moved again. Again we marched through the town, going down the hill this time. There was the same performance as when we arrived, again the children, at personal risk, gave food to a fortunate few. We went back through the arch, and stopped at the railway siding not far outside the arch. Among the Germans was a Yank shouting in his best Yankee English, being well sworn at by the British and swearing back.

The trucks were about 8 feet wide internally, and maybe as long as 50 feet; they were made to take 8 horses and 16 men. They were French trucks and there is plenty of information available about them. There were 50 of us squeezed into each truck. There was no way that one could lie down properly; perhaps if it had all been well arranged we could have lain down with our knees up, but it was impossible to stretch out. We were in the truck for five days and I think five nights. All my notes were lost. In spite of everything we put on a show when marching through the city, both coming and going, singing *Tipperaray, Keep the Homes Fires Burning*, and other army songs.

The trucks had wide doors (of course kept locked) and at each of the corners were windows high up, and fitted with grilles. There was a four-gallon petrol can for water and one for human waste, which was almost entirely liquid by this time. We could stand and look out of the window one at a time for each window, being about a foot high and about two feet wide they were good for ventilation only. When the can was full, the custom was to shout '*achtung scheisan*' and empty it out of the window.

The Australians were not very disciplined in their ways and they would not wait until they were clear of the station; when a German passed they would do their throwing first and shouting afterwards. I understand that this came to a head at one station; the German refused to take it, and he fired at random into the truck. Two Aussies were reported killed but again the incident was not seen or heard by me. In another truck they removed floorboards, and some were shot going out; there were no reports of successful escapes.

The five days I was in the truck I ate nothing except when we were allowed out at Belgrade, where the people had prepared some food for us. I ate the stew they gave me because I could not carry it otherwise, I kept the little maize loaf they gave me until three days after we were in Austria. It was about five inches in diameter and two inches thick, and it was solid. When eventually I ate it it proved to be excellent food. I had unfortunately been allocated to a truck with a large number of movement control who were a company of RE composed of well-educated, high-class Londoners, with very high opinions of themselves. The senior man in the wagon was the RSM of that lot; there were one or two remounts – one of these was a boy from the Cameronians – three or four of my own company; and others from different regiments. I don't remember any Aussies or Kiwis.

The RSM took charge immediately, and said that there would be five rows of ten. He then marked out ample space for himself and his cronies, leaving the rest with less space than their fair share. There was little we could do but accept, because he was senior and he and his men were organized; but later when I saw them lying out full length, with room to spare, I stretched out and let them do what they liked. They complained to the RSM and I suggested to him that he should try dividing the place out fairly. From then on I stretched out as often as I felt like it, and was not disturbed – a fair divide would have curtailed the RSM's space. It is apparent that I have underestimated the width and overestimated the length of the wagon.

We left Salonika going west and gradually, in a long slow bend, turned northwards. We had no idea where we were going but we stopped at a place called Monastir, which is also known as Bitola. We were halted at the platform for about two hours. The place was crawling with Bulgarian troops, they were unpleasant looking people. We were not allowed off the train, and in fact they did not even open the doors to let the smell out. We moved north from there towards Belgrade, and at one place, after dark, we halted in a siding to let a train past. As the train passed there were people singing, beautiful choral singing. I had no idea what this was and enquired from a German soldier. He explained that they were Croatian exiles going home; their singing was lovely, it reminded me of Gaelic music.

The Cameronian lad was in the last stages of dysentery, he was passing slime and blood, and in army language he was dead; nothing more could be done for him. He smelled a bit but then no one was fresh. Everyone smelled a bit, some more than others, but the Cockneys would not let the lad rest; they kept pushing him and telling him to take his stink somewhere else. They were like a pack of curs at a wounded animal. Since then, if there was a candidate, I have never voted other than Scottish Nationalist. The boy was still alive when we parted company, four days later. It seemed to me that his tormentors would not let him die in peace.

A sergeant Punshon and I had some arguments; really he was a likeable chap, and at another camp we got on very well. He told me that there had been no 60-pounder guns in Greece; this was at variance to what my friends had said, and in the course of the argument, it transpired that he thought that if something had not come through Athens it had not entered Greece. I thought that if these people were so good at movement control they should have done something about the diarrhoea and dysentery. By the way, Punshon was very well educated indeed.

At this point I should say that the Albanians, Yugoslavs and Greeks fought, when many larger and more powerful countries did not. The whole campaign took Jerry some five or six weeks, and a few months later he was within three weeks of taking Moscow, when that wonderful winter of 1941–2 froze him in his tracks. Even at this late date I think that we should say 'thank you' to the Greeks and send the Elgin marbles home.

Our next stop after Belgrade was Budapest, where we were not allowed out of the wagons. The Danube was in spate and I was very interested in the way the ferries described a very steep curve upstream in order to arrive at a landing stage exactly opposite that they had left. I have not been able to establish whether we were in Buda or Pest, not having a map of sufficient size. The Danube was not blue. After a short stay we travelled westwards and then stopped at Marburg, as it was then; it is now Maribor. Approximately half of my company were left there. Archie Campbell from Ardrishaig died about this time; some say it happened in Salonika, and others in Marburg. The cause of death was dysentery brought on by starvation.

After spending some time on the train at the station, we moved on to Wolfsberg, and left the train there. One could smell the Stalag from the station, it had a distinct and disgusting smell. From Wolfsberg we marched over a bridge and into the Stalag. As we entered, the Belgians and French were playing the British national anthem. Each nationality was forbidden the playing of its own national anthem, but they had not thought of them playing the anthems of their allies. Our lads usually played *Rule Britannia*.

During the whole nightmare journey I ate nothing solid except the stew at Belgrade. I drank as much as I could and as far as I could judge, the dysentery was gone, and my only problem was weakness from dysentery and starvation. Then I ate what we had been given for the journey and had collected *en route*; it took a very long time to eat at sixty chews per bite, and after an hour the dysentery returned. Immediately I returned to the starvation routine; two days later I was able to pass solids – the dysentery did not return.

Jerry seemed to have some difficulty in counting. We were always paraded in ten ranks or five ranks, usually five – they would shout out 'funf und funf'. We were marched past a window on the right-hand side and the right-hand man was handed a small loaf for the five men in that file. Then a few yards further on a small piece of sausage was handed to the left-hand man, again to be divided amont the five men in the file. The Australians, in particular, immediately worked out that a whole loaf was of more use to one man than his rightful share and a small piece of sausage, and even on the first day we saw several times four Aussies chasing a fifth, and somewhere else nine Australians all fighting for a share of one loaf.

The first day they worked out how the loaf should be cut up. One man was delegated to cut the bread as fairly as possible, then with his back to the others he would take a piece in his hand and shout out, 'Whose piece is this?' This method stopped most of the disputes about food. The same method was used to divide cheese and sausage. The food now was adequate to keep body and soul together, but we were still ravenous.

The Stalag was divided into several compounds; nearest the gate was the German soldiers' compound; next was the French and Belgian compound; then there was an open compound which contained an assembly area, showers, medical and delousing. When we arrived there were a number of very long tents in the assembly area, with a two-feet-deep layer of straw covering the floor. They were really quite comfortable compared with what some people had to go through. Beyond that was the main British compound where we ended up after being deloused and checked in with details all taken, including photograph. We were in the main compound for two or three days and then went out to working camps.

Whilst I had cured the dysentery, deficiency diseases were beginning to appear. I had a small boil on the back of my neck which refused to go away. Others in different places would come and go, but there was the beginnings of a real beauty in the small of my back; it did not inconvenience me at the time, but it gradually grew and grew. I was sent out in a group of 500 to a place called Zeltweg, to a Luftwaffe training aerodrome. The Luftwaffe treated us very well and there were no complaints whatever about them. The German soldiers also were correct in their treatment of us. However, some of the civilians were not so correct.

There was a Canadian civilian who ran about on a motorbike. He had been living in the place for some time before the war and had stayed on. He was nice enough according to reports, although I personally had not spoken to him. Most of our boys were Aussies and Kiwis, although all our various groups were represented, and I became acquainted with some of the English lads. There was in particular, a Dorset lad named Lance-Corporal Stone. I don't know his regiment, but he was an unofficial medical orderly and he was very good with me when the carbuncle began to give trouble.

Being a training 'drome there were trainees lost very frequently, I had noted that the number killed was one or two every day. They made no difference to us because of that. We saw one day a lovely, slim twin-fuselage plane but that was the last that we saw of it. Two or three years later we were told that the British had bombed the factory. It was reckoned to be a Fokke-wolfe 110, but I could not be sure of that. It was a lovely plane, much nicer than the Lockheed Lightnings of the Yanks. The remains of one – apparently shot down – is shown on one of the newsreels from Stalingrad.

We were building a main runway for the aerodrome, which had been a civil 'drome taken over by the *Luftwaffe*. It was some runway, of great length and width. The main drain running down the centre line was fully a yard in diameter. There were several side drains in the width of the runway, which ran through 'solway kerbs', which are effectively concrete pipes with a continuous slot along the top to allow water to enter. Nearly all the British soldiers were employed in a series of pits and different apparatus, preparing material for concrete aggregate, and mixing concrete. These were arranged at the perimeter of the airfield. First there were some pits of various depths for extracting ballast, which conveniently was the basic subsoil – a mixture of sand and pebbles of various sizes. From there it went to a series of mechanical riddles which spewed out the different grades into different lorries, for distribution to the various groups of ten men each serving concrete mixers. We worked out ways to slow the work down, and sometimes we were very successful. We required more rest than we were getting, and of course we were doing a little for the war effort. Sand was built up into large heaps by continuously moving bands fed from the foot, each by one lad with a shovel. If another chap helped, and both worked quickly, they could jam the machine in about thirty seconds. It would then smoke at the top of the band and, if the Austrian foreman did not see it, it would catch fire. This would give us a very reasonable rest. Usually the foreman was furious – perhaps the cost was deducted from his wages.

Everything had been worked out exactly; for instance, there was a fixed number of shovelfuls to be put into each barrowload. There were always several boulders, a foot or more across, and some much bigger, lying around. The revolving drum was four or five feet across, and if one of these boulders reached it, it could be destroyed in a very short time. One day I had just filled my barrow with sand when I noticed a very large boulder lying beside it. An English lad beside me said, 'Do you think we should try it, Jock?' I said, 'OK' and we managed to lift it and to drop it into my barrow, where it dropped out of sight in the sand. I then in my turn managed to wheel it to the machine and drop it in but unfortunately the Austrian in charge saw it before it could do any damage. I think that he was for shooting me; I'm not sure; but he started after me, shouting out something, so I stood and looked at him. The Austrian soldier in charge was in turn very annoyed. What exactly he said I'm not sure, but the two or three words I picked up were to the effect that if he wanted shooting he could go to the Russian front and get more than he wanted, but in the mean time he would leave men alone.

The concrete from these machines was put into jubilee wagons, and made up into two trains pulled by diesel locomotives and run down alternately direct to the runway. The trains were crewed by Australians and they were first class; they managed to derail the trains at least once a day, and would be changed for others when this happened. There were two of them killed in one of the derailments which were achieved at the corners, or crashing the trains by other means. At least once a day we would get half an hour's rest when the train was being put back on the rails, and this did much for us. Two or three men died in the big holes where the ballast was being extracted. We lost several men at Zeltweg and were there about six weeks altogether. We succeeded occasionally in placing boulders in the skip but never again one as large as the one the Austrian foreman had discovered.

When one of these boulders reached the skip it could be heard hitting the blades as it rotated and could quickly destroy the drum. The Austrian civilian was looking specially for things like that, and while I was there he always stopped the machine in time. The problem in the pits where the lads died was that they were already very weak and overworked in great heat. One subcontractor in particular was very hard on them.

One day after having my boils and carbuncles dressed I was late for my usual job and I finished up in the contractor's pit. At that time it was frosty in the morning, but we were baked when the sun rose. I had taken my greatcoat with me and was so pleased to survive the day that I quite forgot it and left it at the site. I was allowed back to check but it had already been stolen. Most of the Aussies had their own greatcoats and one or two had in addition small sleeveless jackets made from cut-down British Army greatcoats; there was an extra one of these the next day and I assumed that it was what was left of my coat. I was now in serious trouble because there were no greatcoats left but a lad had been killed the previous day and after a long argument I was given his coat. This was an old Greek Army greatcoat, and was very good. I used that until the Red Cross arranged a supply of our own coats. Without the Greek one I would have been unlikely to survive the Alpine winter.

There was no doctor at the site – serious cases would have been treated by the *Luftwaffe* doctor – but we were looked after by our own Medical Corps. There were two New Zealand medical orderlies, and one or two volunteers. My carbuncle had been causing me trouble for some time. I couldn't see it but I could see my mates looking at it as it was being dressed, and even the medical orderlies had asked if I was fit to carry on work but it did not trouble me when I was working. At the same time a boil was growing at the back of my neck which was not going away. All that could be done was to clean the wounds, dress them, and hope that they would cure themselves. There was little else that could be done in a working camp; there was not a great variety of medicines available. The time was approaching when I would need to go to the Stalag, and at that time the whole camp was closed down by the Red Cross who had pointed out that the Geneva Convention forbade employment of POW in such situations.

There are one or two anecdotes about the Zeltweg camp that I would like to relate. There were frequent concerts, and many of the lads gave their party pieces. There was a lad by the name of Robertson from Perth, who gave us some songs, he was a very likeable person. He stood up one day and sang *The Bonny Earl of Moray*. It was the first time that I had heard it and it immediately became one of my favourite songs, but the effect on one of the guards was electric; he was entranced, said that it was the loveliest song that he had ever heard, and asked for the tune and words. That was the guard who had taken my part in the 'boulder' incident.

We were well looked after in every way required by the regulations, but we were short of vitamins and unable to replace what we had lost at Corinth, and the effect of Salonika and the journey up, when we were at our lowest ebb. The room that I was in, a smallish barrack room, held also the survivors from the cruiser *Gloucester* mentioned previously. The red-bearded one gave me a graphic account of the battle of Jutland. When the frost first started about the beginning of September, the *Luftwaffe* gave us schnapps in our coffee each morning, for which we were very grateful.

We fed in an open grassed area in front of our barrack room. There were two tables to serve from and to hold the very large cooking boilers from which the food was doled out. The dishes were about two feet six inches each way. As I said we were still very hungry; in fact we were hungry from the time we were taken until about Christmas time when the effect of the Red Cross parcels began to be felt. By that time we had had these for about a fortnight. There was one very large soldier, about six feet two inches I would think, who particularly suffered from the effect of hunger. The big dishes would be very well cleared out by those serving but every day this chap would descend on them before they were removed for washing up. I don't know how he managed to get anything out of them but he was there for a quarter of an hour every day scraping away at them.

The navy boys were particularly hard on this lad; they had been captured on Crete at the end of the battle, had been a short time at Salonika, and had not been at Corinth at all. They did not know what starvation was; long-term abstinence was unknown to them. One of them shouted at the soldier, 'Go on, pig, get your feet in.'

During the advance in the desert, when we were on 'iron' rations, each man received three packets of biscuits a day – 48 biscuits – and consumed them without difficulty. In addition he received three 12oz tins of bully beef per day, plus many extras, and he could take as much Italian food as he could pack away. As prisoners we received the same biscuits at Corinth and Salonika, up to a maximum of eight per day, and very little else.

Corinth Walk – tune Lambeth Walk

Prison life is very tame,
Till you learn the social game,
Of dodging the Jerry guard,
Down at the market yard.   'AUS'

See the chap without a pass
Get up bayonet up his arse,
From the Jerry guard,
Down at the market yard.   'AUS'

Old major Hicks gets shirty,
'Cos things are dear and dirty,
But you must buy your cheese there,
Beans there, and greens there,
Out in the Grecian sun
Have your daily bit of fun,
Oh dodging the Jerry guard,
Down at the market yard,   'AUS'   'AUS AUS'

Calamity Day 29 April 1941. Tune 'Three Little Fishes'.

Way down south of Calamity bay
Sat ten thousand men who were trying to get away.
The navy came and took the wounded and the ill
And the rest of us crept back in to the hill.
Boom Boom, Clatter Clatter, came the crack of the guns
Of the bombers and fighters of the evil-eyed Huns.
All the next day we lay perfectly still
Hidden in the ditches in Calamity Hill.

All the next day they repeated the dose,
The planes flew low and the bombs fell close.
Nightfall came, we assembled at the Bay
But the ships that appeared there were sweet BA.

Dot dot dot, dash dash dash, dot dot dot,
Oh hark to the cry in wailing morse,

Where in the H-l is the Royal Air Force?

Monday night was the end of the fun
Cos instead of the ships came the Bloody Hun.

Swim said the brigadier, swim if you like,
But damn it, said the Adjutant, I'm a-going to fight.
Bang bang, clash clash, Bl-dy MT.
Bang bang, splash splash, chuck it in the sea.
This we did without any fuss,
Cos we've got the Dunkirk habit in us.

Tuesday we were prisoners of war,
At least that's a thing we've never been before.
Since then life hasn't been too sweet
With nothing to do and B-r all to eat.

Sleep sleep, eat a little and more sleep,
Sleep sleep, eat a little and more sleep.
Each day passes in the same old way,
To commemorate the doings of Calamity bay.

Song first heard in Western Desert September 1940, recorded at Corinth, June 1941. Tune unfortunately forgotten.

I'm a lone Royal Engineer, and I'm stationed at Matruh,
And I've got a little dugout in the sand,
Where the fleas play tig around me as I settle down at
    night,
In my flea bound, bug bound, dug-out in Matruh.

Oh the windows are of meshing and the door is four by
    two,
And the sandbags let the howling sand storms through,
You can hear those blinking Ities as they circle round at
    night,
In my flea bound, bug bound, dug-out at Matruh.

The place is strewn around with tins of bully and meat loaf,
Of marmalade and jam there are but few,
Still I'm as happy as a clam in this land of lice and sand,
In my flea bound, bug bound, dug-out in Matruh.

I wish I had a pretty girl to keep me company,
To relieve me of this mess that I am in,
Oh the angel how I'd love her, if she'd settle down with
    me,
In my flea bound, bug bound, dug-out in Matruh.

CHAPTER EIGHT

In the Austrian Alps

O N THE CLOSURE OF THE WORKING CAMP, AT ZELTWEG all the 500 men were sent in the first instance back to Wolfsberg, to Stalag 18A. In a few days most of them were out again at other working camps. In a week or two the camp at Zeltweg was taken over by Russian prisoners of war. When speaking to some civilians later who had worked at the place, we were told that after the first winter frosts the whole piece of runway we had done had to be relifted and done again. They said that one could walk over it anywhere and see the outline of a pick here and a shovel there, showing almost photograpically through the concrete. The Russians eventually completed the runway.

When I reached Wolfsberg and settled down I reported sick. Doctor Munro was in charge and there was a German surgeon available as well. The first thing Munro said was, 'We'll put this man on a course of prontocill,' which was one of the new German drugs, a red dye. The pills I had been given were to be taken every four hours, one at a time, until they were finished. I then went back to the doctor every day to have the discharge dressed. I was unable to see the large carbuncle in the small of my back and indeed I had some difficulty in feeling it. A circle about five inches diameter was very hard and painful. The boil on the back of my neck was rather more than an inch across. It was bandaged by passing it across my throat, crossing it over and then taking it round my forehead.

The Austrian under officer in charge of the daily working of the guards treated me with great respect; knowing the man he would have done that anyway, but he apparently thought that I had a head wound. I did not make him any the wiser, because the thing on the back of my neck was bad enough, but that on my back was atrocious. I had a reasonably good time while I was there. I was there for three weeks. After the prontocill there did not seem to be a great improvement, but at least it was no worse. Munro then put me on a course of Epsom salts to 'clean me out' and that it certainly did. Then they started to attack the wounds from the outside, dressing them so many times a day with hot lint fomentations; the lint had to be made perfectly dry after sterilizing in scalding water. They had a special way of achieving this and the relief was immediate when it was applied. After about a week of this treatment they were able to lift out little bits of matter with tweezers and cotton wool. After about ten days they were able to remove the core of the boil; it came away in one piece about an inch cube. They were then able to clean out the hole with spirits and other sterilizers. It cured from then on. The carbuncle took much longer, but they cleared it out eventually; when it began to heal a little I was left with a dressing which was to be undisturbed until it fell off.

Then I was sent out to another working camp; but before that, about the end of October or the beginning of November, the Russians came in. It was a terrible sight; I was standing looking at it and I still could not really believe it. However, I have the photographs and they speak louder than words. They were marched in, many of them already dying, and I was told by the lads who cleaned out the wagons that there were bodies in the wagons covered by two or three feet of filth. That may have been an exaggeration, but there were indeed many bodies. The men were sent down to the delouser and made to undress; it was snowing at the time, although it was not lying. They were put through the whole operation; hot shower, deloused, and clothes deloused in the big steam boiler. As they hit the hot water they collapsed in hundreds. Starting in the early afternoon, and continuing throughout the whole afternoon, there was a constant stream of stretcher bearers, provided by our boys, from the delouser to the barracks where the Russians were housed. Half of our barracks and compound was split and given to the Russians, the Russian part being that further from the administration centre. When we went through in the beginning of July we were housed in tents in good weather, the Russians who did not go through the system in the afternoon, were left in the compound all night. Some at least of them died and I have photographs of two of them.

One of the Russian dead found in the huts next morning had had his liver removed, for obvious reasons. After the large number of deaths when they first arrived, the Russian prisoners were dying off, several each week, until the end of the war. At the beginning, for the disposal of the dead, each one had his own rough coffin, but this was thought to be too expensive and they were then buried two or three to a coffin. Soon that was also too expensive, and the camp joiners made a special coffin with a hinged bottom. This was placed over the grave with two or three bodies in it, a rope was pulled and the bodies fell in. The coffin was then removed ready for the next supply. Even that became too much trouble and the final solution was a very large lime pit.

What I remember most about our own delousing at Wolfsberg was what it did to some possessions. Many of us had fancy leather belts purchased in Egypt; some were foolish enough to leave the belts on the trousers. When the lad in front of me received his belt back from the delouser it had shrunk to a circle about five inches in diameter and was about half an inch broad. It would have made a fancy collar for a Cairn terrier.

The nucleus of those of our troops who were running our compound in Wolfsberg was now established, and had connections in the town; many of them worked there. One of them had looted a camera from an Italian prisoner of war in the desert. It was rather like the modern disc camera. It fitted inside his shirt and there was a lens that looked like a button; it was with this that he took the photographs. I remember showing them to people in Dunoon who, while they had been in the army, had been nowhere and seen nothing; but they knew everything and the photographs had been faked, according to them. Another thing they said was that no camera made could do what I had said had been done. About three years ago there were two programmes at different times on TV on different channels which showed the camera exactly. These were programmes on the history of photography. And these are the type of people, themselves practised liars, and therefore unable to believe others, who say that the holocaust never took place. There are many like them around.

One of these was the vindictive creature who succeeded in causing me some damage. This was the architect who had called himself a surveyor in order to avoid military service. He succeeded in doing so for several years while another took his place, and women and children of Europe were fighting his enemies.

The photographs were printed in the town, by people with whom they had become friendly. On a visit to the Stalag much later I found that my former mate was well established and he offered to get me prints. They cost me thirty marks. I put them in the top of my left boot, covered them with the small gaiter and walked out like that. On that occasion I was not searched. I was in regular but infrequent correspondence with that mate, Owen Davies, until he died at Christmas time 1993.

Some time after my return to the working camp I showed these photographs to our French friends, those who stayed under our floor, or more correctly on the next floor down. We spoke at cross-purposes for a short time, until it became obvious that they thought the photographs showed our boys as they arrived at Wolfsberg, and they said that was exactly how we had looked. I thought that they were exaggerating, but maybe not.

That conversation reminded me of the first few days in Wolfsberg. Every day we received an issue of small biscuits. They were about two inches by one inch by three eighths of an inch thick. It was a long time after that I found out that these were a present from the French POW from their own rations, and had been baked in France.

Now for a bit more about the carbuncle (and it was definitely not a precious stone). The centre was about the size of a large egg, and the whole area round about was raised and very hard and painful. When I left for the small working camp it was still quite painful. Any time we had a cold snap it became more painful, and at that time the severe winter of 1941–2 was about to begin. I was at the working camp for some time before the dressing fell off, and after that I really had very little trouble with it. About a year later a piece of dead flesh fell out; it was about an inch and an eighth long, carrot shaped, and three eighths of an inch thick at the top, tapering to a point. It was many years before it ceased to be painful during cold snaps but it was no more than a slight inconvenience.

About the end of November I received a medical parcel from Reggie, my brother. I am quite unable to remember all that it contained, although three items proved to be of great importance. First was a thirty-day supply of multivitamin capsules; these I took one a day until they were finished, and they caused, or appeared to cause, a pronounced improvement in my health. There was a bottle of ferrous sulphate tablets, and every time I had even a very small boil I would take a tablet and it would disappear as if by magic. There was also a small packet of Bicarbonate of Soda, about two inches long and an inch square. This was very useful later. The Red Cross parcels arrived before Christmas, and in a very short time most of us lost our feeling of desperate hunger. Referring again to the carbuncle I was left with a scar which looked like a bullet hole for very many years; it may still be there.

I went to the small Alpine camp at Bodendorf in November, just a guard and myself. The guard's name was Jan Mazourek, the same as a famous president. He gave me his name and postal address when eventually he was sent east. It was: Mazourek Johann, Brunn – Beamtenhes'n, Fouskastr. 27.

The guard took pride in his English, which was not all that good, but for one who could speak no German, I was in no position to criticize. We went by way of Knittlefeld, Zeltweg, and a place called Katztall. We called it catstail. It means Cats Valley, and had been in the Middle Ages a well-known robbers den. Eventually, very late at night, we arrived at Murau, and discovered that the train would stay there for the night, and that there were still several miles to go.

The guard then led me round one place after another; he tried the jail but they refused to accept me, he then went to a small POW working camp that had been established in Marau, and they would not have me either. Had I been able to speak German I would have suggested that I might go to Oban; but nothing seemed to do. A request to a convent was brusquely turned down, and then he had a brilliant idea: we would walk. We then set out, and I kept asking how far it was, but there was a language difficulty.

He obviously knew what I meant but did not know enough to reply. He kept repeating, 'Stunde, Stunde,' which I found out the next day meant 'an hour'. There was a bright moon shining, ground covered with frozen snow that we did not sink through, and I was weak, tired, and carrying all my worldly possessions. After what seemed an age we passed through a small village, and about a mile further on came upon a complex of farm buildings.

A very large St Bernard came running out, barking and growling at us. The guard immediately shouted, 'LIEDE' and 'Nieder, Liede, niede.' It began to wag its tail, and that was the first time that I saw the owner's dog. There was a great deal of frost on it, particularly about the face; the very large eyes were framed in frost and shining in the moon. I was then taken into the camp and given a bed in the corner. By the time I arrived all the lads were in bed and I did not speak to them until the next day. The next day must have been Saturday and I was given the morning off and told to stay in bed.

The medical parcel had also contained calcium lactate tablets, for a defence against frostbite which was prevalent at that time, and of which I had very little. Fortunately I had socks; most of the men had footcloths only by that time. I had kept my socks well darned but I could not go on for ever, and when they were beyond further repair a parcel arrived from the Uist folk with socks and other items. The old socks had large holes in the heels and I made to throw them away when Len Bigmore asked if he could have them. He put them on his very large feet back to front and they were much better than his footcloths, and they did him until his own personal parels arrived, the first one being a month or so later. The holes on the heels of the old socks almost closed when they were turned round. With the foot cloths we had been given wooden shoes, our boots were about worn out with holes through the soles and other defects. But to return to the medical parcel, by the end of the war there was probably more than half of the ferrous sulphate left. I had used them only about four times and the other lads could use them any time they required them.

About a year after I arrived in Bodendorf, the camp size was doubled, the room across the corridor being added, and another eight men arrived. With that lot was a Yorkshireman called Joe Frodsham. I don't have his address and do not remember exactly where his home was. He was a very reasonable chap, some years older than the majority of us, perhaps in his early thirties. He remembered his father's return from the First World War; he had gone straight to the pub instead of coming home, and Joe had been sent to fetch him from there and bring him home. Joe had a bad stomach and he came to me one day to see if I had anything that would help. He chose the Bicarbonate of Soda, and I gave it to him. He returned in a few days with what I thought was the whole packet. He said, 'That was very good, I'm OK now.'

I said, 'Why don't you keep it? You might have another attack.'

'No, it's your stuff, you hang on to it. I'll come for it if I need it.' He said he required very little, and he took it in water or tea. That packet served him for the time we were there together, approximately two and a half years, and there was more than half of it left at the end of the war. You will understand that the medical parcel was a very useful parcel indeed.

There were in the camp when I arrived two Australians, McLarty and Bigmore, first-class lads both of them. McLarty had been shell shocked and was just beginning to get over it. It took a very long time and he still shook a little. You were told about Bigmore earlier; he was the lad with the damaged spine. There were three Kiwis, Bob Judd, Gunner Judd (often addressed as Gonorrhoea Judd) and Arthur Higginbotham (again an older chap, probably in his early thirties). He kept very much to himself, and was very quiet; he had an overpowering hunger until the end of the war, and had very few teeth left. There was apparently something wrong with his metabolism. On one particlar occasion, in the autumn, we were walking to our work, and were passing through an orchard between our camp and the next farm. There were many windfall apples on the ground and most of us picked up two or three, but Arthur managed to get himself fourteen, and by the end of the day he had demolished thirteen of them. Lack of teeth was apparently no drawback, and he earned himself quite a reputation. At that time it took us between two or three hours to reach our working place high up on the opposite mountain. On the return journey it took us not more than ten minutes to reach the bottom of the hill on our sledges, the record being seven minutes. There was also Charlie Beale from Invereargill, and Leslie Michael James O'Sullivan, a remarkable man from Dunedin.

Willie Hamilton from Peebles – one of my own company – was also in the camp. He was, at the time, very ignorant in book learning, but a first class countryman and woodcrafter. He taught me a great deal. He was also a first-class navvy and knew in particular how to do the maximum amount of work for the minimum expenditure of energy, and this was very useful knowledge to have. He was a very useful person to have around. There was an English Welshman who went to school in Mold but lived in Buckley, Chester. There was also a Liverpudlian Welshman, very much more Welsh that the other, who spoke the language very well, and thought of himself as Welsh. This was Owen Davies, who was my mate for a long time; from him I learned a great deal about Welsh history and how to play chess well. He was effectively a Liverpool Orangeman, worked for Cunard, and had been captured in Crete, where he was in a specialist group of Royal Engineers

– a 'Docks Group'. Others there at that time were Ronnie Fraser, from North Shields, Alex Brown from Salford, and his pal Ginger Buckley also from Lancashire, and for a rather short time Alex Mather from Dundee. When food became more plentiful, the lad from Buckley lost his hunger. He then stopped telling us interminable yarns of the huge meals he had in Civvy Street, and told us instead of his conquests of the lovely high-school girls from Mold. There was also Fred Cooper, 4th Hussars, from Nottingham.

From the Aussies and Kiwis, I learned much about woodcraft and working with an axe. The Australians particularly were very good axemen and I never reached their standard. I was by far the best of the British home troops, and I enjoyed axework but when I came home I found that there were no trees to cut. The lad from Buckley, Chester, was a member of 580 Army Troops Company, Royal Engineers; he was a clerk, but the company was a highly specialized base unit. What their exact job was, I was never able to find out. It was said that the General in charge thought that AT meant anti-tank in all cases, and they were immediately dispatched to the front, before anyone discovered the mistake they had suffered several casualties. They were then sent to the rear and finished up on the Hellas as I have said before.

Another of the originals in the camp was John Joyce, from Glasgow. He was known as Yoikee – the way the Germans pronounced his name – and was from No. 512 Field Survey Company, RE, whose particular job was to survey for the artillery. He worked for the Ordnance Survey before the war and his whole office staff were moved into the army at one fell swoop. He was a very good comrade.

At this time the German Army had a crude but very effective way of dealing with frostbite. Two buckets would be placed on the floor, one containing boiling water and the other freezing cold water. The victim was sat down on a chair in front of these containers and had to place his damaged foot first in one and then immediately in the other. He had to move very quickly because he would freeze in the one and scald in the other. It was not meant to be a refined form of torture, and their own sufferers were treated the same way. Over long periods at this time the outdoor temperature registered 30 degrees below zero, centigrade. There was an iron latch on the door, and when we rose on the morning we would leave little pieces of skin sticking to it if we forgot to wear gloves, or hand shoes as the Germans called them. One time was more than enough to forget. When walking along the road we could see breath from our pals quickly building up as frost on their moustaches, eyelids, eyebrows and even on any hair below the eyes.

Those of us who had been in the desert and had learned the Arabic squat were better off than the others; we were practised in squatting and in controlling it. This was very useful in deep snow as at least we had some chance of keeping our bums dry and avoiding piles. The others were unable to sit down.

Our boots were taken from us at night and were locked outside the room; we had to make do with *holz pantoffels*, wooden shoes, from then on. They were quite good, they were warm on the feet at least. Two buckets were kept in the room at night, one for solids and one for liquids. There was quite a cursing when anyone had to use the solids receptacle but the other was well used. So in the morning there was usually one three-quarters full and one empty. Swift from 292 Company got up in the middle of the night and we heared him cursing and swearing and then saying 'got you'. It appears that he was using one bucket when a mouse jumped into the other and he put the lid on it. We could hear it running around for a while before going to sleep. In the morning Swift lifted the lid, and picked up the mouse by the tip of the tail. He was able to hold it out horizontally; it was frozen solid.

Gunner Judd specialized in making mousetraps, a kind of box with a very ingenious deadfall lid on it. He was never able to catch anything, but we managed to buy a spring mousetrap, and we heard it going off during the night. When we looked in the morning there was nothing in the trap, but two feet away we found a black rat, only just alive. It was a beautiful animal, with lovely purple-black shining fur; but I had heard about black rats before and was very careful with it. There were no visible fleas on it, so I handled it with gloves and drowned it in the horse trough. Then I gave it to the pigs.

Mentioning the pigs reminded me of another incident. For a short time we had a big Scottish chap in the other room, who was very quarrelsome and difficult to take. He was always complaining about things and had fallen out with the locals. It was his turn to collect rations for the room, and he had been given a large dish of soup; he said that it was nothing but hot water and grease, that he was not going to dish it out to his pals, and he took it straight in to the pigs. It may be that he was too lazy to carry it up two floors. The pigs were farrowing at the time, and there were many piglets in the place. The next thing that we saw was the vet's car arriving; he ran in to the pighouse and gave many of them injections. He was successful in saving them all. The vet had a little West Highland terrier, which he called 'Jock'. We saw a great deal of that animal.

Another day we were given some extra cheese, we were quite well fed at the time. The big lad did not like the cheese (without trying it) and he went down to the kitchen and complained volubly. It was skimmed milk cheese and that gave it a rubbery consistency. There was a blond girl in charge of the kitchen, Frau Schmidt, daughter of the owner, and married to an officer serving on the eastern front. She was stand-offish, but a nice lassie. Some of the boys had an uncomplimentary name for her, 'the iceberg', or something to that effect. They had an argument and our lad threw the cheese hard on to the floor. It bounced up to the ceiling and came down again, and rose again nearly to the roof. Fortunately, he was one of the new ones from the other room. Where they had been I don't know, but they had not been to Corinth.

Some time later I went down for the rations for our room. I met the same girl and she gave me the food, for which I said *Dankeschon*, which means thank you very much. She replied *Bitte sehr*, it's a great pleasure: it's the first time I heard the expression. So many of the husbands were killed or died on the eastern front or in Norway, or other fronts, that I can't remember what happened to her husband. I don't remember ever seeing him, and she had no children. She was still there when we left.

Eventually the Kiwi gave up his attempts to make his trap work and gave it to me. I adjusted the working parts to make the action more delicate, and at last had it to a stage that a beetle would have chance of tripping it, and it worked from then on. At that time we were all trying to design traps that worked, but the 'Kiwi Box Trap' was the only successful one. I baited it and put it above the ceiling of our room, and two nights later we heard it going off. Carrying it in my left hand I took it down to the horse trough in the morning. I had a bar of wood in my right hand. I dropped it into the water and thought that it would drown the rat, but the wooden door floated off and the animal escaped. It then swam the full length of the trough, and was climbing out at the right hand end when I hit it with the bar of wood, I felt very sorry for the beast.

After that, any time I had a catch I held the door and the box under the water until the bubbles stopped. One night when the guard was out hunting, we heard a great commotion from the room across the passage, it sounded like someone was being murdered. In the morning, when we asked what had happened, we were told that a rat had appeared in the room, and they were chasing it backwards and forwards with bayonets, knives, axes, and everything that they had hidden away. We were two storeys up, and it must have been summertime because it was bright and the window was open. At last the terrified animal took a flying leap out of the window. It landed on the dung heap beside a pig. The pig accepted it gratefully and swallowed it in two bites.

There had been searches occasionally by various people, and as the war progressed they grew more strict. In one of the earlier searches, the first one in which the Gestapo was involved, the other room was given a very

IN THE AUSTRIAN ALPS

thorough going over. First they pulled at the notice board and a bayonet and a hacksaw fell out They then really got to work and found all sorts of forbidden articles. Flushed with success they then searched our room and found nothing. I had everything too well hidden. My main cache was in the thin gable wall between the room and outside. This wall was about seven inches thick overall, timber framed with wood lining outside and a type of thick white cardboard inside. I removed a large sheet of this inner lining. There was a small skirting at the foot, and I removed the whole section; fortunately at that point it was only about four feet long. At the same time I removed the section of cardboard sheeting and found thin timber boarding behind it. I shortened the nails in the skirting and nailed the cardboard to it at the back. Then I shortened and greased the other nails and was able to lift off and replace the section in a matter of seconds. Then I removed a piece of the inner boarding about three feet by two feet and the place was ready. I had a large area to work in, although it was only about five inches wide. Then later when the searches became more frequent and stricter, I placed black-out paper behind the tins so that there was no possibility of them being seen through the chinks between the outer boards. Nothing that I had hidden was ever discovered.

Later, on request, I made another cache, to take bigger items, and things that were not so valuable to us. In the first cache I took care of all the tins that required to be hidden. I took no payment of any kind but one thieving treacherous person stole one of my tins as I was checking them in and out. Fortunately I have no idea who did it, just some poor soul who thought that he had more right to live than me. The opening into the second place was made the same way as the first one but it was made into the triangular space behind the uprights at the side of the roof. There was a large space and we could if necessary go round behind the guard's room to behind the other barrack, or if necessary hide someone in it. My photographs I packaged carefully and slid up behind the pasteboard on the slope of the roof. The nails were not loosened in any way.

The Gestapo became more security conscious and put a network of strap-iron on the outsides of the doors and bolted it through. It was a rather stupid piece of work. The iron was outside the doors but it was in darkness unless one of the three doors was open. The guard's room was in between the other two. We had a chap from Birmingham, who was a blacksmith by trade, in the other room. Winter was on the way and he decided to make a sledge. He took a strap of iron from each door, and that was never discovered. The iron had twisted the door and loosened the hinges; one side of the hinge was a long spike with a right angled turn on the end to take the other part of the hinge. The spike was merely hammered into the door frame, and was inserted from the room side. When they were placing the strap iron we noticed that the spike was far from secure. The next night that the guard was out we pulled the spikes out, greased them, and replaced them. We could then open the door (from the wrong edge) at any time, and no one would know from the outside that the door had been interfered with.

Our regular work was the construction of a forestry road up the moutain on the opposite side on the valley. It was being built on the sloping side of the hill, and we had to excavate the high side and fill the lower side. The road was two metres wide. Filling had to be well done and compacted otherwise it would sink in the spring when the frost went. We worked on this road almost the whole time we spent at Bodendorf, although at different times we helped at the farm, and on other work. The farmhouse was also a guest house which sold beer, coffee and other things. There were some great concerts there, which we could hear from our rooms. Up the hill a short way from the guesthouse was the pighouse. This was an extensive building; the piggery being on the ground floor. The French lager was on the middle floor, as well as some storage space. Our place was on the next floor, in the roof space. Access to the upper floors was by means of stairs and a timber gallery on the side remote from the house. At the end of this gallery was the toilet, simply a little cupboard four feet square. There was a board with a hole in it, which was the seat, and down the left hand side was a piece of timber, five inches square, inclined downwards to the back, and with a deep V cut out of it. This was the urinal. At the first frost an icicle would begin to form, hanging downwards from the end of the trough. At the same time a pillar of frozen solids would begin to build up below the hole in the seat. The Aussies were laying bets on whether the icicle would reach the ground before the pillar came through the hole. I think that the column had a narrow win, but in any case we had to send in an Aussie with his axe to fell it, and it was again approaching the hole at the end of that remarkable winter. With the arrival of the thaw the Frenchmen were sent in with long-handled shovels and an ox-cart to carefully collect everything and spread it over the fields.

In the guesthouse stayed Blasius Murer, the owner and the boss, a man aged about 45 and with strong Nazi sympathies, his sister Anna, a very fine woman, (who eventually married one of the guards just before he left for Russia, it is likely that she never saw him again), and several others. Before Anna was married she had a son, who was about twelve or thirteen. He was always addressed as Hirsch (deer) or Hirschel (little deer), it may have been his correct name. He was at a private school near the Italian border, and almost at the end of the war he was coming home by train, when the

American planes shot it up on one of the Alpine passes, and the boy was one of those killed. Anna's attitude to us did not change as a result of her loss. I had been quite friendly with that boy.

Now one or two items out of context. The Russian prisoners came from Smolensk. Now about John Joyce. I was in a moving, crowded lift in the high building, in Hamilton, and a voice behind me said, 'You were in Klagenfurt.' I said, 'No, I wasn't in Klagenfurt, but I recognize your voice; you went over the wall.' When the lift stopped there was Yoikie, looking much the same after all these years, still with the Ordnance Survey, and at that time working in Hamilton. Later he transferred to Inverness, and was still in Inverness when I came north and I saw him once or twice. He died about two years after he retired. Anna's son was an intelligent young boy who used to come to me to identify various objects. He brought me a moth that was between two and a half inches and three inches long, I thought it was a death's head, but I had no way of identifying it. He also brought me a young bird and other unusual objects. He had an interest in chess and I think I had one game with him. His English was quite good.

About 75 yards from the guesthouse was a large building, I think of three storeys. In the ground floor the cattle wintered. The floor above was principally a grain store; there was hay there as well, but the main hayloft was in the roof. Just outside our window, about seven yards away from the entrance to the pigsty, was a little building with a horse trough in front of it, it was used as a drying room, and we used to go there to wash. There was always hot water available. Old Nanna worked in there; she made the bread and did the washing up. The room was primarily a washhouse, but the right hand side seemed to be blocked off, and it dawned that this was a large oven. There was a little metal door for the oven, where the bread was baked every week. In the loft above stayed Anna, the cowgirl, who lived in sin with the cattleman. She had a little girl, about two and a half years old. She was a little blonde lassie who was usually smiling and very cheerful, but when she was annoyed with something she would scowl at us, turn around, lift her little skirt, and point her bare bottom at us.

When the war had almost run its course the cattleman would be about forty. He had been invalided out and told that he would not be required again but in late 1944 he was called up again and was given a nice safe posting in Norway. Three weeks later we heard that he was dead, and that he had been killed by the British 'Bandeserai'. This was their propaganda name for the Commandos and it was about the time of the 'heavy water' raid. Anna and her little girl were still there when we left some months later.

At last the ladies in the guesthouse became tired of rudeness and complaints about good food (they took the same food themselves) and they had a small cookhouse built for us at the end of the washhouse. One of the boys was appointed cook, and we did not eat so well from then on. We were given our rations, all of them, without extras. The food now was 'good English food', as they called it, but many of us could see clearly that we were getting much less. This went on for quite a long time and I think that then there was a change back again but on that point my memory is not very clear. At any rate by that time the Austrians were themselves hungry.

The Austrians in Steirmark (Styria) spoke German very differently from the normal German, or Viennese, or the educated people; for instance, *ja* became *jo jo*; Klagenfurt became Clognfoort. Where in Scotland Malcolm becomes Malkie, the diminutive in Styria would be equivalent to the English 'le', so instead of Malkie it would be Molkle. When we arrived at first we had an oldish civilian in charge of us on the road; we did not know his age, he looked to be about 65 or 70, but it could just be general dilapidation. His name was Sebastian Stack; in Bodendorf he was called Sevostian Stock, and usually 'Vostle'. He lived with washhouse Anna, who washed linen, and baked bread and did very much more. They were reputed to have a large family of sons, of which we knew four. We had Vostle for about a year, then the bosses became dissatisfied with his work and he went back to working on the farm. On one of the searches a cache of donnerite (the German equivalent of dynamite) was found in the toilet, and I am quite sure that Joe Frodsham had put it there: later in the war we made some hand grenades, and Joe was one of the moving spirits. In this case Vostle was blamed – it seems that in his wild youth he had been in the habit of fishing the Mur with explosives. We thanked him profusely when we left the place and I think that he had no idea why we thanked him.

One day I was in the washhouse when Anna received a letter saying that one of her sons had been killed. At that time we had been there about a year. Approximately a year later another son Blasius (Blos) came home wounded from the Russian front having been told that he would not be required again. Six months later he was back in the army, and again I was in the washhouse when a letter arrived for her. Immediately she began to cry saying, 'Again I am a son short.' She was unable to read but she opened the letter and an Iron Cross fell out. There was the usual message; 'Your son will not return, Heil Hitler,' or words to that effect. Later I will have something to say about her younger sons who were there nearly all the time: Fritz who was about twelve when we arrived, and Adolf who was about ten. The youngest boy was called Florian. Washhouse Anna was one of the few people who was really nasty to us. This was understandable but she had no great power in the place, and was not in a position to do any harm.

Fritz was sixteen two months before the end of the war, and was called up. He went towards the eastern front through Dresden; there he met the fire raid and was not heard of again. Adolf was taken away at age fourteen, and was put to work with the Hitler Youth, building defences in Yugoslavia. There he suffered attacks from aircraft which he called 'Bandiserai' aircraft, which were in fact British. He came home some six weeks before the end of the war and was there when we left, so he, at least, survived. He was a likeable lad.

Most of the valleys in Austria run east and west, and by good fortune, according to the geology of the place, the steeper slopes face north, lying on the southern sides on the valleys. The northern sides had the gentler slopes facing south, and were generally farmed almost to the top. It takes a good hour to walk from the valley floor to the topmost farms.

We were constructing a road on the forestry side, and this meant that we had to cross the Mur by the little bridge called Cecilia Bruche, where there was a railway halt, and climb up a bit to the start of the road. We started from a crossroads where another road went down to St Lorenzen. One day for some reason we went to the smith to get our drilling irons sharpened. We used these irons for hand drilling into the rock. The smithy was a lovely place, like something dreamed up by Walt Disney. All machines were worked by one water wheel. When one lever was pulled the bellows worked, another lever worked the small lift, and a third lever worked the trip hammer. This was some hammer, it delivered short, hard blows in very quick succession. It was essentially a log secured eccentrically, being pivotted perhaps at a third of its length. A hammer head, adjusted to hit on to an anvil, was fixed under the short end. At the other end was a large wooden cogwheel, which rapidly raised and released the log. When it was working the whole place shook. It was quite a comical place and well worth seeing, if it is still there.

We took our drills in there and left them to be collected in the morning, then left the place to go home via the St Georgen crossroads. As we walked up to the crossroads we passed a little waif of a girl, who stepped off into the deep snow to let us pass. This was the little Polish girl, Marie, and that was the first and only time that I saw her. She was heavily pregnant, her time must have been very near. She looked to me about twelve, probably she was about fourteen. We never saw, or heard of her again; no doubt she was put down shortly after we saw her. There were a number of Poles in the area, boys and girls, slave labourers; some we became well acquainted with. I talked to a young lad called Peter, who was on the hill with a horse and sledge to remove something or other, and I asked him how he had managed to end up in Austria. He said, 'When I was fourteen, my mother sent me to the shop for some messages. Jerries grabbed me and put me on the train, and that's how I happen to be here.'

You will gather from what I've said already that the first winter was horrendous even in the barrack room. For the next winter we were better prepared. The owner had called in the maurer and the mauler (the bricklayer and the plasterer). They extended the brick-built stove into the room (up to firebox level) about two feet six inches each way, and covered this with an iron plate, which had a removable circle about a foot diameter in the middle. We could then make the plate red hot if we so desired, and boiling water was no trouble; the room was comfortable at all times. Unfortunately, the room also proved to be comfortable for the bugs, and they moved in, in force. Bed bugs are little flat insects, known to the Americans as mahogany flats, roughly three-sixteenths of an inch round, almost clear when hungry; but a mahogany colour when they had a good drink of blood. When well fed they had a disgusting smell. They went out hunting at night. The room was lined internally with sheets of softboard, and as soon as the light went out we could all hear them scraping about behind the sheets, pushing out and dropping on us. This did not suit me at all. After the first day I managed to obtain strips of paper and obtained flour by some nefarious means, made paste and covered the joints round about my bed. That was my problem solved but this did not suit at least one other man, who claimed that I was not taking my fair share of the bugs, and attempted to make me remove my protection.

Instead of removing my protection he got a flea in his ear to go with his bugs. I took the view that if he was not so lazy he could apply his own protection. However, a complaint was made to the boss, and one of the boys was given a day at home to tape up all the joints in both rooms, and indeed he made a very good job of it. He saw no point in doing the guard's room, and the guard had to sleep with the lights on all night.

November and December 1941 was the time when our clothes were in the poorest condition; clothes were falling apart and in many cases there was more darn than cloth. I even managed to darn a complete new stern in my trousers. Shortly afterwards I obtained a spare piece of cloth from the remains of a damaged piece of uniform, and replaced a circle nearly one foot six inches round. To my mind I made a very good job of it. Every now and then we were required to put a new patch on our left trouser knee where the shovel rubbed against it.

British Army clothes sent through the Red Cross arrived about the end of March 1942. We had received issues of German underwear, foot cloths and other items. Mostly they seemed to be poorer quality than ours, but the German long johns were better designed if the material was not so good.

They formed a lining against the trousers, were tied to the socks, and were much warmer than ours. The British ones were tight against the legs, irritated the skin, and neither kept the cold out nor the heat in.

The foot cloths were said to be better than socks for keeping feet healthy, giving fewer corns and other foot troubles; they lasted a long time, but were inclined to shrink. Even at this time, ten months or a year after Corinth, many people still had severe dermatitis and were finding it very difficult to cure. I think that it was not cured in most cases, but was contained by massive doses of vitamin C which the Germans managed to obtain somewhere; for the worst cases they were injecting it. Jerry had a special ointment, which reminded me of the Lion ointment of my childhood. It was a green colour and was used in all dermatitis cases and in almost every case it caused a marked worsening of the condition. They would have done much better by keeping the affected area dry and hot.

There was the odd case of serious illness, not too many among our troops, but the Russian soldiers were going rapidly downhill, and some of the Russian civilian workers did not look well. There were three girls from Kiev in the complex, they stayed in or near the guesthouse. As well as I can remember and reproduce the sounds, they were Anka, Olcha and Maritchk – called Anna, Olga and Marie by all and sundry. By that time they were about eighteen, the oldest being Marie, next Anna and youngest Olga. They had simply been removed from the roadway and turned into slaves, very far from their homes. We spoke to them frequently. Marie had been training to be a teacher, and could make herself understood in English. They looked a great deal older than their years, seeming to be about 30 and all had been raped several times. They all told the same story. Before coming to Bodendorf they had worked as labourers on road contracts, and Anna had a photograph of herself working with a long shovel, and with her dress tucked into a very large pair of ugly bloomers, which looked as they had been made from an old blanket. The girls were delighted to be working in a place where most people treated them well and courteously.

There had been a girls' school near Kursk, for girls fourteen to sixteen years old; there were several of these girls near us. They said that all the girls in the school had been moved west. Some of these girls were quite attractive; the hardships they had suffered did not yet show on their faces. There was one called Catle (that would have been Ecaterina), and there was an Anna in the next farm to us; we knew that pair fairly well.

There was a small farm across the river from St Lorenzen, which could afford only one Russian girl, who became very friendly with the farmer's daughter. The Russian became fluent in German, and at the same time the

Austrian girl became fluent in Russian. It was a surprising experience to hear these two girls speaking to each other.

Every working camp divided into pairs of prisoners who could trust each other. Occasionally there were larger groups, but usually these broke up quickly; there were one or two triples which stayed together but not many. For example, it was an advantage to both to open only one packet of tea or coffee at a time and they looked after each other's interests, so that they had double the protection of a single. It was a particular advantage in the case of tinned perishable foods, one tin at a time being opened. Of course there had to be complete mutual trust. My mate was Owen Davies, and we were together for about a year. After he was invalided back to the Stalag I stayed on my own; this I thought was safer and the rest were already paired off in any case. Owen had been quite a ladies' man from his youth, and he had been friendly with a girl called Jean, her second name I have forgotten. They had a disagreement about two years before the war, but parted on friendly terms, and Owen had another girl who was writing to him. While at Bodendorf he received a letter from the first one, and arranged for one of the lads, Alex Brown, to write to her. This friendship blossomed and after the war they married. About a month later, when the next mail arrived, Owen had a letter from his current girlfriend. Briefly it said that she had found a fireside fusilier and had ditched Owen, who was shattered. He had chronic dermatitis, and it flared up again at that time. I don't know if the way he felt at the time had anything to do with it but the medics were unable to control it. The Ukrainian doctor at Murau could not help and Owen was then returned to the Stalag. After that I saw him once or twice on visits to the Stalag then he was sent out to the big camp at Klagenfurt.

I saw the effect of this kind of thing on several chaps over the course of the four years I was in Austria, people receiving letters saying that their fiancées had found someone else, and occasionally even being told that their wives had children, perhaps two years after they were taken prisoner. This type of thing was not entirely one-sided. For example, a happily married Kiwi who worked out of the Stalag, became friendly with a girl, whether Austrian or slave worker I was not told, but he finished up with VD. He had no intention of going home to infect his wife, so he walked to the fence and began to climb over it. He refused to stop despite shouted warnings from several of the guards, and at last he was shot.

It should be understood that all the Anzacs were volunteers, and while most of them had joined for normal reasons, many of them had joined because of marital problems. One of our room mates belonged to the South Island somewhere, and, when he was fifteen, having successfully fertilized a young girl, thought it necessary to 'get as far north as possible'. There he was befriended by a farmer who gave him a home and a job. While there, he contracted 'infantile paralysis', which is now called polio. He was successfully treated in hospital by draining his spine and other methods, and was then sent back to the farm to convalesce. The farmer's attractive young wife made an excellent nurse, until he fertilized her as well. His options were then severely limited and he joined the army. He had made a complete recovery and was in (I think) the First Echelon. The farmer was so disgusted with his wife and the man he had befriended that he too joined the army, but this time in the Second Echelon as an officer. Officers and men were kept separately, but they met briefly at Salonika, and there was no conversation but a bitter look spoke volumes.

There was another Kiwi in the camp, Leslie Michael James O'Sullivan, whose people had been mill owners and had been burned out in the troubles in Southern Ireland; then they emigrated to New Zealand. They appeared to utterly hate the English. We heard all the rebel songs and stories of ancient Irish kings. I learned much from him. He had mother-in-law trouble. He had married a girl called McConnochie, whom he adored, but mother-in-law was trying to convert him and he was a staunch Catholic. I think that is what the trouble was. We heard of nothing but quarrels, and at last he left. He was one of the escape party, and I'll come to that later. He was in another camp which caught fire while it was locked, and while the guard was out at a dance. There were one or two killed, and Leslie was badly burned, but recovered. Some time later, on the way out, I met him at St Johann in Pongau. He was much quieter and left me with the impression that he was one of the finest lads I had met. He was looking forward to going home to his wife.

The big Australian, with the damaged back, would have joined the army in any case but the catalyst was a girlfriend he had. He described her as a very nice girl, family friend, and both families were in favour of marriage. But our friend was not sure enough to commit himself, so he joined the army. I have not heard of him for 50 years.

The other Anzac I mentioned, also a very fine chap, was Charlie Beale from Invercargill, which lies away down south near the tip of the South Island, and only a few miles across the water from Oban. From him I learned much about the history of New Zealand, and he helped me with axemanship, woodcraft and a great deal more. I don't remember where we parted company, but I think that he was with us until the end of the war.

Charlie, and indeed all the Anzacs, gave me a great interest in farming. At least one of them was interested in the difference between husbanding and farming. He insisted that the Austrian Alpine folk were the best husbandmen he had seen anywhere, but that they were not good farmers. First-class husbandmen they were, but I could not wholeheartedly agree that they were not good farmers. Everything was used and recycled, and nothing was wasted; in that manner they were without doubt very good husbandmen. The hay was perfect, great care was taken in making it, and every little piece of fertile ground was used for something.

There was a beautiful stand of experimental wheat (taken from the Ukraine); every stalk was the same height, with large heads of bearded wheat, large grain stuff, and I would have said that it was barley but was corrected by the Anzacs. There were fields of poppies which were used to make margarine. Forestry was centrally controlled as a long-term renewable asset, and the high pastures (in effect the sheilings), were worked with the low ground, perfectly complementing each other. I would have said that they were very good farmers. There was also an efficient and very well-organised veterinary service.

About the beginnings of March 1941 the Czech guard took the lad from Buckley and me to the Stalag to collect the Red Cross supplies, and I think that we stayed the night there. There was one set of battledress for each man, there were cap comforters, boots, and I'm sure that we received greatcoats also with that delivery. There was not a great deal to report from the Stalag; there was not much doing, there were a number of Russians about. We returned by the same route which we had used the first time, and again the little train had stopped for the night by the time we reached Murau. This time we managed to get into a British working camp, and we were given a couple of bunks at the end furthest from the door. The occupants were asleep at the time. When we awoke in the morning the place was full of Scousers, and very nice lads they were. By this time I have forgotten their regiment but they were very Bolshie. When we awoke, I was immediately asked, 'Are you a Jock?' Then the questioner shouted out, 'We've got a Jock here at last. We'll get this place sorted out now.'

I said, 'No, I'm sorry, we're from another camp up the line.' One question led to another.

'What are you here for?'

'We've been to Stalag to collect clothing – British Army clothing – sent through the Red Cross.'

'We've got nothing like that.' At this point the guard came in, a quiet country bumpkin type, called Carl, to whom he said, 'Where are OUR clothes?' Carl's reply was brief and to the point: 'Nicht': none. Then they had a discussion about it. There was a newspaper photograph stuck to the wall of British Guardsmen marching past, and they had put a large caption under it 'REAL SOLDIERS': above it was a photograph of the 1940 Fire of London.

Carl came back to take them to work and they said to him, 'Nicht f-ing hosen, nicht f-ing arbeit, f- off, Charlie. No f-ing trousers, no f-ing work. F- off, Charlie.' Charlie turned round and walked out of the room, and about ten minutes later a sergeant-major arrived, and he said that the clothing would be supplied very soon. There was no shouting or bawling and they agreed to work. That was the last that we saw of them. Every time I think of Charlie, I feel sorry for him, he had such a mournful face, like a dog that had been whipped. I'm sure he had no idea what the war was about.

We had a pair of boots each with that supply of clothing: they were British Army boots and my pair served me very well for three years. Then, six months from the end of the war, we received each a pair of Australian boots; they were a different shape but very good and comfortable. The first pair I received I had to restitch at least once a year. In the spring and autumn there was often hard frost on top and soft snow underneath. At these times we frequently broke through the crust, and at last the stitching would cut. I would do the stitching myself and get the local *schuster* to resole them with leather and wooden pegs. Hobnailing round the edges I also did myself. Nailing was done round the outer edges of the soles and heels, and one nail on the leading edge of the heel, which was an excellent thing to stop slipping on ice. There were no nails on the inner faces of the soles because this caused the snow to stick to the leather where it was very difficult to remove.

That clothing supply was most welcome, and I can't remember when we received further replacements. During all my time there I received four clothing parcels from home and they too were most welcome. There were different things in each parcel, the most unusual being a knitted blanket. These knitted blankets were communal efforts: a group of women and girls would knit as many squares of eight-inch side as they were able, or until the supply of wool ran out. These were collected at a central point and sewn together by volunteers. The army uniforms came via the Red Cross and from then we always had something to work on and were never again cold to the same extent, and were always well shod. For back-up we still had our wooden shoes.

One day our interpreter, and the nineteen-year-old lad from the potteries, had an altercation near the buckets. The rest of us were fed up and several of us told them to stop, and this they did but not before they had kicked over the urine bucket. A good part of the contents went over my wooden shoes, and having warned them in ample time before the disaster, I said, 'Well which one is going to wash them?' Neither of them would agree to clean up, so I said, 'Well I'll just need to do both of you, one after the other.' I didn't know how I would get on but they would be more careful in future. The potteries boy and I got on very well and did not want to fight, so he said, 'All right, we'll wash one each.' So they washed one each and hung them up to dry, and that was the end of the affair. These squabbles were usually about nothing – they flared up and disappeared just as quickly.

An evening in that camp was a confusing affair. I would be sitting at the end of the table, writing out information about architecture, building construction and civil engineering. In the general confusion and noise there was no other way that I could fix the facts in my mind. Most books I wrote out four times each and knew the contents back to front and inside out. Arthur would be sitting beside the fire; there might be one or two fights, or at least squabbles; Australians playing 'two up'; the bridge fiends shouting 'double and re-double'; two playing with dice, and O'Sullivan singing *Don't run down the Irish, if you do you'll make me sad*, and altogether a fine, quiet home we had.

CHAPTER NINE

More Memories of Austria

Probably the best news we ever received over the grapevine was that of the Japanese attack on Pearl Harbor; there had been very little doubt before, but now we knew that we were going to win. It might take some time but the outcome was now certain. When the Russians were drawn in I was sure of ultimate victory, but thought that it might take a long time, perhaps ten or fifteen years. When Germany declared war on the US, the probable time-scale fell to a few years.

Now another item out of chronological order. There was in the western desert, when we first arrived, a company of soldiers who travelled up and down the road on pushbikes. I think that they were signallers but at this late date I am not sure.

There was one other method by which we received news, which I have not mentioned before, and this was by means of British and American leaflets. Towards the end of the war this was quite common. A plane would be seen travelling over at high level, and we would see what looked like a mist coming from it. This was the leaflets being ejected. About four hours later they would reach the ground. I have one or two of these leaflets. In the last few weeks of the war they took the form of a newspaper, dated every second day, and of that I managed to retrieve only scraps. It was called *Red White Red*, the colours of the Austrian National flag. There was a great deal of news in it.

It was a shooting offence for a civilian to pick up one of these leaflets; but the regulations were so framed that it was the picking up that was forbidden, and one civilian was prepared to read it if I picked it up. As the war progressed the turnover of guards increased in frequency, they seemed to last for a very short time. We had one called Hackenschmidt, a Viennese chap who had a 56 or 57 inch chest, a very broad man, in his early forties. He was very powerfully built, and about five feet ten inches tall. His amusement in civilian life was swimming the Danube, this was acknowledged to be a great feat.

Hackenschmidt took me to Wolfsberg on one occasion, and that was the last time I went to the Stalag: I remembered it for two reasons. First, I met Owen again and, second, he managed to obtain the photographs for me. As usual when we reached Wolfsberg we could smell the Stalag, it stank horribly. There was a little boy on the bridge over the river, about twelve years old, with a very long thin pole to which he had attached a snare at one end. He was attempting to catch a very large fish in the river just below him; it looked like a salmon, and I never found out if he had caught it.

We were in the Stalag to collect Red Cross parcels, gifts from the homelands, clothing, etc. After this collection they were sent through Scheifling. There was not much to report from Wolfsberg; there was the latest reliable news from the BBC, and the usual crop of rumours. The Stalag had been damaged; the Yanks had bombed it one day and killed some eight men. They were not very popular at the best of times, but this made it worse. It was about midday, and they were about 30,000 feet up; I keep repeating this but they did not have much idea where their bombs were going. The camp had very large red crosses on the roofs, which could be seen for miles. It is unlikely that we will ever know the reason for the bombing. I was given one gruesome detail – a piece of skull, about four inches square, lay under the wire until the end of the war.

About this time we were given a certain amount of propaganda in an attempt to persuade us to fight on the German side, in what was called the 'Bulldog Brigade'; there were all sorts of sweeteners promised. Only two from our Stalag joined. One of these was a man called Courlander, Courland is a district in White Russia; his people had been murdered by the communists and of course he was not fighting for Germany, he was fighting against the communists. He was given a fifteen-year sentence. His case is reported in one of the *War Illustrated* volumes. There was a sergeant-major as well who joined for some personal reason; these were the only two from our area. Out of the 150,000 or thereabouts British POW in German hands, there were less than 150 in the 'Bulldog Brigade'.

You may or may not know that the Southern Irish sent at least a battalion to Russia and they were photographed several times. There was a war history broadcast on TV, I think that it was in the sixties, and I have a shot of a battalion marching past, singing, '*Wrap the green flag round me, boys*'. Against this we had some Irish Nationals fighting on our side, and I personally met several of these. All those I met and spoke to were first-class lads. One of these, Paddy Riley, stuck it until he reached Wolfsberg, and then he gave the Jerries a great deal of trouble. He told them that he was a neutral and that they had no right to hold him. I don't know what kind of yarn he spun, but he gave them a great deal of trouble, and many of them were very annoyed, much to our amusement. I expect that he was sent home, at least I never heard of him again. He was from Dublin, and a good comrade.

I met two or three others; all the names are forgotten, but I am quite sure that there were many more on our side than on the side of the Nazis. I have always been very interested in Irish history, especially early history, because they were our ancestors as well, and I learned a bit from one of the boys who was in the next camp for some years. I think that he too was from Dublin. He had a great interest in the ancient Irish kings and also could speak a bit of Gaelic. On the way back to Bodendorf on the last Stalag visit, Hackenschmidt, another lad and I stopped at Scheifling. Again the train had stopped for the night, and again we started looking round for somewhere to sleep, but this guard wasted no time and took us to the jail. There we were locked in a double-bedded cell, and a real good old-fashioned cell it was. It had a wooden bed, wooden pillow, no blankets, no heating, no frills. Every time we woke up during the night (and it was a very cold night), we were comforted and amused to see the guard trying to warm his hands at a hurricane lantern. He was sitting just outside the door, so that he could always see us through the grill. Hackenschmidt was a good helpful chap, and most of the guards were excellent. We did have one who was a bit of a rascal, but he did not last very long. He was sent to the Russian front because of the break-out. During this last trip to Wolfsberg we were halted at the station where the main line changed to narrow gauge. The guard was away somewhere and we were sitting at the station waiting for him. There were two Russians a short way along the platform. It would be about two years after they had arrived at Wolfsberg. These were young men, soldiers, and they looked about 80 years old. Their clothes were in rags, and there were no soles on their boots. When they moved they shuffled about with very short steps like very old men. All we had were cigarettes which we were carrying from Wolfsberg. We gave them a packet each; I kept guard while the other lad passed the cigarettes over. At the time it was all we had to give. The sight of these degraded human beings was quite a shock to us because at that time most of our boys were quite healthy, most of those who died were already dead, and it was a fairly prosperous time in Germany with plenty of food about.

One of the guards we had was a chap called Burisch, also from Vienna. I think that he was of Hungarian extraction. He was an amiable chap; tall, angular, and very thin. Every night he would come to the door and shout, 'Macklayan zwei partie' – MacLean two games – then he would come in, put his cap on the bench, a very hard bench, to cushion his bony behind. Then he would sit down and we would have two games of chess. He was an excellent player, the best I have ever played against, and from him I learned many of the finer points of chess. Unfortunately, with the passage of time and lack of practice these have been forgotten. He always beat me until the last game, when I managed to manoeuvre him into a kind of fool's mate; really, in his class, he was not used to such simple moves. I was moving to the checkmate when he rose and said that he had to see his Frau.

I said, 'I thought your Frau was in Vienna.'

'Oh, yes, but I have another Frau here,' and as he reached the door he turned and said, 'Oh, and another in Scheifling.' That was the last game we played.

There was another Viennese guard by the name of Joe Vebric; he was a tram driver in civilian life, about 35 and probably the best guard we ever had. Twice, before going home on a week's leave to Vienna, he went round all the lads and asked if there was anything we wished to purchase from Vienna. We were paid in a kind of camp money called *lager gelt*. It was quite legal and could be used to purchase things that were not vital to the war effort. I had amassed a large amount of this stuff and would have liked to acquire drawing instruments – some of the best were made in Austria. I gave him all that I had. He returned in a week and was very apologetic; he had had a beautiful set of Reifler drawing instruments in his hand, had paid for them, and was making for the door when he was asked for his *schiene*, which was his authority to acquire them. He had no *schiene*, and I did not obtain my drawing instruments. The money would have been spent on items much less desirable; but I did get two Austrian pipes, one of which I brought home. The rest was frittered away. We did not have Joe very long; he was sent east, to where so many, good and bad, had gone before him, and had melted away. We heard no more of him.

At this point I should mention Granberger, another Viennese and another gentleman. He looked to be in his forties, and we had him for quite a long time as I remember going to various places with him. We took a sick man to the doctor in Marau, and I was at least twice to the dentist in Tamsweg; different dentists each time. The first one was a very attractive young girl, but a confirmed Nazi. She displayed her venom by removing a perfectly good tooth and leaving me with the aching one. The other dentist was Swiss. He filled the gap and I had that tooth until the sixties. That was the dentist who asked me for a 'Chesterfield' and I didn't know what he was talking about until one of the other lads told me that it was an American cigarette.

On another visit we arrived very early at Tamsweg. Tamsweg is a little village to the west of Bodendorf. It is in Salzburg province and among high mountains. Having arrived early, Granberger decided that we would go to the guest house. The pavements were icy and slippery, so we walked in the gutter which was not so dangerous. I was at the rear, next to the guard, and there were three or four of us altogether. Granberger tapped me on the shoulder, and said, 'This lady would like to speak to you'. There was an older lady, probably about 40 and a younger girl who led me into a place which turned out to be the toilet. She immediately apologized in English, and said that there were people watching from the house across the road. She asked if I was English first of all, and I said 'no' first of all, and began to say Scottish, then said 'yes' because most of them did not know the difference anyway. Then she said, 'You're Scottish?' and I said, 'Yes.'

She said, 'Where are you from?' and I replied, 'Oban.' She said, 'I failed to reach Oban; we went through Glencoe.' She came out with a long story about this, and she wished us well and hoped that we would be all right. During the whole exchange the young lady just watched and I assumed that she was her maid. She went away and I went in to the café, had some coffee, played a game of chess, and had some schnapps. Every pub and café had a chess board. That was all we heard at that time.

About a week later a tea chest full of books arrived at the camp. These were the lady's English books. There were all sorts of different subjects; the book I remember best was one about St Kilda. Since then I have not been able to find a copy of that book. Some of the other books were old fashioned and very interesting. She also sent items of food, items that were not rationed; in brief, she was very good to us. The next time we met the men from the other camp, Alex Barlow, an artillery man from Glasgow, told me that he too had spoken to her and she was a countess who lived in the beautiful fairy-tale castle above the village.

As long as we had Granberger we continued to receive gifts of various kinds. He seemed to be in accord with her and they knew that they could trust each other; but at last he left and we heard no more of him. When I was due to retire from my council job, the Revd Barbour was on an official visit to Wick, and I was one of those detailed to see him. I sat with one of my outdoor staff watching and listening. The moderator's wife was also sitting looking on and she came over to speak to us, and asked me where I was born. I told her where I was born, and she said she was born in India, and asked, had I ever been to India? One thing led to another and she finished up digging into everywhere I had been, and I told her about the countess. She said, 'That's interesting, she's a friend of mine, I am going to see her in a fortnight's time.' I said, 'Please thank her for me.'

The Countess's name was Countess Wassilie, and I hope that is the way to spell it. She was at that time 78, and still doing well. She must have been 38 when I spoke to her, 40 years earlier. The Countess could have done herself severe harm by helping us, she had a great deal to lose. Of all the people who put themselves to personl risk in order to help me, out of the goodness of their hearts, the Countess is one of a very small number I have been able to thank.

This reminds me of Joe (and I apologize if I have mentioned him before), who was for a short time in charge of us on the road. He had been a POW in Siberia for six years during and after the First World War. We had extra lads on the road at times; they used to come and go. Joe spoke to one of them and asked him where he had been before, and was told that he had been working for Count so and so in a large house 40 miles away. At this, Joe questioned our lad very closely, then he went to Pouchy and told him that he would be away the next day. The day after that he was back, he went up to our mate and told him that the Count was the man he had worked for in Siberia for six years. Sometimes I wonder if that count was the husband of the lady who helped us. Joe gave me much information about Siberia – I tried to learn from everyone I met, and from every situation in which I found myself. Joe got rid of many preconceived ideas I had about Siberia.

Now for the story of Alex Maver who was a lad from Dundee and in the Service Corps. He had a pronounced cast in one eye. He looked after himself very well, his boots always well polished, and kept his clothes in very good order until they wore out. He had a valet set with him, which he had managed to retain. In this set was a large nail-file about ten inches long. We were forbidden knives and he had turned his file into a knife. He had made a very serviceable grip with a long leather shoe-lace, and carefully sharpened both sides and the point; it was a very good weapon. He and I were friends for eight or nine months. I used to watch him on the road in the summer (that was the very good summer of 1942). He did not do much work, he was always leaning on his spade with the end of the long handle tucked into his armpit. One day he was studying intently a very large tree stump. There were many ants emerging for their mating flights. They were climbing up the stump and using the top as a take-off runway. Alex would wait until they were half-way across, bring down the edge of his spade exactly on the waist and then watch the six-legged part running away. One night we were in the camp talking about this and that, when a Kiwi asked me where I came from. I said Scotland, and he asked where that was, and I said about 1,000 miles north-west. Alex then asked him where he came from and he said about 10,000 miles straight down and he pointed to the floor. I could see that Alex was disturbed about this, but he said nothing until we were outside. Then he asked me about it and he said, 'I thought the world was flat,' and it was quite obvious, one could see that it was flat. He'd never been told so I gave him a short lesson in elementary astronomy, which he had no difficulty at all in understanding, and I had a book on elementary astronomy which he studied carefully.

He told me that his father had died in an asylum, not long after the First

World War, and I understood he was there because of the war. He himself had never been to school; he was taught at home and there were large gaps in his education. He was good at French and there were one or two other unexpected things that he knew about, but there were always these gaps. The first or second night that I was in that small camp, he was called in to the guards' room and was there for a very long time. When he emerged he said that his mother had sent a reply-paid telegram, arranged by the Red Cross and via Switzerland. This was a unique occurrence, and unheard of in Stalag records. There had been no contact with his family up to that time. That was odd but I thought no more about it.

Near the winter of 1942–43 he told me one evening that his skin was drier than usual. No doubt it was but I did not see much wrong with it, but he had evidently seen it as a sign; he knew that something was wrong, so he went to the doctor and he did not come back. In the course of time, and to his cost, he finished up in the same camp as Adam Currie, who took a sadistic pleasure in making his life a misery. One night after a particularly bad session of nagging, sneering and teasing, Adam woke up in the middle of the night, to find Alex standing over him with the knife in his hand. Fortunately, someone else had seen him or he would have died there and then. I hope that Adam learned a lesson.

Alex was removed from the camp, and hospitalized in Graz, where it was reported he was kept in a cage. Later I found that this was not quite correct; the cage was round his bed, and was locked only at night. They were strict with him certainly, but they looked after him well, and knowing the Austrians he would be treated with respect. He was there until the exchange of prisoners started. He was then designated LZ (*Lazaret Zug* – Hospital Train). In most cases this meant that he had a very limited time to live. People so designated were sent home and exchanged for a Jerry in the same condition. The Hospital Ship – the SS *Gripsholm* – sailed from Sweden. I made no attempt to trace him after the war; many of us did not wish to be reminded of what we had been through, and Alex had more reason than most to feel that way. So I heard no more of him, although I have not forgotten him. He was home a long time before Adam Currie.

There was one other lad from our group designated LZ. This was when the war had almost run its course, and from the condition he was in I don't think that he would hold out to see his home. This was Fred Cooper from Nottingham, a quiet, dark-haired chap, a regular soldier: he told me many tales of fighting on the north-west frontier and other interesting anecdotes. He was the cook for a time but for some reason or other he did not want to continue at the job, and he came back on to the road. This was the last winter 1944–45. He had very great difficulty in climbing the hill, and had to stop frequently. He was not much more agile than I am now, but we managed to keep him with us – he was about 30 at the time. Obviously he was very ill. We noticed in the camp that someone was rising early and emptying every water container. We all kept some water in the camp; I had a bowl which took about two litres, and even that was empty every morning. We discovered that Fred was the drinker, he had a most extraordinary thirst.

We took him to the Ukrainian doctor at Murau, and the interpreter was present at the consultation. When they came out Fred asked what was wrong with him and was told, 'I'll tell you when we get home.' When we arrived back at the camp he was told that he was in a very serious condition indeed and that if he was careful he might still live, but he was to take very little water, in fact no water at all; only a stated ration of very weak tea. The rest of his diet was also strictly set out. It was much as what he was already receiving. He stuck to his diet for two nights then the thirst became too much for him, and all the dishes were empty in the morning. He was moved to the Stalag to be sent home.

We were felling trees at the back of the camp when we first noticed that there was something seriously the matter with him. One large tree had been badly felled; it was a cherry tree with branches all over the place, and many of the branches had stuck into the ground and had to be removed, and the tree then sawn into logs. Fred and I were above the trunk on the cross-cut saw, the 'don't push, just pull saw'; we had become quite expert at that. I was sent under the trunk with my axe to cut the branch, this was accomplished with three blows. Then the trunk jumped three feet upwards and caught Fred on the face, breaking his nose. I noticed later that the swelling on his nose refused to go away, and it dawned on me that the swelling was no longer related to the break. Then I consulted my little Penguin book, *Human physiology*, and there it was; Bright's disease, all the symptoms were exactly described. That was my own book, sent from home via the Red Cross.

Fred had a particularly nasty tale from the north-west frontier. He was in the Hussars, either the Fourth or the Tenth, and they had light tanks patrolling in the Khyber Pass area. There were some infantry with them, and the force was attacked and pinned down during the day, and were then attacked again after dark. The Hussars were all right, the tribesmen couldn't get into the tanks, but the infantry underneath were all murdered during the night, and then they were horrible mutilated. They managed to get away when daylight came. Fred said that the Afridis could see in the dark.

This boy Cooper was very dark. The owner and he detested each other so when the chief entered the cookhouse one day there was some kind of squabble and the chief was forcibly ejected. He did not like this and he began to shout at the top of his voice, 'Communista, Schwartz Zigeuner,' and very much more. In the chief's view, communists and gypsies were death-camp fodder, and by that time the gypsies had been exterminated. It was at this time that Fred left the cookhouse. He at least had the pleasure of throwing the man out of his own cookhouse.

There was, endemic throughout the Alps, a thyroid deficiency, which caused a great many goitres and deformities, and a significant number of deformed cretins could be seen about the area. The cure had been known for a long time before we were there, and what we saw were probably the last remnants, the last generation to be affected. For example, there were two with very large goitres, almost as big as their heads. There were two little women, twins, who were very pleasant little people, always smiling, but not very intelligent. There were a great many claw hands and feet shrivelled on one side causing the sufferer to limp on his toe. At the guesthouse lived a girl who without this disease would have been beautiful, she had dark hair, lovely face and a good figure (nearly); her calves were twice the diameter they should have been. She was known, rather cruelly, as 'dresser legs', by our folk. She always had a scowl on her face, quite understandably.

There was a man who made his living by hunting: his right arm was shrivelled up, he held it close to his side with the claw hand up, it was always in this position. He must have been a good hunter because he made his living by it. In the last winter, which was a rather severe one, one of our boys broke out; I think that he had a girlfriend at the top of the hill. He was from the adjacent camp, the ones who worked on farms. He was at one of the highest farms and had become drunk before leaving to go back to camp. He was too drunk, and collapsed in the snow, and there the hunter found him relatively close to death. The hunter wasn't a big man but he carried him on his shoulder for a mile and certainly saved his life.

There was another very sad story. A girl who lived at St Georgen often came up the forest road with an ox-cart. She was a beautiful, smiling blond, about twenty years old, always bright and cheerful. She had a sister who was one of these cretins, thin and shrivelled up, and of course she was sour faced. I am reasonably sure that the girls were twins, in any case Suzy worried about her a great deal, and was always sad faced when speaking about her. She had an older sister as well, who was I think married to one of the soldiers from Schiefling; we saw them occasionally. In the spring of 1945 Suzy, her older sister, and the husband were at the pool on a Sunday when we were also there. Suzy was talking to one of our boys about his family, and all went well until he spoke of his sister, then Suzy said, 'Meine

Schwester kaputt': my sister is ruined, and she hurried away. According to my little Penguin book on physiology the whole of the Alps had this problem. It is treated with thyroid extract, and according to our friend Meier it was caused by an iodine deficiency.

There was a young lad who worked occasionally on the road, we knew him for about a year. His name was Franz, but was better known by the affectionate diminutive Franzel. He was about sixteen the last time I saw him, a fair-haired lad, and a very pleasant character. About a fortnight before the end of the war Meier was noticeably quiet and unhappy; I asked him what was wrong and he said, 'Franzel, he was interfering with the field post; he'd been stealing parcels from it. They took him in to Graz and hung him.' We worked out later that it was probably our parcels he had been at, but that made no difference, it was still field post.

A little girl came to work at the guest house a month or two before the end of hostilities. She was just out of school, or perhaps working her school holidays. She was called Elizabeth, and known as Lisel. She came into the washhouse one day when we were all there. She was carrying a very sick hen, it was opening and closing its beak and gasping for breath. It was obviously dying. She went round the lads one after the other saying to them, 'Tod machen'. She had been sent to kill the animal, to put it out of its misery, as I thought. 'Tod machen', means 'make it dead'.

After she had been refused by several others she asked me, and I decided to take pity on her and drew its neck in a fraction of a second. She looked at me with a look of horror and disgust on her face, and at that moment I remembered that in Austria they always killed poultry by chopping their heads off. I'm afraid that it was too late then. There was a flock of turkeys kept somewhere in the complex which was presided over by a large turkeycock; it appears that he was not satisfied with the number of wives he had and was always chasing the chickens. A chivalrous cockerel went to their defence, and he fought bravely for three days and then died. He just kept attacking and having his head bashed. The first couple of days he would circle the turkey at a distance and employed hit and run tactics; he was a great deal faster than the turkey, but once the larger bird managed to get a grip it did not let go, and on the third day he managed to catch the weakened cockerel by the comb and hung on until the smaller bird died. The turkeys looked very well in the evening, roosting ten feet up in the trees, and silhouetted against the setting sun. The Austrians had two words for *Turkey*; these were *Trauthun* and *Indiana Vogel* – Indian Bird.

Some way back I mentioned different ways in which the time passed in winter evenings. This depended on the number of people present, there might be simply men from our own room, more usually men from both rooms, and frequently men from two camps. With a full complement there would be at least eight persons playing bridge. I might be playing chess with someone from the other camp, but usually I was working. Aussies were singing *The road to Gundie Guy* or occasionally *Waltzing Matilda* and O'Sullivan rolling dice or singing *Wrap the green flag round me, boys.* The dice were rolled to get a double six. The usual Aussie pastime was 'Two up' – two coins were tossed and bets made on which double came up first; often the game was speeded up by using three coins, giving a result every time.

The bugs never annoyed us again, but I don't think the guards ever had an undisturbed night unless they slept with the lights on. The swallow, in all its varieties, has from ancient times been a holy bird in Austria. In summer there was always a swallow's nest on the pendant light in the guesthouse entrance passage. These were chimney swallows, but house martins nested under the eaves on every house. There was a nest just above my window and I could reach out and touch the young birds if I wished. One day I was lying on my bunk and I noticed that the young birds were almost as big as the parents, and that there were one or two bugs crawling among the feathers. They could be seen crawling in and out of the feathers, and the birds were in no way disturbed. On consulting my reference book I found it recorded that some birds make a habit of picking up ants and placing them under their feathers, it being thought that they receive some pleasing sensation from the formic acid. It may have been something of the same kind with the house martins; but I have found no confirmation anywhere.

About half way through our internment a young Jewish lad arrived; he would be seventeen or eighteen years old. He had been brought up in Syria with his family. For some reason a cousin, a girl fourteen years old, was sent to stay with them, and our new comrade had given her a baby. As he put it, 'Papa was very angry, so I ran away and joined the Foreign Legion.' I don't know where he was captured; he had been with the Yugoslav partisans, but the details escape me. I said, 'We work on a road,' and he said, 'Work, what, ME work?' He stopped, and tried to speak to, every girl who passed on the road. He lasted about ten days. His native language appeared to be French.

Arthur was sitting by the stove as usual, with his billy full of hot, weak tea. He said that milk spoiled the taste and that was the reason for taking it weak. Our new friend asked Arthur for some tea and Arthur said, 'Why don't you make it yourself?' 'I don't know how to make tea.' 'Well, all you do is put water in your billy, put it on the fire, wait until it boils and put some tea into it. I'll tell you how much to put in.' A few minutes later he was back at Arthur saying, 'How do you know when it's boiling?' 'When it's bubbling up and down.' 'Well it's nearly jumping out of the pot, and I don't know if it's boiling or not.'

That young lad gave us a great deal to talk about for the few days we had him. Everything about him was mysterious. If, as he claimed, he had been in the Foreign Legion he should have been in a French camp, and he should not have been in Yugoslavia. Nothing about him checked out, except that he did seem to be obsessed with girls. He was not with us long enough for me to sort out his story.

It was very noticeable that there was a marked increase in irritability, squabbling and fighting, when cigarettes were scarce or unobtainable. There were fifty with each Red Cross parcel, and the issue was one parcel a week. The cigarette issue was not nearly enough for some of them. In addition, I received a hundred and fifty John Cotton cigarettes a month from the Argyll Prisoners-of-War Relatives' Association. These I handed to my mate as long as he was there. After he left I don't remember who I gave them to but I didn't make a profit out of them. There was, in addition, a small ration of German cigarettes – not being a smoker I don't remember how many there were. They were called Junaks and were made in Poland, and were not well-liked. They were about four and half inches long, the first three inches an open white cardboard tube, attached to one and a half inches of powdered 'tobacco' in thin paper.

Occasionally Yugoslav cigarettes could be purchased in the village store at St Lorenzen. They too were intensely disliked by the pundits, who said that they were filled with cabbage leaves. Part of the Yugoslav plain was reputed to be very fertile; I know that they grew maize there, and I think that growing tobacco would present no problems. The John Cotton tins were very useful – those were used by Frodsham and myself for the grenades which I made, took apart and never used. We kept the parts in separate places but I always had ready the fuse with detonator and match attached. The length of fuse was such that when the match and detonator touched, there were three seconds to explosion after the match had been struck. I had these measured out and tried, without the detonator, of course. The detonators were very difficult to steal. The parts were hidden in very good hiding places. On the road the detonators were hidden in a little round tin in the foreman's pocket. When blasting he prepared each shot before doing anything else. The little detonator was secured to the end of the fuse, the fuse cut to length, and the match slipped on to the outer end. They were then inserted in a cartridge of donnerite and carefully placed in the hole, usually on top of a number of donnerite cartridges, and carefully taped down. As he prepared the fuses he counted the detonators he had used and those he had left; they had to tally, and usually they did. One man would distract his attention and another would take a single detonator. Over a period three were taken, and we considered this to be sufficient. When we had the detonator we would watch him checking, counting and recounting about three times, then he would scratch his head, shake his head and forget about it. The donnerite could be picked up at any time; it was not checked, nor was there any difficulty with matches and fuses. The matches were hollow cylinders of cardboard that fitted neatly over the end of the fuse. The seconds were then counted to the explosion. From memory the fuse was a minute to the foot. Here is a little story of the blasting.

Our foreman, Blasius Meier, had pouches under his eyes and was called Pouchie by us, and plain 'Meier' by the natives. He was in charge of us for two and a half years and was a gentleman. He had been one of Dollfuss's boys, who had tried to prevent the Anchluss, and was a marked man as a known anti-Nazi, so he had to be careful in everything he did. He had been in the army, perhaps in France, and had been invalided out; he was not a healthy man and was on some sort of medication. He had a little dog; a queer looking thing, it looked like a Scottish collie with its legs shortened, perhaps a cross between a dachshund and a collie. This thing was always with him, and on a particular time he had set the fuses, a very deep bore in the bed of a stream, there were about ten cartridges in it. The water above contained it and always gave a very effective explosion. The dog wandered away and was just beside the shot. Meier always shouted loudly, 'brennan wertz, drei mal, brendt schon' or something to that effect. That meant something like, 'I am going to fire, three times, they're burning now' and this could be heard at the guesthouse which was several miles away, down the hill, of course This time the dog was too near when it fired, and it was blown over the edge. It wasn't injured but was badly scared, and after that time it would begin to shake when Meier started to shout – it refused to run away and instead ran to its master, standing shivering beside him until the shots had all fired. One day, after a series of blasts, one of the locals, whom we had never seen before, came running up the hill shouting and swearing in high-speed Steirisch, most of which we couldn't follow, and there was a long, bitter argument in words I understood little of, before the civilian stamped off downhill. I asked Meier what was wrong and apparently the man had been squatting down making a deposit, when a largish piece of rock had landed beside him, and he had deposited rather more than he had originally intended. He maintained that Meier had not shouted a warning. Meier never found out what the man was doing in the woods – he had no good reason to be there; but he wanted to be sure that someone paid for the fright he had been given. He had no case and Meier heard no more of it.

At one time we had a guard from Luxembourg for a few months and we all got on very well. Much against his will, he had been conscripted into the German army. He had worked on the Luxembourg railways and had been all over Europe with his trains. All non-Germans were well-watched; those in the army were usually in the storm battalions of the SS. He was due to go to the Russian Front, safely out of the way. He had been to a dance and had heard that he had to return to headquarters immediately to prepare for going east. He left in such a hurry that he had left his guardroom key with somebody, probably the girlfriend, and he was therefore unable to reach his rifle and other kit. He came into our room to see if we could help and allow him to work in our room. There must have been a train running at night. It may be that one went eastwards.

First of all he picked up the poker, a rather short, thin apology for a poker. He cut it shorter, using a hammer and chisel on the edge of the stove. Then heated it until it was red-hot and bent the first inch and a half at right angles, using one hammer as an anvil and forming it with the other; then he flattened the projection and went to check it against the keyole. The hole was S-shaped and he formed the 'S' in a very short time, and tempered the red-hot metal in a bucket of water. It worked easily first time. Either he was very fortunate or was a first-class craftsman – I suspect that he was a bit of both. He handed it to me and said *Schlussel fur dich*, a key for you, then he was away. I hope that he survived, in spite of the odds against him. I hid the key along with the rest of the contraband, I didn't require to use it very often. Once, one of the Birmingham boys borrowed it 'to collect something important' and it 'worked like a charm'.

We had reasonably good intelligence: we had BBC news sometimes a few days late, but, by hook or by crook, it reached us, and we knew reasonably well what was going on. There was other intelligence which came down the line from various people; not as much needed for a good escape plan, but different kinds of things. Towards the end of the war there was a very strong rumour that Hitler had ordered that no prisoners should escape and that all were to be killed before the end of the war. It was at that time that we began to make our plans. First of all, there was a rifle in the guards' room and the key was essential. But the first objective was the rifle. There was a little arsenal in the guesthouse. Murer, while he had been very good to us, was a long-established member of the Nazi party, having joined before the *anchluss*, and was one of the party chiefs. The plan was to use the rifle and grenades, go up into the hills somewhere and at least take some of them with us.

There was a farm about a hundred yards away which employed a Frenchman, a tall, likeable lad from Nancy, and he had access to a radio which he had adjusted to receive BBC news. We usually had the recent intelligence from him, but we did not see him every day. In any case, the *Stalag* news was more reliable; there were a certain number of agents in *Stalag* who could pick up coded pieces of news. When first in Austria, there was a Walloon who passed on reliable news to us, but I can't remember if this was at *Stalag* or at *Zeltweg*.

Many of our people made a habit of moving from camp to camp; they would be sent to a camp, and if they liked it they might stay for a time, until they got bored. Usually they did next to nothing. Some made it their business to upset the camp as much as possible, then they would report sick. They had some method of hoodwinking the doctors, or perhaps they were genuinely sick. It is even possible that doctors sent in a report saying this is a malingerer, send him to the worst camp you know about. News received from the travelling people was generally accurate and recent. We were working the crops about fifty yards from the road, when a couple of lads marched past, accompanied by a guard. They were making for another camp and they shouted over 'Italy's surrendered'. A lad called Jock Foy was working next to me, and he just got up and walked away. I shouted after him, 'Where are you going?' He replied, 'I'm going home'. He waited a long time before he reached home, but he went back to *Stalag* from the next sick parade. It should be understood that NCOs and WOs were not forced to work, and there were a certain number of people who had promoted themselves. These were known as barbed-wire sergeants, and it was said that there was one of these in *Stalag* who had stitched a piece of barbed wire above his stripes. Exempted people could volunteer to work, but I don't know if, once started, they were permitted to return to the exempted classes.

On the next farm, where worked the Frenchman with the radio, lived also one of the young girls from Kursk, 'Kursk Anna'. She was an attractive girl and this was unusual in light of the way they had all been treated. They all had very harrowing experiences. She helped us as much as she was able, would give us what she could get and always gave us a smile as we passed on the way to work. However, she permitted one of our number, a man from Birmingham, to get too close to her and she became pregnant. Our lad was a married man with children, a joiner by trade, who seldom worked on the road, being hired out to various civilians to practice his trade. She then was a liability in the slave labour force and not worth the trouble of permitting her to live. With great difficulty her employer succeeded in saving her. She was by this time back at base, where there must have been someone with a spark of humanity left. The foetus was removed in small pieces, and she described the operation in such detail that I think she was conscious throughout. She returned, a shattered girl and, after telling us all about it, she never looked at us the same again, and I can't say that I blame her.

Stalag was a remarkable place because of the number and types of people in it and attached to it. One could get information on just about anything, and experts on just about everything in present knowledge. It was reckoned to be as good as any university. Of course, there were all sorts of things to learn, particularly about explosives and methods of escape. If one was serious and had a good plan, even a map was obtainable; but then one had to be resident in *Stalag* to get the advantages. There the greatest problem was getting out of the *Stalag* itself, whereas our problem was knowing the best time to walk out and in what direction to hike. It would have been easier with maps and intelligence, but the greatest problems were fluency in various languages and passing as being of a different nationality.

By this time in the *Stalag* they were making their own wireless sets and these were growing ever smaller. It was said that they could now fit three inside one Canadian Red Cross parcel. The Canadian pack would be about one foot long, four and a half inches deep and eight inches wide. This would make the set roughly eight inches by four inches by four and a half inches, a tiny container for a valve set. The Germans knew that there was a receiving set in the *Stalag*, so these sets were hidden in various places round the camp. There were searches and, when these became too frequent or too close, they would let Jerry find one and stop listening for a time, but all the time there were ways and means of receiving news.

Now a little more about Anna (Kursk Anna). At the time of her terrible ordeal she was under nineteen years old, twelve hundred miles from home, did not know where her family were, or even if they were alive or dead. As a Russian slave-worker, her life hung by a thread anyway, and our man knew exactly the danger she was in. He never expressed the slightest regret, remorse, or compassion for the girl. The difference between him and the farmer was like the difference between night and day. To put it mildly, the farmer took a certain amount of risk in pleading for the girl's life.

In the last few weeks of the war the *Volksturm* (equivalent to the Home Guard) were called up. There were some queer characters among them – anyone who could crawl was in it. They constructed a strong point at the foot of our road up the mountain and it was a remarkable piece of work. I regret that we did not have the opportunity to examine it closely. It was built on a slight eminence across the river from the road and was to halt anything coming from the east. It was occupied day and night until the war finished, but was never used for the purpose for which it was constructed.

Our friend from Birmingham was out one night for a stroll; by the end of the war he was going anywhere he liked and was getting quite callous about it. On one occasion he was out at dusk, walking along one of the lower roads on the inhabited side of the valley, when a machine gun from the strong point began to fire at him. There were several bursts and he ran the whole way home dodging here, there and everywhere. He arrived back in an exhausted condition, quite white. He maintained that they were trying to kill him. I think that they were giving him a fright. But, then again, it may be that they were trying to kill him. Perhaps there was someone behind the gun who wished to make another pay for what he personally had suffered. Whatever the reason, I hope that he sometimes thinks of Anna.

There were in the adjacent camp two Kiwis, brothers, each well over six feet tall, but the older was bigger, stronger and nastier than the other and, more than that, he was taking care of his younger brother whether he liked it or not. We were leaving the place, having had the choice to go west or stay. Most of us decided to go west, there being a fair chance that the Russians would take over that part of the country. We were not too sure of them, at the very least they were trigger happy. The Russians in fact stopped at Judenburg, a few miles east of Murau. We went west. We had a chance to go to Pongau and were on the platform waiting for the train when the two brothers began to fight; the younger one wanted to stay. It wasn't much of a fight; the younger one was out-classed, and he was told that he was going home whether he liked it or not. He was a bit distressed and came over and told me about it. It went like this: he was friendly with an Austrian girl, he was very fond of her, he had left her with a child, and he did not want to leave her. The older brother's attitude was that he felt responsible for the younger, and he was going to take him home to his parents. After that he could do what he liked.

There were one or two farms on the lower reaches of the north-facing slopes, where the ground began to flatten out towards the floor of the valley. On one of these was a young Russian lad called Peter. He was about fourteen when we saw him first and perhaps sixteen and a half when we left. He was the only Russian male civilian that I saw in the area, although of course there were any amount of prisoners of war in the cities and towns. There were many Polish boys and men, together with Frenchmen, civilians and soldiers, and most nations were represented one way or another.

The set-up on the road was this: there was a small gang of British to do the work, at the best there were never more than fifteen of us. They were overseen by Wosel Stock, a pleasant old gentleman as I've already mentioned. Above him was a nasty little person from Murau. He was known as Herr Lintner, called himself the engineer and was in fact the clerk of works, and not a very good one. After a rather short time he managed to get rid of Wosel, who was replaced by a bearded old man whom we called Noah. At times he could be nasty as well; but at last I got on very well with him because I began to understand the way he spoke, which certainly was not the usual German.

I had tried for a long time not to learn German. I thought that there was enough in my mind and had no wish to learn it anyway; but I required an axe, and there were several types, including an older one always used for cutting roots. I strolled up to Noah and said '*wurzel hockie brauchen*' meaning 'I need a root axe'. Correct German would have been something like *Ich brauch das hacken fur wurzel*. However, he pointed to where it was, and I picked it up and walked back to where I had been working. There was a row of lads standing with their mouths open, and they said, 'What did you say to him?' I said, 'I just asked for the root axe'. After that I had no problems communicating with them. One day there was a girl on holiday from Vienna who asked me to translate for her, and I managed an adequate translation. It was her first day on holiday and she had difficulty with the local accent.

There was a man from the Pyrenees, who stayed on the topmost farm, and who would come down to visit on a Sunday. He had a very peculiar brand of French, which reminded me of some of the middle-ages stuff we had in school. I could understand him better than the Parisian French could and on a few occasions did some translating; but I was far from happy with his brand of French. He was a true mountaineer – he could run up the mountain.

One day on the road there was a stand-up argument between Noah and Lintner. I don't know what it was about, but Noah got the sack. Then we got Pouchy to look after us. Shortly afterwards, Lintner tried to get rid of Pouchy and, instead, got himself the sack. A few days later, the real engineer arrived. He was a lovely old gentleman, probably between sixty-five and seventy, and staying in Murau. He spoke a fair bit of English and was a very pleasant character altogether. He took photographs of us without our knowledge and then handed prints to each one in the photograph, without any cost to us. He was knowledgeable on all sorts of subjects and very intelligent.

During the first spring there was a disaster on the road, and this may be why Lintner was sacked. Every time nobody was watching, we would find a patch of deep snow and cover it with earth. This saved us work and prolonged the job. In parts there was deep snow under the road surface and when spring arrived the road collapsed in many places. It did not appear to worry them very much; they just had us fill it in again. Pouchy knew how to build the embankments and we got on very well with him, without too much physical effort on our part, and they were quite happy with the arrangement. So were we.

During summer and winter there was always something interesting to see on the road. We saw what they called a *hirschkub* – a long word for a hind – a red deer hind. Another day we saw a chamois, very low down on the mountain. We saw them twice; the second time they were down on the valley floor, striking animals. Roe deer were fairly common. Now, the birds – the nutcracker crow was very common – as was the hen harrier in the summer and probably in the winter, although I don't remember it so much then. There were all kinds of woodpeckers, again mostly in the summer. There was a large one that looked black, a green one and the two spotted varieties; crested tits and almost any bird one could think of would be seen at some time in passage over the Alps. Now back to the animals, red squirrels and what looked like black ones, and foxes were common. We saw one wolf and Meier was as surprised as we were. He said it would have come up from Italy. Badgers were common, on the valley floor at least.

One time, just after a large bomber raid – a thousand or a five hundred – a single plane came up the valley. By that time they had shot the opposition out of the sky and single planes were not uncommon. This one was preceded up the valley by a dark arc as though the plane was in the centre of a circle. It looked to be about six-feet wide and three hundred yards from the plane. Most people don't believe that we saw it, and I have never had any explanation.

The last spring came suddenly. It came with a southerly wind. The next day we were climbing the hill and everywhere we went there were little black things like fleas jumping about on the snow. Every now and then there would be a little red spider. The Austrians were not surprised. They said, '*cum mit wrm wind von Africa*' – they came with the warm wind from Africa. Apparently this is the dust disturbed by desert sandstorms, sucked up and brought over at high level to drop on the Alps. It was said to be not uncommon. It was uncommon to us.

Twice I saw the Zodiacal light, at about two-year intervals. This looked rather like a long, thin searchlight beam, very pale. It began at the western end and ran up and round the path of the zodiac, until it faded out about three quarters of the way across. Usually the stars were bright and clear in the wintertime. There were at least two spectacular eclipses, which we were fortunate to see, not having any previous forecast.

A flock of lovely little birds arrived one day towards the end of the first winter; birds larger than sparrows but smaller than thrushes. They were working at a tree with berries on it, many of them were upside down. They very quickly stripped a tree and then moved on to the next one. I asked a local boy what they were, and he said *Schnee vogel*, snow birds; But I had a bird book by this time and found that they were Bohemian waxwings.

We saw them on two different occasions. Flocks of long-tailed tits were fairly common. Hawks were seen occasionally, sparrowhawks were common and kestrels could be seen now and then. There was another bird which I had thought was a kestrel, but it had a beautiful clear and loud whistle. Meier called it a 'Turm Falke'. There were no rabbits that I could see, but there were any amount of hares. On the river bed one could see, any time one looked, water ouzels, or 'water crows' as Willie Hamilton called them. Also common were Ring Ouzels (stormcocks), this a type of thrush with a white band under its throat. There were a great many foxes, but I had been there nearly a year before I saw one. One day in conversation with Lionel Bigmore he said, 'There are lots of foxes here; you see them almost every day.' 'I've never seen them yet,' I said. 'You'll need to learn to look properly. Look further ahead than you're looking,' Len said. Then I began to look well ahead, and saw very many of them.

There were Red Squirrels and what seemed to be black squirrels; but these may have been tree dormice. One of these animals was playing well up in a thin pine tree, when Meier said, 'Look at this,' and he took his stick and began to tap regularly on the trunk. This clearly excited the animal; it began to circle the tree and gradually came lower and lower, until it was almost at the tapping stick.

After the desert and Greece, the quiet and peacefulness of the Alps and the better food we were getting, restored me to full strength, and probably I was stronger there than I'd been before in my life – that is after I had recovered from my boils and carbuncles. I had no further trouble with my health until towards the end of the third year, when a large red patch suddenly flared up on my right leg. Willie Hamilton, speaking from experience, thought that it was phlebitis. However, the boss apparently knew what it was and he ordered me to bed, saying 'bleib ruhig', keep still, and after two days it was completely better.

CHAPTER TEN

Comments on Austrians and DPs

IT WAS JOE FRODSHAM who one day told me that he had seen a budgie on the hill. It was very difficult to believe, but one winter, in a very bad cold spell, a flock of birds settled on one of the pine trees, and Joe shouted out, 'These are the budgies, Mac'. They were crossbills and they made a very good job of stripping the pine cones. Each one would perch on a cone, working round and round it until it was empty, then it would go to the next cone, and all the time there was a shower of falling waste; this had the appearance almost of rain. Pouchy said that they were called *Kreuzschnabel*, an exact translation of 'crossbill'. At different times they became very common in the forest.

We had news of a sort from the *Camp Illustrated Weekly*, of which I brought home six copies, and still have at least one. This was the German English-language newspaper, prepared specially for internees and POWs. The news was heavily tinged with very skilful propaganda, which was blatant in the final years of the war. There was a resumé of the news each week and always the Germans were advancing strongly in the face of bitter resistance; but, over the course of some weeks, the advance would take place much further west. For example, at the beginning, the fighting would be to the east of Kharkov. Then there would be bitter fighting round Kharkov, and the next report would be of strong advances west of Kharkov. Apart from that kind of thing, the paper was quite good. A large part of it was written by British prisoners, different poems and articles, and also some good articles by the Germans. There was a very enlightening article by the German forestry service, and some others I remember. There was a poem by somebody from the Western Isles which was very good, but that one I have lost. There was a comical incident one week: a sentimental poem by a man to his wife, which started off, 'You are always in my heart though parted we may be'. Next week there was another poem under the same title – the first poem had been from a man called Phipps. The second poem began, 'You are always in my heart, though parted we may be. You cribbed those sacred lines, Phipps, with no apology', and it continued in this vein for several verses then finished with proof that he had written the first poem also. There were no further contributions by the first man.

Pigs contributed a great deal to the economic life of the Alps; every farm, small or big, had its supply and it was quite an occasion when a pig was killed for food. Every family killed its own pigs. When working on the hill we would perhaps hear a pig squealing on the opposite slope, probably two or three miles away, and there would be comments about this. At the guesthouse, all the executions took place immediately below our window, and we made a habit of watching these carefully. The owner, the patron, was very skilful. The pig would noisily squeal its protests as it was being dragged to the place of execution; then Murer would kill it instantly, cutting the jugular and piercing the heart with one short thrust. He used a short knife with a broad blade about three inches long. His sister or cousin would stand beside him with a very large wooden bowl. There was a gap in the pig's teeth in the upper part of the jaw. A rope loop was put in that gap and tightened over the snout, and I think that the pig was in agony when being dragged along by the rope. It was hoisted on to a kind of table, made of poles at about four inch centres. The knife was thrust and there was no sound after that apart from the blood pouring into the basin and the woman stirring it quickly to prevent it clotting. For two or three days we were very well fed with black pudding, which some of the lads refused to eat, apparently thinking it beneath them. But it was very good food

After the blood had been collected and well stirred, the pig was placed in a previously prepared trough and cleaned. Two or three days previously, they had collected a supply of pine-tree resin. This was now mixed in a trough of hot water, a chain was placed in the trough and then the pig. There was a person on each end of the chain, which was pulled back and forward, while moving it along the trough and back again. This removed all the hair, and the pig then was a lovely, clean, pink animal. There were various little presents for the kids – small, tasty, pieces. The insides were removed and parts not considered edible were made into soap – quite good soap.

One day Aussie, Clem, McLarty and I were leaning out of the windows, looking at the performance down below. At that time we had a comical little guard, an under officer, who had two stripes. He had a little pistol of which he was proud – it looked like a Beretta. He asked to be allowed to despatch the pig. He shot it through the head, more than once, and still the pig refused to die. At last, after about ten minutes, the owner arrived and did the job properly with his knife. Much of the blood had been lost, and altogether it was a very poor job. McLarty said, 'You know, it's all very well studying all that down there, but if that shower down there was really hungry, they would do the same to us'. Berettas were Italian pistols, which were easily obtained in the desert.

Another fine evening I was leaning out of the window 'having a Hing' in Glasgow parlance, when Marius, one of the Frenchmen, passed below. He was not the handsomest of men. Young Fritz approached him and said 'Marius, *du bist nicht sehr schon*' and a furious Marius replied '*Sale Bosch, Ich nicht brauchen schon*'. Now for a rough translation – Fritz said 'Marius, you're not very beautiful'. Marius replied 'Dirty Hun, I don't need to be beautiful'.

One afternoon, when we came down from the hill, we went in to the washhouse to clean up. Fritz and his parents were there, Wosel and Wash-house Anna, and they had a sack. Something was moving in the sack and I enquired what it was. Wosel said '*Katz, prima essen*' – cat, first-class food – I must have looked a bit amazed, so he stirred it with his foot and it meowed. I thought that he was having us on, but next morning I was in again for the morning wash and Fritz again was there. He had a little balloon about one and a quarter inch diameter with which he was playing. He showed it to me proudly saying '*schau, von Katz*' – look, from the cat – This was the cat's bladder, and I was rather horrified: But they had always eaten cats because they liked the taste. On the road next day, I had a word with Meier about the eating habits of the Steiermarkers and started with, 'Old Vosel down there and his family ate a cat last night'. He looked at me and said, 'But cats are good, first-class, just like pork – but dog's a bit strong'. It took a minute or two for this information to sink in, then I thought, I'll see what I can find out from him. There was a hen harrier passing and I asked him what it tasted like, and he told me that it was not too good. Then throughout the remainder of the lunch hour I asked him about every living creature I could see – for example, the pigeon was good and the squirrel first-class. Another day I tried him out on the plants, and he knew every one. Most were edible but some were poisonous. There is a large, spotted mushroom which is edible if skinned.

As the war progressed, there were different signs of decay and disaffection in the German strength. The first thing we noticed was that all the guards and people on home duties were relieved of their modern weapons and re-equipped with French rifles. These were the rifles with the long spike bayonet but they took only three or four bullets and were not really very good in modern war. It was noticeable that the previously universal greeting of *Heil Hitler* was no longer universally used. For example, in the disaffected areas on the Yugoslavian Border, *Drei Litres* was used instead, which was like saying 'three pints' in a British pub, and this insult to Hitler became common in these areas. A song with a lovely catchy tune became popular about the middle of 1944. It went *Jetz is alles veruber, Jetz is alles vorbei, Mein man ist in Russland, Mein herz ist ganz frei*. That was one of the cleaner parodies of it that were current at the time. I have been trying to obtain a copy of that song ever since. This song became so common that it was banned; people were liable to be shot if caught singing it, especially while in groups.

There were rumours of machine-guns being set up in the streets of Vienna in order to keep the population in check, and I had no reason to disbelieve these stories. There were quite a number of desertions – the first hard news came from one of our number returning from *Stalag*. At Murau he saw a small detachment of eight or nine SS leaving the train and running up into the hill. They had been told that a deserter was staying up there, so they went up and shot him without further ceremony. Personally, I met two of them myself on the mountain. They were walking westwards along the tree-line, making for home, about two thousand feet above the bed of the valley. They were very jumpy but were carrying no visible weapons. I walked down towards them and could see them put their hands in their pockets, so it may have been that they had pistols but I was making for my small pack which contained some food. I spoke to them on the way past, they acknow-ledged and walked on. A couple of days later Meier said to me, 'What did those deserters say to you?' I said, 'What deserters?' 'You know those men you spoke to the other day'. Evidently there was a flood of them coming through at that time, about six weeks before the end of the war.

Even before the bomb attack on Hitler the old Austrian greetings were coming back. It was then *Gruss Gott* and *Firte Gott* – God's greeting and go with God, almost an exact translation of our 'good bye' – God be with you. These greetings I had not heard before, and I notice from TV features that they are still in use.

The Dambusters Raid, which was earlier, caused a kind of panic about the place. All were very jumpy for some time. I think that it might have been at that time that we noticed the rifles being changed. There were new orders to the guards and all sorts of restrictions. The people were very uneasy. I think that they had just then realized the extent of the bombing, and many of them knew nothing at all about it. In the autumn of 1943, and particularly in the summer of 1944, we began to get more visitors from Vienna and the other cities – Linz, Weiner-Neustadt, for example. Most of these visitors were young women, their men usually being in the East, although one or two had never been married. There were also a few boys who came with them at different times. The summer of 1944 was very good, and we saw much coming and going at the guesthouse. A couple of young boys came into the camp to see me. They had been enquiring about 'chess' and had been directed to me by someone, but it turned out that 'chess' was the way they pronounced Jazz, so I passed them on to the interpreter. Before leaving, one of them came back to me and gave me a little edelweiss.

The women were fine people, quite willing to talk and to speak about world issues. The only thing that I could say against them was that some of them appeared to despise the locals, whom they thought to be uncouth and ill-educated. It appeared to me that if this was true of some of them, they more than made up for it with other qualities which were more important.

My hearing was very acute at the time I was in the army. Usually I was the first to hear anything that was going on and I remember particularly the first mass bomber raid that we saw. I heard the drone at least five minutes before anyone else was aware that something was amiss. We were sitting down at lunch-break when I rose up and began to walk to and fro, staring at the sky. The others kept asking what I was looking for, then I saw a thing away to the south-west, across a corner of the sky a broad line of white trails, almost like a road opening up in the sky. That was the first, and about a week later they came directly overhead. They were in great diamonds, I think about five hundred in each. There were at least two of these diamonds. There were two planes that looked black from the ground and intelligence was that these were the command planes. They took about ten minutes to cross, from coming into view on the south to disappearing over the hills to the north, and in that time three of them were shot down. We noticed puffs of smoke in a straight line close to the sides of the planes and at first thought that it was unbelievably accurate *ack ack*, until it became obvious that it was vapour from the guns of the planes, all being fired at the same time. This was the first sign that an engagement was going on, nearly six miles above us. The fighters were too high up to be seen. We found out from the civilians that for every bomber shot down, Jerry lost two fighters. In the succeeding raids the bombers were accompanied by increasing numbers of long-range fighters. These were Lockheed Lightnings and Mustangs. The Mustangs were reckoned to be rather more effective. Gradually the fighters were coming over low enough to be seen, and latterly at tree-top height. We could see the extra fuel tanks being jettisoned and leaflets being dropped.

One of the Fortesses, which did not appear to be damaged, came out of the formation and began to fly eastwards along the valley, at about twenty thousand feet. Then a row of white dots appeared, below and to the rear of the plane, and there was some discussion as to what these might be. Then, as they came lower, a black dot appeared beneath each larger white one. It became obvious that we were watching the crew descending by parachute. The canopies seemed to be deeper and narrower and the cords much longer than those of the British parachute. We counted nine men in all. They came down at Judenburg, several stations down the line to the east. On a later raid a Fortress came down on Lorenzenberg and the crew were buried on the top there. I don't know whether or not they lie there yet. One of the parachutes, from the first plane mentioned above, was caught by the wing and came down with the bomber.

On the second raid, after the main flights had passed, a fighter appeared over the hill behind us. It did not seem to be damaged but it was very low and was probably making for Zeltweg. This was the new *Fokke Wolfe*, a very efficient plane, whose radial engine gave it a very flat, cut-away appearance. It was doing a great deal of damage at that time. By the time the bombers had reached their targets they were far out of sight, and we would hear two or three bursts of *ack ack* fire and a load of bombs, then another load of bombs and the whole lot would then come down like hailstones on a tin roof, all within half a minute. This became a common sound. Before long, the bombers were coming and going as they pleased, and the mass raids stopped. A few planes at a time would be sent in, as required, and there would be fighters at tree-top height, chasing trains up and down the line and shooting everything that moved on the roads, from bullock carts to men on crutches – anything that moved was shot at.

There were several night raids. It was said that these were all carried out by the RAF using Mosquitos. The intelligence from *Stalag* was to the effect that the British did more real damage at night in a very short time than up to ten times the number of American planes did during the day. I don't know if that claim was true, but the Americans did have a major success in a daylight raid on Knittlefeld. By good fortune, they caught three shifts together at the factory – there was a group ready to leave, one just arrived and ready to start – and a third group in mid-shift. They were reputed to have killed five thousand out of the total workforce of eight thousand. This had been a major factory for the production of ballbearings and their production was crippled, at least for a time. There was one particular night raid when some bombs fell quite close to us, two or three fell on St Lorenzen and at least one on St Georgen. There had been blanket bombing on Klagenfurt, which must have been done by the Americans, because, at that time, the British did not do blanket-bombing.

In the morning I went as usual into the washhouse, where I met young Fritz, who was visibly shaking. He was weeping about the bombing of Klognfurt, as he called the place. He said that during the night it was just like rain, *so wie regen*. This could not have been more than a year before he was sent away himself and was caught in the fire-raid on Dresden. It may be that he had some kind of premonition. He was in a terrible state.

We heard Mosquitos every night for some time, then gradually they stopped and we did not hear them again. Then, until the end of the war, we saw mainly long-range American fighters. While there was great activity in the air, sun dogs could be seen almost any day. They appeared to be little bits of rainbow, below and to the left of the sun. When we were flying home at the end of the war, we flew over Munich and one other large city which I took to be Stuttgart. The destruction of German property, as seen from the air, appeared to be complete; it had to be seen to be believed. For a short time we had in the camp a man from London, one of the 'travellers'. When being chivvied by a civilian about the way our side was conducting the war, he was told, 'This bombing is no way to treat civilized people'. He replied, 'Well, you started it. My mother and father were killed by your bombers in London, about four years ago'. That was the end of the conversation. Weiner Neustadt, where the complainer stayed, I think, was a kind of remote suburb of Vienna, some twenty-five miles from the capital, and much of Austria's newer industries were concentrated there.

The Lightnings usually patrolled in pairs and were often at a lower level than us. They would fly up and down the railway track and pay great attention to tunnel entrances and exits. They would go away for a few minutes and return hoping that there had been a train hiding in the tunnel that could be attacked when emerging. They would then try the next tunnel; but from our vantage point we never saw a train being hit. Young Fritz brought in clips of bullets from the fortresses. These would be from the one that crashed on Lorenzen Berg. These were heavy bullets, like little shells about 0.6 inches diameter, and I would think that any plane hit with one of these in the right place would come down. These were the only bullets I saw. There may well have been belts, or different calibre ammunition on the other guns. The fortresses had twelve machine-guns on each machine.

As 1944 progressed, it was clear that most people had accepted that they were going to lose the war but some were prepared to insist that they were going to win in spite of everything. None the less, there was a general relaxation in the way we were treated. Of course we were still locked in, but the rules could be bent much more easily. There was an attempt to put us on parole in order that the guards could be sent to the nearing front, and an *ausweis* – a type of passport – was prepared for each man. This had a photograph and all relevant information. The snag was that, to get this additional freedom a declaration that there would be no attempt at escape had to be signed. That would have been contrary to 'King's Rules and Regulations'. I knew of nobody who signed. However, that summer we did have much more freedom, and one weekend Pouchy took us to the top of the mountain. It was a lovely day, a wonderful climb on a very attractive mountain, and Pouchy was a very good guide. He was very impressed by the agility and mountain craft of an Aussie called Cuthbert, who was from the other camp. I don't know what particular part of Australia he hailed from. The mountain-top was a large, flat plateau. Pouchy said that all the mountains in the area had tops which would allow a plane to take off or land. He said that the partisans had been doing just that. The tree-line was about two thousand feet from the top, but there was much of interest above the trees. There were gentians almost to the top. There were no edelweiss in the area – they grew only on limestone.

There was a small type of rhododendron, which could be seen growing almost at the top. I have been told since then that this is known as the alpine rose. There were some large burrows at the top of the hill. Pouchy said that these were dens of *Murmeltier* - marmots – they seemed to be quite common. They were killed for food when they were available; it was said that they were very fat.

Once or twice, as the thousand bomber raids were coming in, I noticed a kind of mist issuing from the sides of the planes. They came in from the south-west and left towards the north-west. This was material that took a long time descending and sent back confusing echoes to the radar after the planes had turned to a different direction. It would at least waste some time and make it that much easier for the attackers. The material was known as 'window' and was everywhere used by the kids to decorate their Christmas trees. The civilians were told that it was poisonous to cattle and, for all I know, it may well have been but I think that a cow would have to be very hungry to be persuaded to eat the stuff. I brought home some of it and have it still.

Now, some of the impressions of farming in Austria. As already reported, the pig formed a substantial part of the local diet, but this was more for its fat than for the muscle. In consequence, the animals were allowed to grow large. In this country and many others including the Antipodes, pigs killed for meat are killed at three months old, that age being considered to be the best. When allowed to live for two, three, or even more years, they grow large and very fat. The locals greatly valued this fat which was called speck and was eaten raw. Every farmer and smallholder would have at least one huge animal, grown specifically for its speck. I used to wonder about the chances of getting worms, but they had a very good veterinary service. They knew about worms just as well as we did and there were no cases of which I had heard. Like the Gallachs, they had an excellent gossip service, and some of us would have heard if there had been any cases. Occasionally we would receive a ration of speck. When we arrived in the area we were given it frequently, but, as the war progressed, it became very scarce. Each man received a piece about one and a half inches square and four inches long. Like our hosts I, and many others, ate it raw. One would cut a slice off the bread ration, cut a thin piece of speck, place it on the bread, and eat them together, *Steiermark* fashion. Most managed without trouble but one of us was so disgusted that he nearly made himself sick every time he tried it. Pouchy obviously was not too fond of it either, he began to take a frying-pan to work with him every day. It was a remarkable frying-pan with the appearance of a very large ladle; the handle was up to two and a half feet long, the pan was about five inches deep, with straight, sloping sides, making it about seven inches diameter at the top. This implement enabled him to cook with comfort on a very large fire. At lunchtime he would cut his piece of speck into half-inch cubes, place these in the pan and melt them. He would then take an egg, crack it on the edge of the pan, pour it into the pan and stir. Next he would lick out the shells and throw them over the edge. He would repeat this process with another egg, stir vigorously, and put another egg in, again and again, until ten eggs were in the pan. It obviously tasted very good. He demolished it without difficulty. The draught animal most commonly used in the Alps was the ox. There were a few horses but they were not so good on the hills; they were faster than oxen but not nearly so strong and speed was no advantage in any case. Most of the draught oxen were very large, and in some ways difficult to control, being much heavier than horses and also much stronger. Yet it was quite usual to see children younger than ten working with them quite happily. The yoke was secured to the horns and there was a short rope secured to the middle of the yoke, which the person in charge pulled on while shouting what sounded like 'Here, Here' and the beast would follow the driver. The drivers could be heard for miles, shouting at the oxen.

On one occasion, the Frenchmen were taking a load of timber up the hill, and for years I could not work out why. Now I think that they were storing timber for building the strong point later. The load had crossed the bridge and passed under the railway, when the ox rebelled and lay down in the snow. Nothing the Frenchmen could do made any difference. They tried kicking it, beating it with sticks, even flicking at it with their knives – it simply lay there and roared at them. So they lit a small fire under it and it moved then, at a fast trot. All the time an Australian was regaling us with stories of the 'Bullockies' in their homeland. At the end of the war draught animals became very scarce and some peculiar sights were seen. A beer wagon regularly passed up and down the valley pulled by two magnificent, perfectly matched, grey oxen, about five feet high to the shoulder. Unfortunately one of these animals became no longer available and it was replaced with a horse, a large draught horse with large hairy feet. At the end of the first day this ill-matched pair worked together the horse was nearly dead with exhaustion; it was attempting to pull at its own speed all day, but it was a very intelligent horse and after the first day it simply held back and let the ox do all the work. The lines to it were always slack and those to the ox were tight. Clearly there were good reasons for the Mosaic Law which said 'Thou shalt not plough with an ox and an ass together'. Because of the steepness of many of the fields ox carts were small, low-set, with small wheels, to prevent them rolling over. The steep fields were ploughed thus: a furrow was turned over at the lower side of the field, all ploughing following the contours. The earth removed from the furrow was carted up to the higher side of the field and left ready for filling in the final furrow. Then again at the lower end ploughing continued each furrow being turned downhill, always ploughing in the same direction, until they reached the top of the field where the earth from the lowest furrow was placed in the gap. While we were there the richer farmers began to use ploughs with two shares, and this enabled them to plough backwards and forwards and still turn all furrows downhill. In the really primitive places the plough was merely a log of wood with a pointed piece of metal on the leading edge. There were two holes on the upper edge, set about ninety degrees to each other. A bar of wood fitted this hole first on one side and then the other, making a primitive but effective reversible plough. Of course they always turned the soil downhill – it would have been impossible to turn it uphill.

Contour ploughing, which has recently been hailed as the saviour of the Tenessee Valley Dustbowl, has been practised in the European Alps, probably for thousands of years. The oxen were shod with metal plates, one on each half hoof, and shoeing them was obviously a very dangerous job. At the St Lorenzen smithy there was a large frame about nine-feet long and about four or five wide. At each corner was a tree trunk, each one being connected or braced to every other at the top. There were two or three windlasses fastened to the top pieces. The ox was walked in and a leather sling fitted under its belly, the beast was then lifted up by means of the windlasses, and each leg strapped to a separate post. The ox would be roaring by the time they had worked on it for a short time, and I had assumed that it must have been a very painful operation. I think now that the ox might simply have been terrified. By the end of the war there was a marked and noticeable shortage of draught animals. Some, of course, had been killed on the roads; but I think that the majority had been eaten. It became not unusual to see people who always had pairs of good oxen ploughing with a pair of cows, or even with one cow.

We didn't see a great deal of the cows. They were in the byre all winter and in the summer they were sent up to the high pastures. So we saw them a short time in the spring, and also a short time in the autumn when the aftermath had been cut. At that time they were allowed onto the fields. In the last autumn, when they had been allowed to graze the better grass, it was necessary to keep them moving, otherwise the animals would stand and gorge themselves on the sweeter grass to be had on the valley floor. One of the Frenchmen was given a whip and detailed to keep them on the move. Whether the Frenchman knew what he was doing or not, he made a poor job of it. Perhaps he was hitting back at his captors, or it may be that he did not care. We were returning from the hill and found six cows lying in the apple orchard, between our camp and the next farm. They were literally blown up and, judging by the disgusting smell, must have burst internally. Their legs were rigid and sticking out as if trying to get as far away from each other as possible. The vet arrived at the double. His main weapon was a knife and sheath, which were plunged into the animals at the correct point, the knife then withdrawn, leaving the sheath, which had hole at the end, permitting the gas to escape. If he was lucky, the animal lived. There were six of them, large, attractive, brown and white cows. It was a substantial loss to the owner. At the same time another Frenchman was detailed to prune the cherry trees, which he did by removing most of the branches, virtually destroying them for some years to come. The French had been prisoners for nearly five years at the time, and it may be that they had developed a hatred of the Austrians. Yet, whatever the cause, there was a great deal of avoidable destruction in the months approaching the end of the war.

When the air raids were taking place, and in particular the daylight ones, all the slave labourers and POWs were smiling and some cheering, while the locals were very glum-looking.

When the graves of the murdered Polish officers were discovered at Katyn, the Germans made great propaganda use of this, and much was said to us about what our friends in the east had done. Pouchy approached John Joyce one day and asked him what he thought of the matter. John replied, 'First, I don't really believe that it was the Russians who did it but, if it was, it is better to shoot a man than to starve him to death.' Having seen a mass grave at Kalamata, when their own dead were unceremoniously dumped into a pit, I thought that it was more likely to be a German grave than possibly a Russian one, not having any experience of the Russian type of killings. But there is no doubt that the Poles believe the Russians did it. It is now generally accepted that the Russians were the culprits.

Another little point about John Joyce: he was a Glasgow Irishman – and a confirmed Roman Catholic. When the Allies were attacking Monte Cassino, apparently the Pope made a bitter attack on the British for damaging his holy place. He made no reference to the fact that at the time it was lousy with German soldiers, spotters and long-range automatic artillery. This report incensed Joyce, so much so that he said the incident would cause a schism in the church, if the Pope could not be fairer in his statements. In the camp up the road there was a Liverpool Irishman with a good Irish name – 'Patrick Michael Collins' – who visited us whenever possible. When at last we left, he was one of the lads who stayed and, before we broke up, he came over to see me and thanked me for various things. Apparently, when he first visited, I was the only one who spoke to him and had made him a cup of tea. I had completely forgotten the incident. He was in the Seaforths and was a regular, so it was unlikely that it was the fifth battalion, and had been taken outside Tobruk. He had a good many yarns of life in Shanghai in 1938 when the Japs were causing some trouble there.

Refugees began to come through from the east. The Austrians had a very emotive name for them, calling them *Die Fliegtling*. I had thought that I would be pleased to see the Germans in the same position as the Arab and Greek refugees, having caused so much trouble and suffering, but, looking at them, it could be seen that there were very little basic differences in the three groups. They were all merely people, moving away from danger and trying desperately to keep their children alive. They were not all Germans: there were some Sudetan Germans, Czechs, Hungarians, all sorts of people passing through. There was a man from Bratislava, who was locally called the Pressburger. He spent a couple of days camped outside the guesthouse. He had a large covered wagon, which had thick wooden sides, perhaps intended for defence, and a canvas top. It was drawn by a good pair of heavy draught horses. He had been a very prosperous farmer but now had nothing but the four-wheeled wagon, his family and the two horses. They came in, in ones, and twos, and in mobs from the East and slowly disappeared to the west. Only odd ones like the Pressburger we saw for more than an hour or two, and the rest were like things passing in the night.

As I said, towards the end of the war, food was becoming very scarce and there were reports coming through from Stalag that 'boys were swelling up right and left'. I myself lost a stone a month in the first three months of 1945 and stayed roughly at that weight until we met the Yanks. It should be noted that many people were worse off than me. With the Yanks I gained three stones in three weeks.

One day as we were going to work the patron was standing in front of the guesthouse with his pal Herr Winkler, who was Susi's father. They had Leidi, the big St Bernard, with them, and Winkler had his gun.

Apparently the bitch had grown too old to produce any more pups and was to be shot. Murer couldn't himself carry out the execution and his friend was to do the work for him. Immediately, Willie Hamilton said to me, 'Well, Mac, if we get any meat with our stuff today, I'm not going to eat it'. At that time meat for us was virtually non-existent. We had some occasionally, very very occasionally, thin, sliced stuff, something that had died by itself. We had rations of German bully beef, which I thought was very good indeed. It came in large tins and was very tasty, but the Austrians said that the quality was not in it. We were very glad to get it. We arrived back at the camp for our meal and I said to Willie Hamilton, 'Well, if I get a large portion, I won't eat it. If it's a small piece, I'll take it.' We had a great big dish of watery mashed potatoes and on top of that was a piece of meat for each of us. I felt that we could not afford to pass anything by, so I took my piece and I think Willie Hamilton's as well. The pieces were about two inches square and three eighths of an inch thick. It was rather tough meat and very dark. I didn't know what it was but it tasted all right. I didn't think that it was dog. Then, I went outside to have a look round the place and I found the skin of the dog hanging up in the shed at the back. I don't know what they had done with the rest of the animal, perhaps they ate it themselves, but it's more likely that it was sent to Murau. What I took helped to keep me going for a time.

In the autumn of 1944, after the first snow fall, we saw girls occasionally on the road with baskets looking for a special kind of tree. I hadn't seen them at it before. It was rather like a Scots pine (European redwood) but the needles seemed to be even longer. The cones were very thick and the seeds in the cones were about the size of a pea and tasted rather like small hazel nuts. I would collect some myself when the other lads were chatting at lunch-time. At that time I always went for a good look round. Just before we left for home, Meier asked me where I went every lunchtime. He had thought that I had a girl hidden away somewhere.

I began to collect nettles. Meier saw me at it and showed me the best kind to pick. That was in the Spring of 1945. Several times I made a nettle stew. I started to pick locks, but the only place not in the direct-line of sight of the guesthouse windows was a large chest at the back of our building. It happened to be full of bran which I used to thicken the nettles and took this for about a month. It must have helped a great deal to supplement what we were getting. Our parcels had stopped – I had my store and ate the contents of one tin a day until they were finished. I seemed to have tins longer than most. There were geese on the farm and I heard one of them making a great noise one day. I knew what that meant and went looking. I had that egg and, after that, it was a race for them. Discreet enquiries to Pouchy revealed that the local geese laid twelve eggs a year. Well, I had six of them, great big things that kept one going for a day. The eggs were laid in the open shed where the dog skin hung up. I had to be quick – the girls from the guesthouse could hear the bird as well as me, but, by the time they reached the shed, the egg was gone and there was nothing much they could do about it. I had it cooked and eaten in a matter of minutes – if necessary I would have taken it raw. At that time we were given mangolds as the main part of our food; they were terrible things. Their correct name being 'mangold-wurzel'; the *Shorter Oxford Dictionary* says that they are grown as food for cattle – they must have been very hungry cattle. It was a very large root vegetable and I can't describe it any better than like trying to chew a piece of wood. But when we were hungry we would steal them from the fields. Each pair of people did what they could to ensure their survival and very many would steal hens. When on the road we would tell the time fairly accurately, by the position of the shadow cast by the mountain on which we were working on the inhabited face. It would climb quite quickly and we knew which farm it would reach by stopping time. Two of our lads were watching the shadow intently and then they said, 'We'll try that one tonight'. Later, we opened the door at the hinges and let them away, built up a very good fire, prepared two buckets of boiling water and waited. They came back with a chicken and it was immediately dropped into the bucket and held by the head for a minute or two until most of the feathers fell off. It was cleaned as well in the same water. The other bucket was half-full and boiling fiercely; the chick was placed in that and was cooked and eaten in a very short time. Feathers and all remaining pieces were disposed of in the fire. All evidence was gone before the guard returned.

All the houses were built on the slope, the byres and chicken houses were placed underneath, so they had to be very careful on their thieving expeditions But they had prepared carefully and knew reasonably well where the chicks were. If they were from 'down under' they were looking for 'chooks'. By some peculiarity in their make-up, it seems that in a row of hens most would stick their heads out on the same side when disturbed in the night. But there was always one, or maybe two, on the other side. They would strike a lighter and grab the solitary one by the neck and jerk it away – and usually this was accomplished without disturbance. This kind of thing went on until the end of hostilities. As already noted, the next camp was very ambitious and was preparing to take a calf when the war ended. I tried dandelions as well, not very tasty, but every little thing that was good for eating helped, and we tried them all. We lifted cabbages from the fields too – they were very large, being about two feet, six inches across. We went in at night and cut the heart from one, positioned two or three rows from the road. Two things helped us: first there were no sheep dogs or cattle dogs about the place, their type of farming made dogs unnecessary, and most of the people showed us great goodwill. These two things made night expeditions much easier.

It was in the last spring that the Burgomaster's worker stole the peacock and at the same time the French workers began to bring in young birds out of the nests. They were cooking these birds one day and I asked them what they were. I was shown the head of one and identified it as a raven; this was from the colour of the eye. They said that the birds had been very tasty and they smelled very tasty. They would mark the nests and take the young birds when they were ready to fly. Willie Hamilton told me that in the Peebles area much the same thing was practised on wood pigeons. As soon as the young birds began to grow feathers their legs would be tied by short strings to a nearby branch. When fully grown, they would be taken for pigeon-pie.

In the autumn of 1944 we had for a short time a particularly nasty young guard. He was from Bavaria, I think. He was a committed Nazi and obviously his family hated the British. He'd promised his sister before he left home that he would shoot a British prisoner. He said that he was not physically fit for the front, so he had no one else to shoot. He had a peculiar, awkward walk and he reminded me of a man in Oban's folklore who walked much the same way and who was known as 'Caca Briogais' a euphemistic translation would be 'messed trousers'. This guard was always picking on somebody or other. On one very cold day we had a huge log fire blazing away. There was a rock-cutting on the high side of the road and O'Sullivan and another lad were on top of that. O'Sullivan had an iron bar and the other lad had an axe, I think. One of the cockneys was on the road beside me and he was being nagged unmercifully by the guard, who was preaching about how great and good Hitler was, until our boy could take no more and said, 'He was a member of the Prussian Master Race, an Austrian Jew who couldn't even produce a child'. The guard exploded at this and said, 'He was wounded in the First World War and that's why he can't produce a child'. Our lad's reply was to the point: 'So, he's just a eunuch and he is going to make the whole world pay for it.' The guard said, 'I promised to shoot a prisoner and it might as well be you.' He started waggling at the bolt of the rifle and at last managed to put a bullet up the spout and pointed it at the cockney. O'Sullivan was standing with his iron bar ready to jump on top of him and the other lad had his axe ready. It was an exceedingly dangerous situation and I said to him, 'Before you do anything else, soldier, and shoot us all, tell me something'. He said, 'What?' I said, 'How many cartridges are in your rifle?' He said, 'I'm not going to tell YOU.' 'Well, I'll tell you,' I said. 'You've put a cartridge from the magazine into the breech and there is another in the magazine. You might kill one of us; you're unlikely to

kill two, and what is left of us will put you on that great big fire there.'
He managed to put the cartridge back into the magazine and quietened
down. Within a week, fit for it or not, he was on his way to the Russian
front and we heard no more of him. After that, I should repeat that most
soldiers we met were gentlemen – there were very few like that one.

Now for another piece of information, out of context. When we were
troubled with dysentery, the Germans treated it with powdered charcoal,
which was very effective indeed, sometimes too effective. I personally had
a packet of powdered kaolin which must have come from Reggie's parcel
and it too was wholly effective. Any time there was any suggestion that
dysentery was recurring I would take some and 'nip it in the bud'. I think
this happened twice.

During the course of the years we saw many hunters on the hill looking
for various wildlife such as Hirsch (Stag), Kirschkuh (Hind), Reh (roebuck)
and Chamois, although Chamois was very scarce in the area. They carried
a sporting gun with two barrels about sixteen – or twenty – bore, with
underneath them and centred was a rifle barrel which looked to be about
0.28-bore for bigger game. It was a very good general-purpose weapon.
They also hunted various types of birds, notably capercaillie, blackcock and
grey hen, as well as various other animals and birds that I cannot recall at
the moment.

About the middle of the last autumn we spent in Austria I began to look
around for something to make a sledge. Eventually, I found a little birch
growing horizontally out of a crack in the rock. It grew horizontally for
about a foot, then curved up to the vertical and grew in the usual manner.
It was like a great white shinty which I took back to the camp and used
to make my sledge. It turned out very well, but I required runners and was
getting ready to raid the strap iron on the door again, when the blacksmith,
Donald Greaves from Birmingham, said, 'It's all right, I'll give you the ones
I removed last year. I have something better, come down and see this'. We
went down into the implement-shed (where later the skin of the dog hung
to dry). Working in there he had taken the cutters of a fairly new reaper
apart. It had been made of good quality steel and he had simply knocked
out a few rivets and removed two choice pieces of steel for his sledge. The
old ones served me very well until I gave the sledge to Meier for his little
girl. Donnie (who was called Tony by the locals) – they pronounce 'D' like
'T') – used the new ones for a few days and decided that they were no
good, so then he took two more off the doors and threw the others back
into the shed. Although my sledge was the best of the home-made ones it
was very far behind those made by the locals and was completely out-classed
by those professionally made in Yugoslavia. The main probem was a twist

caused by using the wood before it had been seasoned. In the spring everyone knew very well that the war was running down to its end and Meier asked me for the sledge. I said, 'Of course you can have it.' He wanted it for his little girl who was under a year old at the time. He asked what *Duart* meant. I had some difficulty translating through three languages and at last I told him that it was the war-cry of my tribe. He intended to dismantle it and rebuild to remove the twist.

When we came to the area first, we started at the foot of the road and worked upwards. We did not over-exert ourselves at first because we were weak and later, when we were a great deal stronger, we produced a reasonable amount of work and still did not overwork. As the road grew we were at the end taking three hours trudging to the top end. All kinds of things were done to relieve the monotony. It was a very slow march every day. Swift of 292 Company (the lad with the frozen mouse) decided to sing and began 'Hi ho, hi ho, *arbeiten ve vill go, mit shofel und mit plug, und a zwei metre stuck*, hi ho, hi ho,' and the next day he had another verse, 'Hi ho, hi ho, *arbeiten ve vill go, mit Noah und mit Meier, und mit zunder fur de fire, hi ho, hi ho.*' Apparently, after that burst of melody, his inspiration ran out. Translation: very roughly, *arbeiten* was 'working'. 'Plug' was a peg for driving into the ground, 'stuck' was a piece or a thing and in this case was a rod of wood two metres long, used as a gauge for the width of the road.

We carried a large can of coffee with us and, it being fairly heavy, we took turns at this, and eventually one of the smart Alecs from the KRR cockneys decided that this was a bit of a 'bind', and he and his mates would cut cards for this (of course he was cheating at the cards) and decided that one of them would carry it up and the other men would have a day off. This arrangement was, with agreement, extended to cover the whole camp. I was in it for a time, until I was sure that there was cheating going on. After that I did my spell, left the general group and carried my own coffee. There was no loss to the others. They carried on as before in spite of the card sharps and I kept out of it.

With that intake was a man called Dow, Trooper Dow, 4th Hussars, from Uphall. He was about two inches taller than me and thought that he was a big shot. As we were preparing for work one day Dow and his myrmidons came into our room 'to sort me out' It went something like this – 'You're going to carry the can today.' 'No, I am not.' 'Oh yes, you are, WE all take our turn at it.' 'NO, you know very well that I have carried my own coffee for a very long time now. Your pals there were cheating in any case.' We were all crowded into the one room with the little guard fussing about at the back, trying to see what was going on. Dow said, 'I'm going to sort you out' and took a dive at me. I was wearing my specs – some time before

I had broken my own pair and now had a pair I received from *Schaffhausen* in Switzerland, by the good offices of the Red Cross. Specs were a necessity, so I snatched them off and laid them on the bunk behind me, just as he reached me and pinned me against the bunk. With difficulty, I pulled my right arm clear and swung at him, hard. Unfortunately his jaw was out of reach and I hit him high up on the cheek: I noticed that on my second swing he was trying to move his head away and the jaw was closer; on my third swing he was really stretching his neck and I said to myself, 'His jaw's in range now. Now I have him'. As I was on the fourth swing a number of lads jumped on him and pulled him off. For the short time the affair lasted the little guard was saying, 'Shentlemens, shentlemens'. Dow's cheek was opened; it was bleeding rather badly and he was marked for about three weeks. All my remaining time there I was not attacked again. After being patched up, Dow came and apologized, saying that he had not know about the arrangement. I told him that he was lying again and concluded with, 'The next time you think you have a soft mark, you had better be sure that he is not a Highlander.' For very many years my philosophy had taught me that I should attack no one without good reason, but that if anyone attacked me I would do everything in my power to make sure that person would more than pay for it.

I have been checking the story of the trigger-happy guard and think that I may have been one cartridge out in the number that the French rifle held but at that time I knew exactly and I told him exactly. I made it my business to know as much as possible about every weapon – where they were kept and what each guard had.

I was always looking for a reasonable chance to escape; a chance of one in three would have been acceptable, but even at the most optimistic forecast never saw anything better than about one in ten. I saw no reason to stir up trouble for trouble's sake. The other boys stirred up the guard and it had been my good fortune to save the situation. It was of course very difficult to know what any person other than one's immediate mates was thinking. For good reasons most of them kept their ideas to themselves – it did no good to spread them about. But there were others, Charlie Beale from Invercargill, New Zealand, Joe Frodsham and perhaps a couple of others, who, like myself, were waiting for a reasonable opportunity – it never came.

One week, *The Camp*, the German language newspaper printed for us, had a whole column of words that could be used instead of German. It was known as – I think – the barbed-wire guide to the German language. They looked patently ridiculous and I paid no attention to them. But a recent arrival from Stalag told me that they all worked very well, and I decided to try them out. The only one I remember was for asking the time. We had the man who had served in Siberia with us and I went up to him and said, 'Fish paste, Joe?' He replied immediately, '*Halb Funf, Halb stunde noch*', that was 'Half past four', literally 'Half five', 'Half an hour yet'. There was another Austrian chap standing nearby and he said to Joe, '*Was sprochensie*', (what did he say). Joe replied in broad *Steiersich*, '*vie spot as ist?*', literally 'How late is it?' A widely used 'German' expression was 'Donkey Shit' – for thank you very much. Another one that worked well was 'water pistol', meaning 'wait a little'. All the rest of these aids I have forgotten.

One of the cockneys was a chap called Bob Baddock, a very likeable chap, smart-Alec like the rest of them, but he wouldn't have done a bad turn to a mate. Someone said to him one day, 'That's a queer name you have'. He replied, 'Oh, I like it, it used to be Badcock until my father changed it by deed poll.' He and O'Sullivan were bored and decided to make things rough for Jerry. One day we had a very light fall of snow and they approached Pouchy and told him they weren't going to work in the snow, that it was not right that men had to work in the snow. Pouchy said, 'If you are not working there is no point in the others working.' So he took us back down the hill and we all had the rest of the day off. There was a great fuss about it but they finished up by getting eight days in the bunker at *Scheifling* on bread and water – and not too much bread. When they returned they were very hungry – but for them that was more or less the end of the affair. There was an order pinned on the guard's noticeboard about their punishment. This I removed and still have. Two or three nights later, when it was snowing heavily, and there was about two inches of soft snow lying, we were awakened at about half past two by very loud shouting by several people. The room-light had been switched on and the patron was shouting and repeating 'SCHLUSS MIT CAMERADERIE', end of comradeship, and 'PISTOLEN CAMERADERIE JETZ', pistol friendship now. He entered the room with a squad of Gestapo Civilians. Neither he nor they had any right to be there in the middle of the night. They took the interpreter outside in his bare feet and harangued him for half an hour in the snow, promised to shoot him and a great deal more, then they let him back in. The interpreter had a Jewish appearance and I think that may have been part of the reason why he was picked on. There were a few other incidents but that was the main part of the affair. The interpreter was the lad from Buckley, Cheshire. He was a fluent German speaker and was a survivor of the Hellas. The Hellas was in his mind all the time and if he is still alive it will still be with him. He was one of the chaps who told me about the Jewish girl, amongst other things. After this barefoot-in-the-snow affair he quietened down a bit and developed a quiet, bitter hatred for the Jerries, a cold hatred the like of which I have never seen except in the Russians and the Poles. He seemed to think of nothing else but getting his own back. There was nothing much he could do but on the way out he tried to get the patron shot. Nothing much happened to Murer. I think he was in jail for a short time but that was all. For myself I was only too pleased to get through with a whole skin, thinking myself very fortunate compared with millions of others.

There was a marked difference between the lifestyle of those living in the bottom of the valley to that of those at the top, many of the latter still working like they did in the Middle Ages. Those on the valley floor had level fields, generally better soil and electric power. All the lower farms had their threshing done by Hydro-electric power, so that they had a great advantage in time and labour over those higher up the hill. Working to a threshing machine was hard work, but it was completed in a few days, while we could hear the flails on the upper farms for weeks after we had completed all the power threshing. The flail was simply two, longish pieces of wood joined at one end with a leather hinge, forming a kind of stiff whip. With this they literally threshed the wheat until all the grain and chaff had been separated, winnowed by throwing it against the wind, separated and stored.

We had an ill-assorted couple with us for some time, probably not for more than two months. One of these was an Englishman who ran a high-class

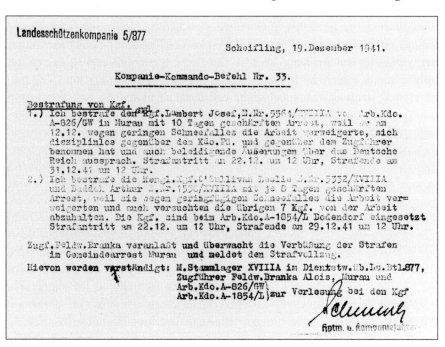

One of the items I stole from the Guard's room.

Gentlemen's Outfitters in Paris. I think that he was picked up in Paris, but could not be certain of that. In any case, he was not in the army and I don't know what he was doing with us. His mate was a cockney, Arthur something, who called himself Arthur double-barrel. He was a busker, made his living by playing the ukulele in the streets and he would entertain us with it. His repertoire included a large number of filthy songs; but he was also very good on the ukulele, playing popular and classical music, and was very easy to listen to. He had been suffering from piles and Jerry had offered him an operation to cure it. They gave him a local anaesthetic and he was conscious throughout, with a large ceiling mirror so that he could see what was going on. I don't know whether they stopped in the mid-operation or not, but he was left with a basic defect, in that he had to sit down to do anything and he was left with two openings where he had been born with only one, and that was his reason for calling himself 'Double Barrel'. He was a very likeable person, a kind of gypsy-type, who entertained us very well for a time, until the pair decided to move on. They reported sick and were returned to Stalag. When with us he received special deliveries of gauze, from Stalag, for filling the aperture which was surplus to requirement.

Within a few weeks of the end of the war there was a delivery to the guesthouse. Two or three large vans arrived delivering bales of cloth and other goods – the cloth I remember particularly. The goods were stored in various buildings around the farm. It was much later that I remembered the incident and began to think about the kind of people who had owned the goods. Perhaps they had been the property of the Austrian Jews, but it was clear that they had been looted from somewhere. Some of the lads had stayed behind to apprehend the patron. They had apprehended him eventually. They had also told the British officer in charge where the suspect goods were stored and these were then distributed to the inhabitants of the area.

During each of the first three winters we spent in Bodendorf we had lost electrical power during heavy frost. The reason was that the pipe feeding the small hydro-scheme was frozen solid. In the autumn of 1944 we heightened the dam by not more than three feet and in the ensuing winter there were no breaks in the supply. In the periods of thaw the lights would be much brighter and in times of heavy frost the lights would be noticeably dimmer. Our camp did all the work on the dam and was at it for a fair part of the autumn. From that and other pointers I concluded that the supply was owned by Murer. There was a mid-morning rest-period which they called 'Yowsnen', (if there is a correct spelling none of us knew it) but that is how it sounded. Food was taken at that time – it was equivalent to the Caithness 'Half yoking'. It was carried to us by Amelia, who was a big, buxom lass, a rather rough character but always with a smiling face. She was employed on general domestic and farm duties. She came to the workforce one day, walking delicately, with a large shallow bowl on her head. It was about two-feet across and because it was heavy and about threequarters full she was forced to walk carefully. She lifted it off her head carefully and spilled none of it. There was a howl of laughter at this. There was a beautifully made, purpose-made cushion, which fitted her head rather like a padded tea cosy. It was required for protection of her head. The bowl was a community bowl and the drill was to put in one's hand and lift out a piece of meat, a lucky dip, then one scooped out a bowl of stew and set to. Jack Feaver had been a little bit further away and when he arrived there was no meat left. Wasel had a large piece hanging from his teeth. He took his knife, sliced a piece off and gave it to Jack, who accepted it graciously. It was on both sides a perfect example of natural courtesy. Jack was a farmer's boy from Kent and took some ribbing from the Londoners who were keen to explain how bumpkin-like were the country boys sightseeing in London. 'Yes,' said Jack, 'but, unlike you, they always had some money in their pockets.' The community bowl was in use until comparatively recent times in parts of Ireland and, for all I know, may still be used there.

One of the Kursk school girls was a bright, intelligent girl whom we called Katie. Her correct name would be 'Ecaterina'. Of all the girls she was the only one who told us that she had been inside a church. She remembered going with her grandmother when she was a little girl. None of the others we questioned had ever been inside a church. She also told us of a special type of 'phone she had used. It was a public 'phone and when it was used one could see the person who was being spoken to. This was rather difficult to believe as that type of 'phone is only now being developed in the west. Maritsch had the same story and there is no doubt that they believed it. The three Ukranian girls who worked for Murer were all in their late teens by the end of the war and they looked about thirty to thirty-five. Really, it had been very rough before Bodendorf.

CHAPTER ELEVEN

Coming Home

THE THREE UKRAINIAN GIRLS were Olga, the youngest; Anka (Alaxandra), slightly older: and known as Anna Pavlova: and the third, a few months older that the others, was Marisch, to us Marie. But to her friends she was Matuschk (little mother) and this was a name with connotations of great affection and respect. Marisch was a steadying influence when they were close to despair and this was quite often. But they were all well a few days before the end of the war and I have every reason to believe that they all reached home safely.

It is now time to tell you what I remember about the breakout. In all, five lads went. These were O'Sullivan, Swift and Copestick from the Potteries, (292 Company R.E.), Joyce of 520 Company RE, and Fraser from the Signals, whose home was in North Shields. They spent a great deal of time working out the details of the escape. I could see no hope in it. However, they completed their plans and all the others gave them what help they could. I gave them some chocolate and other things that were easy to carry and, at the same time, I said that if I thought they had any chance I would have been with them. They were not pleased at what I had said. They believed in the power of positive-thinking. Two or three other people held the same view as me. The chances of getting out were remote. The two most popular places to aim for were Switzerland and Vatican City. I heard of no one reaching Switzerland, although if some films are to be believable, some must have done so; but a number made it to Vatican City, where they were stuck until the end of the war. The same thing would have been true of Switzerland. The result was that German guards were exchanged for Swiss guards and the only real benefit was to the Germans.

Another possibility was to go down into Yugoslavia and join the partisans. But there was very little future in that; no one could speak the language and there were no maps available to us. It would have been simpler to board a train and go east out of the frying pan and into the fire. There was one of the Alpine passes which the trains climbed at walking-pace and some managed to board and jump off somewhere in Northern Italy. This might have been a good idea for some of our comrades with spaghetti roots, but I personally would have trusted no Italian who was unknown to me.

There was some argument about the best way for our boys to leave the camp. Had we let them out of the door there was a slight chance that a civilian might see them. Our window faced the guesthouse and there were high-tension, uninsulated cables fastened to the wall below. It was agreed to let them down by rope from the other room and land them on the pigs' dunghill. This was done on a Friday night and there were three clear days before the escape was discovered. There was a holiday on the Monday. Young Fritz maintained that he had been speaking to them on Sunday night. That was impossible, but he believed it and we made them no wiser. There was a great hubbub and we had holidays while it was decided whether or not to close the camp, or what else to do about it.

Pouchy told me what had happened: they had reached about fifteen miles up the valley in five days, then had walked out of the trees into a village and waited to be picked up. It was an abortive exercise and all it did was alert Jerry and make it more difficult for anyone else to get away. However the boys had done their best and finished up in punishment camps, in different areas. After serving his time in punishment camp, Fraser was sent to another camp further east and, at the end of the war, he went east to meet the Russians. We never heard of him again – probably he had been shot. There was one incident in which a number of French prisoners ran out to greet the Russian tanks and were simply run over for their pains. It was a dangerous operation to surrender to the Russians. I met Swift after we came out and had a long talk with him. He had had a very rough time of it for a while, but in the end managed to get posted to a decent camp. For some reason I was unable to find out much about Copestick, but I did establish that he had reached home. O'Sullivan's punishment-camp was Castle Grophenstein. It was a very severe camp.

The escape took place in the spring, or early summer, of 1944. Spring handicaps was our name for the rash of breakouts that took place at this time and the Germans were beginning to get very touchy about them. There were people going walkabout all over the place and the *Wermacht* issued an order saying that breaking out of prisoner-of-war camps had ceased to be a sport and that the high command had designated certain areas known as death-zones and anyone found in one of these would be shot on sight. Where these zones were was not stated or defined. In effect they could shoot anyone, anywhere, and say that he was in a death-zone – a licence to murder. It was about that time that fifty men broke out of an Oflag and fifty were shot. We knew about that case at the time.

The real possibility in going east was to get to Turkey, but we were not sure of the kind of welcome we would receive. In fact I was sure that it would be anything but a welcome. At the best, there was a probability of internment and, at the worst, a good chance of being shot, or of being handed over to the Jerries. Of course one had to pass through Bulgaria to reach much of Turkey, and Bulgaria was very pro-German.

One of the leaflets I picked up on the hill gave a very good description of Hitler's last redoubt. It was an accurate description. The redoubt was to the west of us. I dated that leaflet when I picked it up and I still have it. The information in the leaflet was borne out by what we saw on the road. One Saturday afternoon, we saw a mob coming in from the east and going away up the valley to the west. As the mob approached us we could see some of them breaking away into the fields, picking up vegetables and returning. It was a mob of Russian soldiers, prisoners, of course, and apart from being ragged and dirty they looked fairly strong. From what we now know this must have been the last six per cent of the survivors of the thousands who arrived in 1941. The guards did not seem to be protesting, as they helped themselves to turnips, potatoes and green vegetables. Obviously the guards could see the writing on the wall.

There were two or three hundred men in that group and we saw two more similar groups. Then two or three days later a mob of British came through also going west; they were marching past us when Johnny Primrose dived out of a group and came over to shake hands with me and Bill Hamilton, and said, 'Come on, what are you waiting for? Come with us, we're going home.' They did indeed reach home some weeks before me. They were still marching west when the fighting finished. Then they stole a car and drove into France. I waited until the Yanks took us home. In hindsight, it was not a very bright thing to do; but in those days I trusted the Yanks. Their own lads were on planes and on the way home the day after the war finished. We were kept for three weeks; but these weeks did help me to fatten up. I think that already I've told you that I lost a stone a month for the first three months of 1945, in the two months from then until the end of the war my weight was static. I had things under control, the weather was getting warmer and we were able to pinch things more easily. Then, while with the Yanks, I increased my weight by a stone a week and went home weighing fourteen stones.

The boys in Poland and the eastern camps of Germany were marching for months on what were really death marches, and that is what they were meant to be. Many died on the march and many others died on the way home or shortly after reaching home – for example, one of the Oban boys died within a few days of reaching home and a lad from Dunoon survived for a year or two. There were many examples of that kind. I heard of several when I was in Buchanan Castle. They stole as much as they could on the way home and the guards were often much harder in these north-eastern areas. The percentage of deaths was not high but there were many health

Österreich letztes Schlachtfeld der Nazis?

Die SCHWEIZER PRESSE schreibt hierzu: "Die Festung Berchtesgaden ist keine Legende. Hitler, Himmler und ihre unmittelbarsten Mitarbeiter wollen von dort per Rundfunk ihre Befehle an die Nazikämpfer erteilen..." (Die Weltwoche, Zürich)

"In der letzten Zufluchtstätte der Nazis, im Norden begrenzt durch Vorarlberg, im Süden durch Bozen, im Osten durch Salzburg, Bad Ischl und Sachsenberg, will Hitler mit den ihm verbliebenen Paladinen der Welt das Schauspiel eines verzweifelten und nutzlosen Endkampfes bieten. Es kann sich nur um einige Monate handeln, bis die Nazis in dieser letzten Stellung zusammengedrängt sind..." (Arbeiterzeitung, Schaffhausen)

DIE NAZIS BEREITEN SCHON VOR: DIE ÖSTERREICHER MÜSSEN IHREN PLAN VEREITELN

Der amerikanische und britische Rundfunk richtete folgende Anweisungen an die Österreicher:

1 Beobachtet die Vorbereitungen der Nazis zur Anlegung von Widerstandsnestern.

2 Merkt Euch die Lage von Nachrichtenkabeln, Munitions- und Lebensmitteldepots.

3 Geht mit offenen Augen durch Eure Wiesen, Wälder und Berge. Ihr schützt damit Eure Höfe und Dörfer vor Verwüstung.

Ihr seid nicht allein: Der Kampf der Alliierten ist Euer Kampf! Jede Angabe, die Ihr später den alliierten Truppen über die geplante Verteidigungsstellung der Nazis in Euren Bergen machen könnt, ist ein Beitrag zum Kampf der freien Welt und zur Zukunft Österreichs!

Picked up in Bodendorf, March 1945

—212—

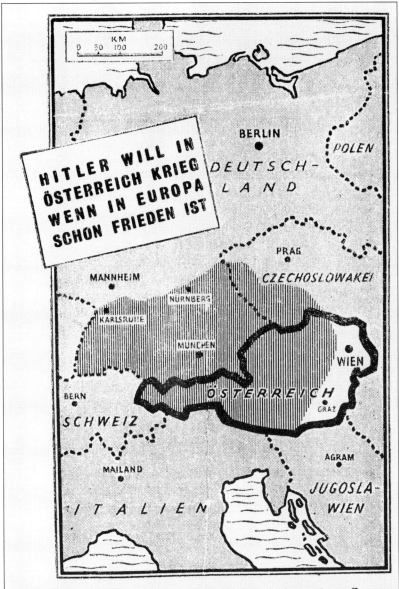

Die schattierte Zone dieser in der amerikanischen Zeitung New-York Times vom 4.2.45 veröffentlichten Karte zeigt das Gebiet, welches nach Hitlers Plänen zum Schauplatz des Endkampfes der Nazis werden könnte.

AU/147

problems among the survivors. The slave workers also were being marched back. No transport was allowed for any of them – it was Shank's pony only. If they were fortunate, the guards might leave them for the Russians to pick up and proceed westwards much faster. Some of our lads reached home by that route. The one I particularly remember was a chap McPherson from Oban, a boy we knew well. The Russians gave him quite a good time and eventually put him on a ship at Odessa. George Kirkpatrick reached home but he was unsettled. We were all in fact unsettled in a greater or less degree.

I don't have the exact date when we started west but we were in St Johann in Pongau before the war had finished, probably on the seventh of May. One day the guard came in to tell us that he had received an order to take us west. We were very doubtful and the guard said that as far as he was concerned we could stay if we liked; but he personally had to go west and he would take with him any who wished to go. Having more or less decided that I was going to stay, I began to assemble the grenades to enable us to arm ourselves and, while doing so, I asked the interpreter for his opinion of the choices. He was suspicious also and he decided to go and ask the guard if there was any truth in what he had said. He replied, 'Oh yes, I'll show you,' and went down to the guesthouse where his own kit was by this time. While he was away I took my key, opened the guard's room and removed several incriminating papers from the notice-board. The total number I forget but I did take the order for punishment of our two lads who refused to work in the snow, the order for punishment of nine Russians who were hung at Judenburgh, for 'Escaping from camp and joining themselves to a gang of ruffians who were terrorising the district', and the order stating that breaking out of camp had ceased to be a sport. These three I definitely had and I think that there were some others as well. I locked the door and returned to our room.

The interpreter returned and reported that he had seen the order to take us to Markt Pongau, to St Joan in Pongau. This being several hundred miles west of where we were, we decided to chance going. Then I opened up all the hidey-holes and removed the contents, taking particular care that I had all my souvenirs and evidence. I gave my spare boots to one of the Frenchmen, said goodbye to the French and to the Russian girls. I had already said farewell to Meier. I threw the bits and pieces of the grenades well back on the roof of our room. They may well be there yet.

When we were marching to the station we met some serving German troops going east. They appeared to be a scouting detail, with motorized tricycles, on which were mounted heavy machine-guns, and I think that they also had a light half-tracked vehicle with them. I saw such a vehicle somewhere and I think that it must have been here. When they saw us they immediately moved into the side of the road, and I think that they must have thought that we were serving British troops. We simply marched straight past them and went down to the station, where two of the New Zealanders had a bit of a fight to themselves. All the men in our room left, but I think that one or two from the other room stayed to 'get' Murer (the owner). Two or three days after we left the British arrived, left some men, and went on as far as Judenburg. The British and Russians met at Judenburg.

The train was slow and disorganized, the route being via Murau and Scheifling. The first real stop was at Schiefling, where we dropped a guard and were left with one only between the two camps. This remaining guard was with us all the way to St Johann and was a very reasonable chap. We stopped at Leoban and were a very long time parked at the station, where

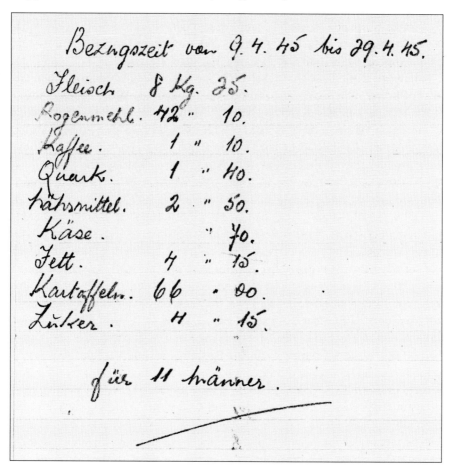

Our last rations at Bodendorf

the scenes were remarkable and unforgettable. There were German troops everywhere, just lying about, a tired, broken army. There was an SS company, doing their duty, divided into pairs, one man a pace behind and to the side of his mate, finger on the trigger of his tommy gun, while the leader examined the passes of the soldiers, one after the other. They were real execution squads. One man was lying on the platform in obvious pain, half his leg was bandaged and blood was oozing out through the paper. He was asked for his pass and he reached it in a hip pocket with obvious difficulty and pain. I am sure that if he had not been able to produce it he would have been shot. The paper bandages looked like little rolls of toilet paper and were more effective than one might think. The main problem with them was lack of strength, particularly when wet. I took one of these bandages home among my souvenirs. It was then that I met the young Hauptman (Captain) of the SS company and talked with him for some time. It was he who said that, 'If the British and Americans would stop now and leave us to it, we would still beat the Russians for you.'

We went from Leoban to Seltzal (The Salt Valley) and from there to Bischofshofen, where we had another very long stop. We wandered about round the station, absorbing everything that we saw. The greatest interest to me was a Bavarian artillery battery. This was a horse-drawn unit, armed with those deadly little, four-barrel anti-aircraft guns. They were beautifully designed weapons. The battery was sitting there, waiting for the war to finish. We chatted for nearly an hour. One of them in particular was very disturbed about the suffering of his horse, which like all the other horses was in a terrible state. They had been continuously on retreat for eight hundred miles, with very little to eat and no time to graze. Most of the horses were blind and lame – every rib could be counted. I asked, and was told, of what they had been through but they did not really say much about themselves – they wanted to see their animals cared for, then to reach home and have a good sleep. Like ourselves they were heartily sick of the whole sorry business. While we were at Seltzal we went for a stroll along the road and were struck by the affluent appearance of the houses. We concluded that it must be a dormitory town for Salzburg. In one garden there was a beautiful model railway and train, with about a hundred yrds of track. Some of the lads would have taken it home if they could have found a way. After two hours we joined the train again and set off. In a short time we were in St Johann and entered Stalag 18c. In this camp were many thousands of Russians, many of them with typhus. There were also two or three hundred Yanks and a thoroughly disreputable-looking lot they were. Compared to the Russians, they were dirtier, much dirtier, less disciplined and seemingly without hope. They had let themselves go and had not had time to get themselves sorted out. We arrived late and were given new British tents to erect and sleep in, and we slept well that night. We were also given some rations. We rose in the morning and were able to go where we liked. The gates were open. There were many beautiful white lorries running about – British lorries. They had brought the tents and also I believe parcels. They had been coming through from Switzerland for the previous couple of months and this was the first we had seen of them. Early in the forenoon, the German soldiers just packed up. I believe most of them threw away their weapons and started for home, and with that the rest of us began to move out. The local farmers had spent the whole previous day planting pieces of potato, as in the old-fashioned method. Every eye and its surrounding piece of potato was planted separately. They had just finished this work when the Russians came out of the camp, went up and down each row, digging out every piece with their hands, and eating them there and then. Then, moving out from the Stalag, they began to take every farm animal they met with. There was not a sheep, calf or larger animal left alive within ten miles from the camp by midnight. Then, they started fishing the river with German ammunition. A good time was had by all.

The first sign of friendly troops was the arrival of a Free French jeep with a patrol of a few men. Then, two or three hours later, the American 86th Airborne arrived and took control of the area. They took the British troops and their own troops out of the camp and installed us in the SS barracks. They then took over the town bakery and every source of food in the place and it was all given to the ex-prisoners. Nothing at all was allocated to civilians. They paraded their own men, those from the Stalag, and I heard them being told that if they were not cleaned up in ten minutes, they would get the British troops to scrub them. They were cleaned up in a very short time and managed to pull themselves together. I never saw such a rabble. I don't know who they were and, to be fair to them, I don't know what they had been through either. They were not the 86th Airborne, who were excellent.

The SS Barracks was set in a large flat area of ground, which was bounded on one side by a steep hill, on which were set rows of attractive bungalows built on horizontal terraces. These houses were obviously the married quarters. On the other side was the river, but the flat area was quite large. I was in a barracks at the foot of the hill, where a long flight of steps came down from the houses. I was in the first room on the right and it was very comfortable indeed. There were eight or nine of us in it. The first afternoon, while I was wandering around outside, a little boy came down the steps. He was about two-and-a-half-years-old. We were on first-name terms in a very short time, then he wandered inside and made the acquaintance of everybody. Soon he was like a mascot to us. In the room were two Maoris, two South Africans and various others; I think I was the only Scot.

One afternoon shortly afterwards, I was sitting on the doorstep, sunning myself and trying to get my stomach used to being full for a change. It was a beautiful sunny day. A teenage girl came down the steps and went from one person to another, hesitating in front of some of them. There were a fair number of lads taking the sun. At last she came up to me and I could see her big, frightened eyes, clenched-fists and white knuckles. She said in a very slow and deliberate English, 'My-little-boy, -where-is-my-little-boy?' I understood immediately and asked if she meant Franzel. She said that she did. I told her to wait and went inside to find the boy. It took me a few seconds before I came out again with the boy hanging on to my hand. The relief on her face could be seen immediately and she nearly ran away from the place. She departed with as much dignity as she could without running, but not before she had thanked me. And that, I thought, was the incident closed. Apparently she was quite happy that the little boy was not going to be eaten and he was back within an hour. He was back and forwards all the time until we left and he gave us a great deal of pleasure. The girl never returned.

We spent much of the time just strolling about and found out that there was a young girl and children in every house. Later, I put two-and-two together and assumed that it was one of the Nazi 'stud' farms that had been reported in this country. However, I am far from certain that my 'two-and-two' would make 'four'. In any case the girl was nice enough and the boy was a joy to have about. At that time they must have been very hungry. They were safe and well when we left.

Two or three of us were sitting on the doorstep in the sun, gorging ourselves when a gang of eight or nine kids arrived and stood in front of us, watching every bite we put in our mouths. We gave them food; we could not have lived with ourselves if we had not. This was a gang of children on their own. There were two girls but the rest were all boys of different ages, some of the parents were dead, some did not know where they were. There was a boy who had placed himself in charge, his name was Erwin (I think). He was from Marburg and had been forced into the 'Hitler Youth'. He had fallen out with the boy in charge of him and had punched him. For this serious breach of discipline he was sent to a camp in Vorarlberg, on the opposite side of Austria, the last province before Switzerland. He had been there for some time, got fed up and decided to walk home. He was about halfway home when we met him. We became quite friendly. These kids were well able to look after themselves and to forage for food. They were schooled in the art of survival. At that time there were gangs like this all over Germany. Anytime we sat down anywhere to eat some of these kids would turn up. They were far too polite to ask for food, but they did not need to ask. We knew only too well what hunger felt like and I never saw a child turned away empty-handed.

By this time we were receiving one Red Cross parcel per day; the intended ration was one per week and together with that we received full American army rations, either 'C' rations or 'D' rations. To add to that we were eating the full output of the bakeries and food-processing plants in the town – and we consumed more than ninety per cent of it, nearer one hundred per cent. Small wonder that we began to expand. I added a stone a week to my weight and was quite bloated when I arrived home. When a person has experienced a long period of sustained starvation, it is very difficult to quit the habit of eating as much as one is able, as often as possible. It was programmed into us, perhaps in case another famine arrived.

This was a very dangerous time for the SS. The Russians shot them immediately when they saw the double lightning-flash on the collar and the Yanks did a bit of this as well. The British were more circumspect but any SS soldier had a very slim chance of survival. When they understood what was going on they tore off their regimental insignia. The Russians simply shot anyone with a torn lapel. It is unlikely that the little boy and his mother ever saw his father again.

We would receive something particularly tasty from the Yanks and would be just starting to eat it, when the starving kids would turn up with their big, magnetic, questioning eyes, they would get it all.

There were Maoris, South Africans, British and the odd Australian in that barrack room. There was a Maori in the next bed to me, who spent most of the time sitting or lying on his bed, carving pieces of wood and talking. On request, he told me something about his early days. He first went to school when he was about eight and rode fifteen or sixteen miles to reach it. He had a rather rough time, but he turned out to be a really fine lad. His name was Tom – the only name he would give us. The South Africans had been captured at Tobruk, a long time after us, and seemed to be very good troops. Of the British troops in the room I have no clear recollections.

The leader of the gang of children was always in and out. One sunny day I was on my way out to sit on the door step, when he passed me on his way in. When settled on the step there was a sudden shout, noise of a scuffle, a scream and he came flying out again. He looked shocked and was shaking. I asked what was wrong, but he had no time to stay. On the way past he said, '*Der Neger, der Neger*'. I went to investigate and apparently Tom had been sitting on his bed with his eyes closed when the boy came in and began to chat to some of the lads. In passing he mentioned, '*Der neger schlafen*'. This was too much for Tom, who did not like being called a nigger. The knife was in his hand but the boy saw him and moved fast. These kids had quick reactions – they needed them to stay alive. Tom threw the knife and it stuck in the doorpost beside the boy on his way out. I don't think that we saw that boy again. Shortly after that interlude I was settled down on the doorstep and I heard a South African and Tom chatting. The window above my head was open. The subject under discussion was a lad known to both of them. Tom said, 'Anyway, what was he, was he an Aussie?' 'No, he was a bloody Pom,' and that is all I can remember of the South African.

Young local boys and occasionally girls would come to see us with things to barter for food and that is how I obtained the SA dagger and other items. The dagger and a Nazi pennon are still here, the pennon with swastika came originally from a German Staff car. The Brown Shirts were suppressed in 1938 and a great many of them were murdered; the leaders were homosexual and Hitler thought that they were bad for his image. It is clear therefore that the original owner of the dagger must have been one of the original Austrian fascists. There were a fair number of them.

MI5 or MI9 (I can't remember which) arrived to de-brief us. They took a rather short time with me, but they received any information that I was able to give them. I told of starvation in Greece and obviously they had heard it all before and knew all about it. Beyond that I had been treated reasonably well. Then I stood outside and waited while the interpreter went in. He was in a very long time and made it very clear that he wanted revenge. He was asked at last if he had any evidence and his answer was, 'No, but my friend has'. He then came out and asked me for the things I had removed from the notice-board. Reluctantly, I gave him the notice about Russian prisoners being hanged and the order that anyone who broke out of camp was to be shot. He promised to return them, came back without them and said they would be returned by the investigators. While they were no doubt returned I never saw them again. There was a photograph of one of them in *War Illustrated* but there is no certainty that it was made from my copy. By the way he had also asked for the photographs. I refused to part with these; there had been a certain amount of risk in removing these from Stalag and hiding them, and I was not going to part with them.

All the reports about Murer made little difference. Later I met 'Pinky' Price from the neighbouring camp, who told me he had managed to help find Murer. He had led the British to the high pastures at Flatnitz, where they found him. They took him down to the valley sitting on front of the jeep, frightened the life out of him and let him go. This treatment was, in my view, quite just, because that is all that had really happened to our lad.

No doubt if I had been stood outside, barefoot in the snow, with three power-crazed maniacs waving loaded-pistols in my face in the middle of the night, I might have thought differently, but I thought that my friend from Buckley should have thought more of his good fortune at his prospect of an early return home in a whole skin, when he was leaving behind so many friends and comrades, than to concentrate on revenge. Some time before this he had been holding forth in the camp, repeating *ad nauseum* 'want to get out of here', then he said, 'I'll give ten years of my life to get out of here'. I said, 'You don't know if you have ten years to give.' For some time afterwards he was as sick of me as I had been of him. Then we became good friends.

There were all kinds of weapons and ammunition lying about in heaps and down at the far end of the camp, beside the river, was a heap of Panzer Fausts. These were the German anti-tank rockets, bearing some resemblance to the American 'Bazooka'. The head was about five-inches diameter and six-inches long, containing a shaped hollow charge such that when it hit a tank the main thrust was forward and everything blew into the tank. To the head was attached a hollow tube about five-feet long, containing a rocket propellant. One day there was a great explosion in the riverbank area and going down to satisfy our curiosity we found one of the American ex-prisoners standing with a rocket tube in his hand. He was all dressed-up in his nice, new uniform. He said that he had been breaking firewood with the weapon when it exploded in his hand. He was a very lucky boy indeed – not a scratch on him and not even shell-shocked.

We got on very well with the airborne boys. I used to study their weapons and was allowed to handle the Springfield rifle, which was heavier than the Lee Enfield. I found it a little bit awkward. However, it was self-loading, which was an advantage, up to a point. They carried their bayonets on their backs and it seemed to work very well. It was interesting to us to watch them training, drilling on the square. In many ways their drill was different to ours. Everything was done to a chant and this was unusual to me. Some were very smart and some rough, just like the British army.

We were watching this unusual performance and a number of kids came along to watch as well. The oldest would be about sixteen; most were fifteen or sixteen. It transpired that these were Polish kids, very bright and intelligent, fine kids, good at the art of survival and very courageous. They were what was left of the Polish underground and the fact that they were in this place meant that some of the SS had brought them out rather than shoot them. The orders had been to shoot them all but some of them had obviously managed to get out. Like almost all the Poles they were very good at hating, and who could blame them?

There was a door on the side of the hill underneath the houses and my curiosity got the better of good judgement and I entered for a look. The passage was about six-feet high and three-feet wide. It went straight in for about a hundred yards and then there was a cross-passage, which was of course in complete darkness. Then I decided to come out. It appeared to be a very good deep shelter but it could have been a magazine. It could also have been booby-trapped, so I was better out of it.

A couple of Yanks came up to me as I was sunning myself on the doorstep. They told me that we were due to go home soon, but that they were to be in the area for some time yet. They said that they would like some radios for their boys and asked if we had any. I told them that there were a few in the building and directed them in particular to my own room. One of the French boys who had been in Bodendorf was standing within earshot and he was amazed. He said, 'You speak to them like it was your own language'. Apparently he did not realize that the Yanks and Scots spoke English.

The Russians were cleared out very quickly. The Yanks could not allow them to continue terrorizing the civilians; they were allowed to run wild for a day or two and then were returned to their own people. How they were treated by their own is anybody's guess. The Russians had been through so much that they did not care a great deal about anything. In spite of what the Germans said about them the Russians had good troops and they were, more than any other nationality, responsible for the destruction of the German army.

These few weeks, immediately after the end of hostilities, was a wonderful time, but there was a sense of anticlimax as well. There was no great feeling of elation, more just quiet contentment. I saw very few people looking for vengeance. There was the lad from Buckley as mentioned above. The Yugoslavs and Poles had lost so many of their people that they could not forget their hatred. Many of them could not see that Germany had suffered too.

When I at last arrived home, I mounted all the photographs in an album, which my mother took and showed to Mrs Mellor of the Red Cross, Argyll. She in turn sent it on to Military Intelligence, who returned it with a letter of thanks. All important parts had been noted. It was marked 6XX.

There was a story that came down the line from Stalag, which I don't think I have noted before, and for which I cannot personally vouch. There was a particularly nasty little Scotsman who loved to make trouble with the English. He made a business of ribbing them and stirring-up strife. A man by the name of Black was in the Stalag at the time and he passed the story on as the 'Gospel Truth'. He was aroused one night by a great noisy disturbance outside, people were fighting and suddenly there was a shout of 'They're bashing wee Jock over here'. The barrack was filled with Aussies, Kiwis and Scots, and the next barrack hut was mainly English. The culmination was a good going riot between the two huts, which required the intervention of the guards, complete with their tommy guns, to quieten things down.

We were deloused three times on the way home. It was not such a big operation as it had been before. There was really no need for it and I personally had not seen a louse since we had been deloused on the beach at Corinth. However I had no objections because of the kinds of diseases to be seen round about and it would have been foolish to take risks. At St Johann the operation was carried out by means of puffing DDT powder over and under our clothes, up our sleeves and trouser legs, and it was left at that. That was the first time that I had met DDT.

We were debriefed four times on the way home, at Pongau, Salzburg, Rheims and Horsham.

All the houses in the area around Bodendorf were finished in a brown colour and I think that they were 'Burnetised'. This was a method of finishing timber houses in which the outside was lightly charred with a blowlamp. It was said to prevent insect attack, fungus and, of course, fire. It seemed to work because there were houses (log cabins) in the area over seven hundred years old, and still in quite good order. They were still liable to fire damage and a three hundred year old house was badly damaged while we were there. Parts of the guesthouse were over seven hundred years old.

St Johann was a pleasant little place and the people were quite likeable. Of course they had no option to be anything else at the time, but I think they would have been all right in any case. I saw my one and only rugby match there. There were scratch teams of South Africans, Australians and New Zealanders. To me it didn't seem to make much sense, but then I knew nothing about it.

One day we were paraded and put on board very large American troop carriers. They took about fifty men each and took them with ease. They were very good vehicles and quite high off the road. We were for a short time on a side road and then on to the *autobahn*. This road took us straight into Salzburg, through the square, past the cathedral and right through the city on to the airport. The cathedral looked very well. Some of our lads said that there had been a bomb through the middle but I did not see it myself. To me it appeared to be undamaged. We dismounted on the edge of the airport and were put into tents in a wood there. We were very well treated. There were film shows every night, hot baths, excellent food and, I think, we were deloused again. They were very particular about their delousing, probably being worried about their planes and when we boarded the planes there were no cushions on them. I suppose that they were concerned about lice infestation. The first morning we were paraded in front of an American Naafi truck, where a big blond was shouting, 'Get in line for your doughnuts and cawfee', and a very well-groomed lass she was too. There were several of them about and they were all beautifully groomed.

The pictures were shown in the open-air. There was a very large screen erected and we waited on the business side of it. You could have heard the sound in Salzburg. The wood we were in was of very tall, thin trees. I was quite sure that they were birch, until one day, when I managed to get an axe from somebody, lit a fire and cut one of them down. This took longer than I had expected and I blamed this on the condition of the axe. I hadn't sharpened it. But when I looked at the grain I found that it was an oak. This was the famous 'Austrian oak', so well-known in the timber trade and used to floor many of our more expensive houses. It was a long, narrow tree, not in the least like the shape of British oak; but a very hard timber indeed. We had our fire and all the rest of it and went for our bath in the morning before breakfast. I had a lovely red and white towel, which came from home, and I had left it on the tent guy rope to dry the previous night. In the morning it was away. I managed to borrow another one and made for the showers. The man from Buckley said to me, 'That looks very like your towel around that boy's shoulders in front'. An English lad it turned out to be, but at that point I was not sure that it was mine, although it looked exactly right. We went into the same shower area. I took my shower very quickly, came out and dried myself on what was indeed my towel. Then the red-headed lad came and began to shout, 'Where's my towel, where's my towel, somebody's stolen my towel?' I said, 'Is this it by any chance?' He looked and said, 'That's it.' I said, 'Can you tell me how it happens to have my name and number on it?' At that he more or less collapsed, turned away and borrowed a towel from someone else. I took my towel home and used it for a very long time. I think it was about thirty years before it fell to bits.

There were many German aircraft parked around the perimeter of the field. One in particular was a huge four-engined bomber. We spent a great deal of time exmining this one. It was a Fokkewolffe Condor, the type that had been used to attack shipping well out in the Atlantic. From our point of view it was a huge plane, it was the biggest I had ever seen close up. I don't know whether or not it was larger than the Fortress – I've never seen a Fortress close-up on the ground. I forgot to say that I made a few pointed and highly uncomplimentary remarks to the thieving red-haired Englishman, but he walked away and our paths did not cross again.

After a few days, a flight of Dakotas arrived and we were put on board. I think they took about thirty men each. There were no parachutes, no cushions, nothing. However, there was a metal upstand about two-inches high to contain the cushions – they had been reserved for superior American sterns. We sat on our gear to keep us, as far as we were able, clear of the upstand. We flew out northwards at first and passed over Munich. We were surprised to see how thoroughly destroyed it had been. At one place in particular bomb-hole touched bomb-hole and shell-hole overlapped shell-hole, over the whole area, which seemed to have been a very large sports ground.

We then turned west along the Swiss frontier and passed over another large city, which I think was Stuttgart. It too was practically destroyed. In fact everywhere where houses were to be seen, they were all damaged. After a few hours in the air we contacted fighters. They would speak to our crew and then descend again. At last we landed at Rheims and were installed first of all in tent city number one, and then moved to tent city number two. These really were cities, huge encampments, with named and numbered streets. We were deloused again and issued with American uniforms. The base soldiers were a poor lot and very far from helpful. They seemed to pick uniforms that could not possibly fit. The trousers were so tight that I had very great difficulty in fastening the fly. The pullover was excellent and I used it for many years. The quarter master was a clown, who had seen nothing. He kept shouting for souvenirs. He received none – we all kept what we had. Then we were allowed out for a time and I walked to see Rheims cathedral, but my trousers were so tight that they were checking the flow of blood to my feet. I was glad to go back. The food served in the tent cities was excellent. It was served on stainless steel trays with three or four sunk compartments, and was served with throwaway knives, forks and spoons The trays were an excellent idea – only a tray to wash and sterilize instead of four separate dishes. I tried to obtain some for a very long time for our summer camping, and at last I did find a source of supply. But by that time I was too old for camping holidays.

By good fortune I had in my travels seen the legendary Arcadia in Greece and I was now in Picardy of the First World War song. It, too, was very impressive, especially when seen from the air. The long avenues of poplars looked well at that time of the year. We were there two or three days at the most and then boarded Canadian Dakotas where we were very well treated. We had cushions for a change. We took off and ten minutes later landed at Laon and for that I have not been able to find any reason. We

took off again and flew over the white cliffs at Beachy Head, landing at
Horsham. That was it, most of us were home; but I was still jumpy. I was
tense, very tense, from the end of the war until I crossed the border. There
was a plane-load of boys who were coming home via Italy lost in the
Mediterranean – that made me think of their unfulfilled, long deferred hopes.

There was a story current about one plane from Italy. It was said that
the lads were ordered to put all their gear in the bomb bay and when they
were well out over the Mediterranean the bomb-bay was opened and
everything shot into the sea. Perhaps they were afraid of souvenir grenades
and pistols, and there were some of these brought in. But I managed to get
all my stuff home.

We were taken from the landing-field at Horsham by our old friends the
RASC Troop Carriers to a camp not far outside Brighton. We were very
well treated indeed, and debriefed again two or three times. Everybody
wanted to know where we had been, what we had been doing, what
happened here and what happened there. We were deloused again – DDT
again – and not too bad. They fitted us out with good British uniforms,
properly sized. Everything was correct this time, all flashes, service stripes
were fitted for us by ATS girls, everything was done that anyone could
think of, and berets instead of the side hats – altogether very good. The
next day they briefed us on how to get home. The medics gave us a very
good going-over. They were going to be very sure that nothing was going
to be wrong with the health of anyone that was not already wrong, and
they would cure what they could. They were very, very careful, and we
even had an X-Ray. There were a number of other tests including psychological ones – in fact the lot.

When we were leaving the officer in charge paraded us and thanked us,
said that most of us had been in the army several years longer than he had,
and at the end he said, 'Don't expect too much when you get home. You
might find them acting a bit queer'. When I reached home I found out
why. The Red Cross had been sending out information on 'how to treat
your prisoner when he gets home'. In effect, they were saying that they
might be stupid. I don't know what the idea behind it was, but it made
many people very jumpy. In that medical I was graded A1. When I had
joined the army I was graded A2. I had a very heavy cold at the time and
that may have been the reason, or perhaps their standards had slipped a little
during the course of the war. Whatever the reason I felt A1.

We were given railway passes and sent north. It was a long journey and
my carriage was filled with Scots ex-prisoners, and when we reached the
north of England there was someone at the window all the time. At last
someone shouted, 'We're over the border.' and we all began to relax. Really

I should have changed at Carstairs but for some reason I had been given the wrong information (probably my own fault) and I went to Glasgow. I wanted to see Seonaid in any case. The first thing I did in Glasgow was check into the Salvation Army Hostel. This was situated at the corner of West Nile Street and Sauchiehall Street. I had a meal then 'phoned Seonaid and I think I saw her for a short time. The next day we went to Rouken Glen and then I caught the overnight train for Oban. The Hostel was well run.

An incident which took place in Glasgow left me for a time with a very poor opinion of Glasgow people. I asked a crowd of them the way to Central Station and all I was given was a load of filthy nastiness, such that I was on the point of knocking the spokesman down, until I thought that I would rather be at home than in the Glasshouse. When I got over it I thought that while my mates were dying these were the kind of things that was raising the next generation and that my mistake was in asking them politely. Then I remembered all the fine lads from Glasgow I had met in the Army.

The train arrived in Oban at some ungodly hour, five a.m I think. Then I walked up to the house and thought I better not disturb them at that hour. So I left my gear on the door-step and went for a stroll. At seven o'clock I returned and knocked, and knocked, and knocked, and the result was no reply, no reply, no reply. So I went away and returned after some considerable time and tried again, with the same result. This time I persisted and at last my mother came to the back of the door and shouted out, 'Who's there?' I told her and she decided to open the door and said that she was not expecting me. I thought that she must have been expecting me. The army boys at Horsham were to have notified her and I fully expect that they did. Perhaps the postman decided that the card was not worth delivering.

It was noticeable that people made of me what they had expected me to be, or perhaps what they had been told to expect. For example, Sandy MacKay had expected me to be weak and half-dead. When I came home after a spell in the second division he said that I was looking much better this time, but there was no difference in me. The army clothing was very comfortable and I was pleased to continue wearing it, particularly boots, greatcoat and cap. These items were far better than the civilian equivalents. But there were some things difficult to accept. The first of these was the sneering of members of my own company, people who had served with me, because I refused to go drinking with them. Apparently this was a sign of cowardice, when they knew, and I knew, that many of them had started drinking only because they couldn't face the war without it. Personally, after the long spell of poverty, I was not going to spend on a useless and potentially dangerous habit, money that was required for far more important things. But there were other things also that were quite unacceptable and I began to understand the bitterness of so many First World War veterans, against many of those who had stayed at home. In particular there was the fishman incident. Before the war I had spent a good deal of time fishing – it was free and quiet. When I was ready to restart I saw a notice in the *Oban Times* that fishing was now restricted to members of Oban Fishing Club, tickets obtainable in the fish shop. The little shark behind the counter told me that all tickets had been sold and I had no reason to disbelieve him. However, I was speaking to Allan McKillop a day or two later and he said to me, 'When are you going to start fishing again? You were always at it.' 'Where am I going to fish? You people have all the places worth fishing and your membership is closed.' 'Who told you that?' 'Him in the fish shop.' 'That's not right. We kept a sufficient number for returning ser-vicemen; I'll get it sorted out.' 'Don't bother, I don't intend to stay here now anyway. I've had enough.' That was the conversation with Allan McKillop, who was a First World War veteran and a gentleman.

I was late for the coming-home party held by the Relatives' Association and was sorry that I missed it. It was a good one There was a disbursement of surplus funds afterwards and we were each given a voucher for £4, which was to be cashed in the Royal Bank. I took it in and placed it on the counter. Clelland took it, glared and slung the money across. I said nothing really. He was just being nasty and impolite, and he threw the money across. There was a pleasant-looking customer standing by me, and he said, 'You're getting quite a lot of these prisoner-of-war things just now,' and Clelland said, 'Yes they've been in here all day like a flood.' I felt like jumping over the counter at him. There was another incident: a young chap who had entered the school just as I was leaving, and who had been captured at St Valery, along with thousands of others, was speaking about the war, and I said, 'You were a prisoner weren't you?' At that, his face went like a mask and I said, 'It's all right, I was one too.' He relaxed immediately and said, 'You'll not imagine what some of these b★★★★★ds say to me, calling me a coward when I've seen more in an hour than they've seen in their lives.' There were a few incidents of that type.

Another common cause of annoyance was the assumption by large num-bers of very ignorant persons that they knew more about the war than those who had served in it. There was one particular case when one woman asked me about Greece and I told her how well the Greeks had acted and had risked their lives for us time after time. She said, 'Well they must have had a sense of the dramatic.' It was great to be in the company of people who knew and understood, and these people were few and far between.

The Salvation Army place I spoke about recently may have been a YMCA. I arrived back in Oban on the first of June 1945, five years and two months since I had last seen it. The repatriation leave was altogether about three months long and I spent a great deal of time just wandering about.

Thomson and MacKenzie were away and I did not see them for some time. I think Archie was the first one of my brothers to come home. Donald was home fairly soon, but I did not see Reggie for a long time. I bought my mother a utility radio and installed it with a very long aerial and lead in. It was one hundred and fifty feet (maximum legal length). I fixed the far end in a large tree across the road. Then I went in and switched on. The first thing I received was a telephone conversation between a man in the US and somebody in Amsterdam. It was very interesting. I picked up some very unusual transmissions on the long wave using that aerial. Medium wave was more selective but there was nothing unusual to be heard on that band. That set was the first my mother had listened to for many years.

I was stopped in the street by 'Tober', Allan Macdonald's father, whose son had been reported missing on Crete. He asked me if I had seen or heard anything of Allan. I told him that I had no knowledge of his son, his reaction was terrible. The pain and anxiety could be seen clearly on his face. Later I met some men from his unit at Buchanan Castle and they were certain that he had been killed. But there was no hard information that I felt I could give to his father. Allan had been an officer in the Argylls.

Many people spoke to me on the street and I don't know yet who some of them were. Conversely I spoke to several people whom I knew very well and who either did not know me or did not wish to know me. A significant number of those who spoke said to me, 'Hullo Reggie'. I found the station bookstall very convenient at times and was not prepared to put up with lectures from Bill Kilgour who had apparently spent the whole war selling papers and cigarettes. He spent about ten minutes lecturing me that I should have stayed in the university. That would have been very difficult because I had never been in the university and the reason was that I had no money. Unlike him, who had money and was short on scholastic ability.

I met Willie Ford and talked with him for a long time. He was another friend who wished to take me boozing. Strangely enough I became friendly with another member of his battery about eight years later, and he said that Ford was always 'roaring fou' when there was danger about. Ford had been my friend since primary school and we kept in touch until he died many years later. I met Angus MacKenzie who wanted to stop and speak, but I remembered when he would not stop to speak to me many years earlier and I simply gave him the time of day and walked on. However, there were some very good times with Hugh 'Cloudy' Bruce, who was still the same likeable intelligent lad he had been before the long years of war. He had gone back to teaching in Oban High School and was having a rough time, probably because of his small size and deafness, and was not being supported. He left to teach in Inverness and died there, or so I was told. I met my old Sunday School teacher and spoke for a long time. For a woman who had at least two brothers in the first war, she had some very peculiar ideas and contradicted everything I said. This kind of reaction was very common, and is still met occasionally.

Eventually my leave came to an end. I was recalled to Horsham and was attached to the second division. Here I was de-briefed again, had intelligence and aptitude tests, was trained on the Bren Gun, Sten gun and Piat anti-tank grenade launcher. We became proficient at all these weapons. We had a five-mile run which caused me some trouble – I was not used to running and probably ran too fast; but I did it – with a great deal of puffing, blowing, and pain. At that place I met a great many people I knew. We had been given leave to visit a cinema in Horsham and were returning in a truck. I heard a familiar voice behind me. I said out loud, 'I think I know that voice. How are you getting on Jimmy Swift?' He too recognized the voice and we exchanged news and views for a time. He told me a great deal about the punishment camp, which had been very hard on him. He told me about all the others of the escape gang.

The next day I met Duncan McCall from Oban. He had been taken at St Valery and had been incarcerated for five years. All he wanted was to be out of the army and home. We were told one night that we were to be gated and everyone would have to stay in the camp, and about ten minutes later we were all out. The instruction did not make the slightest difference, but it did sicken many of us. McCall in particular said to me, 'I've had enough of this, I'm getting out'. He reported sick next morning and ten minutes later I saw him, with all his kit walking down the road out. Two or three days later he was home. At the time I thought that he must have told them a very persuasive story, because he did not look ill to me. Recently I have been told that he lost a large piece of his heel in the fighting around St Valery and he should not have been recalled in the first place. He returned to the cottage at the head of Loch Feochan and to his prewar job. Much later I met him in Caithness where I was for some time a Director.

In his school days Duncan would insist that his name was MCCALL, and definitely not MCCOLL, who were a different branch of the clan and were undesirables. This kind of thought was very common among the clans and families of Scotland and was certainly not confined to the McColls.

We were equipped with the new Number Five Lee Enfield Rifle – The

Jungle Carbine – and it was a beautifully made little rifle, with rubber recoil pad, flash eliminator and a shortish blade bayonet. It is now very scarce indeed, and even in the museum at Fort George, where they did have the rifle, they had been unable to obtain the bayonet. It must have been obvious that I was taken with the rifle because one appeared on my bed after a group had left to be demobbed. I don't know who left it for me, but I seriously considered taking it home with me. However, it was useful only for shooting people and deer and I saw little prospect of that, so I handed it in and received a very grudging thanks for it. It may be they thought that I had taken it. We were completely equipped for jungle warfare and were told that we were bound for the Far East. Then we were transferred to Fort Shibden in Halifax and joined No 250 Field Company. Before joining the Company we were for a day or two in one of the Halifax mills, where there were about a thousand of us. Our parade ground was an old churchyard in the town and we did squad-drill on top of the gravestones, with which the whole area was paved. There were about a dozen ex-prisoners with them. They themselves had been fighting in West Europe and had

Keepsake from a good comrade. March or April 1945, from one of the French P.O.W.

been the first troops into Belsen. They were a good set of lads and I made several friends, the names of most of whom I have forgotten. The Company was in the 49th Division. Fort Shibden was a peculiar place, very small in area, and only one door into it. This opened on to a peculiarly shaped 'square' which, as in all military establishments, was sacrosanct, and no one was permitted to cross it unless properly dressed. Unfortunately, the bárracks and the washing facilities were on opposite sides of the square. The consequence was that we all had to rise in the morning, clothe ourselves fully and correctly, walk across the square, divest ourselves of our clothes, have a shower, wash, shave reclothe ourselves and walk back. It was a very annoying place. The Fort Sergeant Major was heartily disliked by all who met him. There was a rumour current that he had been nabbed by some of the lads, bumped on the railway lines and then thrown into the canal. If that had taken place it made no difference to him – he was still as rotten as ever.

We transferred from there to Inveraray, which for me was very good, it being quite near to home. I am sure that the brass hats thought that it was within walking distance of Oban, as indeed it might have been had they filled in a few lochs and bored many miles of tunnels. I was very pleased to be there and we had a very good time. Oban was outside the limited permitted distance to take an amenity truck (better known as a 'passion wagon'), but one day there was a notice on the Company notice board saying that anyone wishing to go to a dance in Taynuilt should arrange for a day's leave and then apply to the undersigned. Without a sufficient number the truck would be cancelled. I went to the lad organizing it and was assured that they were going no further than Taynuilt. I asked what they would do when they arrived, and was told, 'Oh, we'll walk about the town and go to a chip shop and that sort of thing.' After persisting for some time I ascertained that they were going to Dunbeg, and they agreed to tak me, provided that I walked from there. In the event, the driver took me into Oban but I had to walk back to catch the truck at Dunbeg when they were due to leave. That is what happened and for the sake of a three-quarter-hour stroll I had an unexpected day at home.

Leidi St Bernard

When I marched into Bodendorf
One cold November night
The snow was thick upon the ground
The stars above were bright.

And Leidi came to look at me
And made me welcome there
Her huge eyes shining in the moon
The frost thick on her hair.

When things went well in Bodendorf
The War refused to end.
A few – with dead sons – hated us;
But Leidi was our friend.

All food was scarce in Bodendorf
In early 'forty-five.
I ate my share of Leidi then,
She helped me stay alive.

When I marched out of Bodendorf
In spirits high and bright;
Seemed like a thousand years ago
I left my home to fight.

In memories of Bodendorf
That dun inside my head
I see the skin of my old friend
Hang in an open shed.

CHAPTER TWELVE

Summing Up

LITTLE BITS AND PIECES: First, about Allan MacDonald. Allan, who was lost on Crete, was the first person I knew who had what I called 'MacDonald' toes, and everyone else whom I knew who had them also happened to be MacDonalds. It had not occurred to me that they may be 'MacLean' toes, even after they turned up on Iain. I had taken that to be something to do with his premature birth, but when they turned up also on Jonathon, I began to say that there must be a very large number of MacDonalds among our ancestors, as indeed there are. A recent Sunday paper article on the subject calls them 'MacLean' toes. It seems obvious that they are from the Outer Isles.

Now for a little item I have just remembered about old Austrian life. All their cabins were log cabins. The newer ones were made with logs about four-inches thick and nine inches high, set on the narrower face, interlocked at the ends and beautifully crafted. The older houses were of logs about eight-inches square, obviously squared with an axe. High up on the hill I saw an old man replace one of the older logs in an older house. That man was reputed to be the last man in the district capable of doing the work. He began with a tree about eighteen-inch diameter at the butt, cut a length about fifteen feet off it and discarded the top end of the tree. He drew a square the correct size on the butt and the same at the other end, then put a nail in each end with a line between. He then produced his axe, like a headsman's axe, the cutting edge being about fifteen inches long and set at an angle to the haft. Different axes were required for right and left-handed men. The angle allowed him to stand a pace clear while cutting the log. It took half a day to cut along the line and finish the first face. The whole job took at least two days.

Now a word or two about 'Red Cross' tins. We became very good at telling if there was any danger in them. A little nick or bend on the seam at the end was very dangerous and the contents were usually rotten. The taste also was a good indicator, but very occasionally it could have been deadly to taste the contents. We did come across one example of anaerobic bacteria. Arthur Higginbotham, the New Zealander, who was hungry throughout the four years of his imprisonment (and he literally was hungry the whole time) would have eaten anything. He had a tin with no sign of any external damage and when he opened it on the road it could be smelled ten feet away or more. Joe saw him as he was making signs of preparing to eat it and said, 'You're not thinking of eating that Arthur?' 'But I can't afford to lose it.' 'You'll kill yourself. Why don't you try a little on the dog first?' Arthur cut a small piece off and put it in front of the dog. Immediately the dog yelped and ran away, and very reluctantly Arthur threw the tin away. I am sure it would have killed him. Because of the large number of break-outs, the authorities decided that every tin had to be opened in sight of the guard as soon as received, and this was the reason why I made the cache. Every parcel I received I managed to hide at least one tin. At one time I had fifty tins hidden away.

Now a little bit about Meier's dog. When food was plentiful, those of the lads who could not stomach garlic, would occasionally give a little piece of garlic-flavoured sausage to the dog, who became very fond of it. But this was not good enough for the lad from Dundee, who would cut a piece of sausage, knock the top off an anthill and place the food on it. The dog would try persistently to get the meat but the ants always won. The dog had no chance.

Outside Fort Shibden there was a hill on which was sited an anti-aircraft rocket battery. The men operating this battery assured us that they could hit anything up to forty thousand feet high, but the war in Europe being finished I had no opportunity to see them in action. They must have had heat-seeking missiles. There were proximity fuses for artillery shells in use before the end of the war. Also outside Fort Shibden one of the sights was a set of stocks, apparently in good working order. It was the ambition of some of the boys to put the sergeant major in these and throw away the key. Their ambition was not achieved in my time there.

Our Company Commander was a Major Sparrow, a fine man, well-liked, and he had been with the Company from D-Day until Belsen, right through. A regular who had done his time, he had now been transferred to another Company. I think in India. The comedians who ran the army replaced him with a Major Partridge, who, in spite of his name, was a fine man also. In that Company I worked in the office and nosed about until I found the result of my aptitude test. The summing-up went something like, 'Well educated and intelligent Scot, co-operative and tenacious.'

Earlier I wrote about the Russian girls becoming pregnant to their very great personal danger and I told you about the little Polish girl who was heavily pregnant. I am certain that she was killed and cremated within days of when I saw her, and before the farmer who employed her knew anything about it. She was never seen again. It may be that what happened to her alerted the other farmer to the plight of the Russian Anna.

One of my friends was a Polish chap called Peter Grom, who died some years ago. He had a young sister who was taken from her home and sent to be a slave, and Peter spent a long time searching for her after the war. He traced her to a farm in Austria and there the trail ended. I sometimes wondered if Marie was Peter's sister. Peter had been an officer in the Polish Air Force, then he served in the French Foreign Legion. Then he was in the RAF until the end of the war.

Becoming pregnant could be dangerous for the Austrian girls as well, especially if their partner-in-crime happened to be a slave worker or a POW. It was not such a heinous crime if he were British. The authorities looked on the British as their own race. They were not so happy about the French, who were reckoned to be a stage lower, but when the culprit was from one of the Slavonic races, the girl was in real trouble. The standard treatment in such a case seemed to be all the girl's lovely hair would be removed and a three-year jail sentence served. But the girl was required to work for nine months of the year and the prison sentence would be carried out in three-month spells, every winter for twelve years. Fortunately for those we heard about, the war ended after they had served one spell only.

When my spectacles were broken by a flying stone-chip, the replacements were Swiss army glasses from Schaffhousen. The broken pieces were sent to the Red Cross and very quickly the replacements arrived. Soon after I returned I was given a pair of British Army specs, the first pair I had received in the army. When on my final leave I went to Collie's in Oban for a civilian pair. He spent a long time testing me and checking his records, and then he said, 'You're not like the same person, the distance between your eyes is now 3/8" wider than before the war.' I went home, found my old spectacles and found that he was correct; my height and weight were much the same but my head was apparently wider. All the plotting and planning must have kept my brain growing, or perhaps there was a mistake in the records.

During this period we were completely re-equipped and re-trained. I have already mentioned the number five rifles. Number fours we had had for a very short time before we went overseas, and a fair number of the lads in No 2 Division seemed to have them. The number five Sten was an improvement on the original. It had a wooden butt, bayonet and safety catch. There was a fault in the original Stens: if a loaded weapon were to be dropped on the butt, it would start to fire automatically.

The only problem with the new gas masks was that they got in the way of the bayonet – they sat on the left hip. Otherwise, they were much better. They were handier and easier to operate and the filter was on the side – not the front. There was no tube to think about on the new ones and no awkward pack on the chest, to keep one four inches higher above the ground when firing from the prone position. We were trained in the Bren and Sten, and then went on to mortars, being trained on all British Army ones. Some of these were excellent weapons, especially the four-inch model. I had the impression that the Piat posed some danger to the firer, unless a hit was scored with the first shot. The same thing applied to the Boys Anti-tank rifle which was by then a long time discarded.

The two pounder anti-tank gun was discarded and a six-pounder was used for some time, but it required a greater range and the seventeen-pounder was brought in. This gun did everything required of it. Then the new ammunition was brought in and this had a greatly incresed velocity. The principle of the new ammunition was the same as for the prewar high speed .22 ammunition. A large pear-shaped hole was excavated inside an ordinary bullet, which meant that it was less than half the weight of the original missile. Then, for the same charge, the velocity was doubled. In the anti-tank missile the same effect was achieved by using a sacrificial ring, fitted in two pieces, round a smaller, armour-piercing shell. The ring fell off just outside the muzzle. The seventeen-pounder then fired a shell about the same size as the original two-pounder, and was very effective indeed. The only problem was that sometimes, when the targets were very close, the shell could pass right through the tank, and perhaps hit practically nothing *en route*.

We were shown all the normal artillery, the twenty-five pounder, of course, the sixty-pounder, which, by then, was called the five-point nine, and a big lumbering siege gun. I think it was a ninety-pounder, its wheels were about six feet in diameter and did not have normal tyres. Instead there was a series of centrally pivotted plates, each about two feet by one foot six inches, around the outer rim of the wheel. It was capable of firing one shell every two minutes. It required two men to lift the shell and load it then the charge was inserted separately. At least one shell in every one hundred exploded in the barrel or just outside it and they had never been able to find the cause. In spite of all problems it was such an effective gun that it was retained.

We went from Fort Shibden to Inveraray, nominally as part of a Beach Brigade who were training for the Far East, but I think that by the time we arrived there most of them were already on their way. Our days were fully occupied, but I have no recollection what they were occupied with – not on any useful work anyway. We were in Shira Camp. There were five or six camps at Inveraray, Shira, Castle, one or two in the Village and two at Battlefield. The Camp we were in was on the road to Rob Roy's house. We had a good time there. On the way to Inveraray we went by train to Arrochar and trucked from there.

From Inveraray we went to Edinburgh and were installed in Morton Hall Camp. We went to Edinburgh in Company trucks from Inveraray. Morton Hall was sited next to a Battle School, was a hutted camp and was very comfortable. Again we spent some effort doing nothing useful. We did have a laugh or two. We were on roll-call one morning and the man who picked the left-overs from the kitchen arrived, an old man with a small cart and a very old horse. There was an Edinburgh lad standing next to me and he shouted out, 'Where do you go from here?' 'Only to Liberton.' 'Ye wad be far kinder tae him tae gae tae Loanheid.' Loanhead was the site of the local knackery.

We had a lad who had taken off at the crossing of the Rhine and they had not seen him since. Then he was picked up in some unusual place and returned to the Company at Inveraray, where for a few days he was kept under close arrest. Then at Edinburgh he was installed in the gate guardroom at the Castle. The guards were very good to him and he repaid them by walking out of the door and disappearing again. The guard swore that he had gone out through the window. The only windows in the guard room were arrow slits not more than four inches wide, and he was really a very thin lad. The guard had full marks for trying and for giving us all a very good laugh. A few days later one of the NCOs saw him in the Royal Mile and grabbed him. He was returned to the Castle and I don't know what happened to him – more than likely a year or two in the Glass House.

We would go to the little post office in Liberton to post and collect Company mail. A little old lady came up to us in a distressed state and said to my mate, 'Tell me it's not true, tell me the Germans aren't as bad as that – those Camps are not true.' My mate had been in Belsen Camp and had seen the lot, but he said, 'It's a load of rubbish.' I was not at all pleased with him, but now I don't know whether he was right to lie. The people ran a canteen, a very good canteen, and they were first-class people. After a few months there we were sent to Redford Barracks for demobilization. Then I was at home for four or five weeks before I had an invitation to go, if I wished, to Buchanan Castle Resettlement Unit for a six-week course. I accepted, became fed up and left after five weeks. Nevertheless, it was a good place and I lasted longer than many. Provided I undertook to become a teacher I was given the chance to go to Glasgow University. Unfortunately I had no wish to become a teacher. One of the professors from Glasgow was quite keen to get me. We talked for a long time. I had all the basic qualifications and much more besides but I had decided that teaching was not for me and that was the end of it. I would have jumped at the chance of studying for a science degree, but that was not on offer at the time. There were many first-class lads there. One of these was a chap from Shotts, by the name of Dempster. He was janitor in Allanton School, the last time I heard of him. One of my friends was a remarkable lad called Struthers, who had been in the first SAS and had been captured in the South of Italy, after a drop in (I think) February 1941. Twenty-six of them were captured and he said that twenty of them had been trained as secret agents. He was confined in a camp near the main line to the East and for four years sent home details of all interesting traffic on that line. He was given a good commendation for it. Apparently Jerry knew very well that intelligence was getting through, so when some important military operation was imminent they would hold back all mail for perhaps three months. My mother would wonder why one letter would take a month in transit and the next one would perhaps take five months. Struthers was sick of war and everything connected with it, and all he wanted was a quiet life. One night we went for a walk several miles through the estate and back by the road. On the way back we passed through Drymen, where we saw the local policeman, who appeared to be simply lounging about in the square. At the sight of him my mate said, 'That's what I'm going to be, a country Bobby, that's the best job going.' I did not find out if he achieved his ambition. There is something ticking away in my memory telling me that I had a letter from him saying that he had married, or was on the point of marrying, a girl he had met in the south of England. That may well be the case, or perhaps I am confusing him with another friend.

It had not been easy to keep in contact with one's mates. First of all, there had been two camps in Salonika and at different times I had been in each. I left half of my company in Salonika number one, and at a stroke lost half of the men I knew. Then on the train it was fifty to a wagon and one was indeed fortunate if there were two or three mates in the wagon. In my wagon there were about six of us. The next break-up was at Marburg. We left half of the Company there. Then at Wolfsberg the fact that I had dysentery meant that all my remaining mates were out in different working camps a few days before I left. I was the only member of my company at Zeltweg and then, at Bodendorf, I found Willie Hamilton from Peebles.

It was clear from the early days at Corinth that cigarette addiction was far more powerful and far more wide-spread than alcohol addiction. This was difficult to believe in the light of the alcohol consumption that went on among most groups of men. But in fact it became very clear than only one or two people had real difficulty in surviving without alcohol; but at least thirty per cent of us would have sold their souls for tobacco, and many could be seen bartering what food they had for tobacco, while their mates were dying of starvation. Later, when we became more settled in camps in Austria, many groups of men began to make different drinks out of various materials. Most groups started on raisins, which was allowed to ferment. Some men liked it, at least they said they did. Some other groups were more successful – they built stills and distilled quite good schnapps. A still was of course very difficult to hide. At Zeltweg, on cold mornings, the *Luftwaffe* gave us a morning ration of schnapps in the coffee. That was very acceptable.

None of the working camps were very pleasant places to be in – even the best of them were much worse than any British Penitentiary, but having said that some were much worse than others. There was one in particular which I have mentioned before. This was a quarry facing south, and in summer the conditions were horrific. In the worst camps particularly, and at times in every camp, people wished to move on in order to find the ideal jumping-off place for an escape. Therefore the idea was to be ill enough to be sent back to Stalag. In order to accomplish this there were many ways of faking illness and I intend to list some of these now. There was a special way of faking water on the knee and this is something I saw attempted, and which in our camp did not work. The method was to soak towels in warm water, wrap them tightly round the knee, then have relays of men hammering at it with spoons, then after a time it would swell up. I had a suspicion that if this one worked there was a good chance of permanent damage to the knee.

Another way was to fake heart disease. This was accomplished by means of swallowing saccharine tablets. A certain number caused the heart to race. The optimum number of tablets had been worked out and was common knowledge. None the less, it was a dangerous practice, not all hearts being the same, and there was a danger that some people would overdose themselves. In the quarry camp there was a machine for breaking pinkie fingers. The finger was placed in the correct position, a lever pulled and the pinkie was broken. This scheme worked for a time until the German Medics became fed up with the game and sent the injured man back to effect his own cure. One new arrival to our camp was completely bald. He had been naturally thin on top and had been told by the camp intelligentsia that if he shaved all his hair off, it would grow back in thicker and stronger. He tried it and it worked, or at least he thought it did. He then tried it again with satisfactory results; but a third attempt left him with a permanent egg head. He was then told that if he piddled on his hands and rubbed the urine carefully into the scalp, there was a chance the hair would return. I knew him for about two years and all that time he was as bald as a coot. He did not smell very well, but he kept up the practice until the end of the war.

The essential difference between the British, French, Belgians, etc., and the Eastern boys was the International Red Cross Society and the Geneva

Convention. The survival rates of the Russians varied. Of all Russians captured some forty per cent reached home, but of those captured in the first push, those in the photographs, only three per cent reached home. Of the Germans captured at Stalingrad only six per cent came home. The basic reason for death was the same on each side – working starving people to death.

The Red Cross was essential in many ways. The fact that we received mail, no matter how long it took, was a great morale booster. In 'normal' circumstances we received a parcel a week and these parcels contained not only welcome extra food but also vitamins and trace elements that we could not obtain otherwise. In periods of famine even one tin of bully beef a week made a substantial improvement to a man's diet. During the eight months or thereabout, between capture and arrival of Red Cross parcels, men generally were very weak; usually much weaker than they themselves realized. During the first four or five months there was the phenomenon which became known as 'wet Wednesday' when we regularly 'rained off'. This also boosted the morale and may well have saved a number of lives.

Much of what I remember of Corinth is triggered by snatches of songs. These were parodies of hymns, popular songs and some original material. There was a bitter content in some of them. Recently I found an old tattered notebook in which I had written many of these down, at the time or not long afterwards. What I have has been inserted in different places, not for any literary value but as part of the history of the time. What I know of the authors is noted. *Rendezvous*, *Chaos*, and some others are my own. There was one poem that a chap repeated at all our concerts, which asked why, after the successful counter attack, the navy had left with a sixth of those waiting on the beach, when we saw, and still see, no reason why all the men were not embarked. There was a song entitled *Calamity Bay* which was a potted history of the three days at Kalamata. It portrays some people in a very good light and others not so good.

There was a song about the market yard and this reminded me that there had been a market yard. At Corinth, prisoners were divided into groups of fifty. There was an appointed representative for each group. If a man had some money or had anything to trade, this was to be handed to the representative who did his best with it and handed the result back to the trusting first man. It did not affect me because I had nothing to trade; but others found that they did not trust the representative and went to haggle on their own behalf. Then, they would be asked to show their passes and were in serious trouble. There was a parody of the song *Easter Parade* which was a graphic description of what the retreat was like, with the Luftwaffe in complete command of the air. I do not have a copy of that one and remember snatches only. It went something like this:

> Grab your old steel bonnet, with your name and number
>   on it,
> And dive into your slit trench for the *Luftwaffe* is 'ere.
> And when they're coming over,
> You can see them cut the clover,
> The Bofors sing a sonnet,
> As they whine through the air,
> Then your name will be seen in the Church Magazine.
> Etc. Etc.

On the last few days before the retreat from the hill above Thermopylae there were infiltrations of parachutists expected. They had been in action not far to the north and later to the south. They were expected in British uniforms and speaking perfect English. The first two nights we had to clip the disc seal from a round fifty-cigarette tin to the hook on our gas-mask haversack and this could be seen at night from a short distance. The next night and a half before we were told to 'walk down that road for your lives'. We wore our anti-mustard-gas goggles outside in, and this left a thin white line showing, which also could be seen from a few feet away. There was a password as well as the distinguishing mark; but that I have forgotten.

In 1943 one of our lads was waiting at a station in the south of Karnten, when a troop train passed through with peculiar looking troops in each compartment. He described these as looking like monkeys and this was the Cossack Division, although I am not sure that I agreed with the description given. Their families travelled with them. They were very Royalist and were fighting against communism and not really for Germany. At the end of hostilities most of those who were not killed in the fighting, or by suicide, were shot by the Russians.

Without the sustained help from the Red Cross, I am certain that less than fifty per cent of our lads would have returned home.

Photographic Collection

Now I intend to give descriptions of the photographs which I have included. They are in several groups, the most important being that of the Russian prisoners in Stalag XVIIIA at Wolfsberg. My best information is that these were taken by one of the Kiwis. Owen Davies, the lad who obtained them for me, died Christmas 1993. The next group is the North African one, which were mostly purchased from Tom Pomphrey. There are one or two photographs of the Argyll boys at Margate, a number purchased in Austria and also in my possession are a few cards purchased in Columbo, Cairo and Austria. Finally, there are photographs presented by various well-wishers in Austria.

Egypt and Libya

The Libyan photographs first: the first photograph is of the entrance to Cairo Zoo; second, the Italian monument at Sidi Barrani, on what they called the 'Victory Road to Suez'. That was as far as they were able to reach; third, of graves of Italians between Barrani and Buq-Buq, who had been killed by a British shell; four, two men of our Company at one of the Italian kilo posts on the new road. The man on the left is Ed Sweeney and I forget the name of the other one; Five, same again at a different kilo post. The man on the right is Lance Corporal Walker; Six, a close-up of the monument in 'Five'. *Chi si ferma et perduto* – meaning, I believe 'He who hesitates is lost' is written below a picture of Mussolini, with the name and company number of the Italians who built the kilo post; the next photograph was of a very useful little Italian vehicle, a 'Spa', with four-wheel drive, four-wheel steering, independent front-wheel springing. Our boys swore that it could run over 'dog tooth' anti-tank obstacles. Next, a general view of Fort Capuzzo and the next again is Gambut Road House. After that, three photographs of Italian dead. These are the photographs that some of our lads had complained about, but by that time they had been taken, and multiple copies made, of which I had a set, so I decided to include them. They had been on an ammunition truck which had been hit by a British shell. They were found and buried by our lads some weeks later. Many people mentioned the awful state of the bodies. I think that the dogs had been at them.

Russians captured at Smolensk

I will now transcribe the introduction to the Russian photographs, which I wrote in 1945. 'Late in October 1941 about 2,000 Russians arrived at Stalag XVIIIA, Wolfberg. They had been taken at Smolensk about three months previously. They had travelled for three weeks in closed wagons and had been paraded through many of the principal towns of Germany. Included were large numbers of civilians. Until they had arrived at Wolfsberg many of them had fur clothing. They were relieved of this clothing at the gate. Snow fell during the better part of the day. These men died in their hundreds during the first few days of their stay at Wolfsberg and thereafter at the rate of two or three every day until the end of the war. A squad of British prisoners was permanently employed in making coffins for the Russians. Eventually three bodies were put in each coffin. Finally, a lime pit was used to dispose of the dead.

These photographs were taken by a member of the New Zealand Expeditionary Force. Now something about individual photographs, one by one:- the first one is a view of the Stalag from outside the compounds. There is a party of Russians inside the gates, the British and Russian compounds in the background, the French and Belgian in the foreground, elevated sentry box equipped with machine gun, searchlight, telephone, etc., in the middle foreground; the next one, orderly table outside the German Barracks; photograph three, French compound with washing tubs in the foreground, snow falling heavily and muddy conditions of the ground can be seen. Many of the men can be seen wearing their number plaques – and the photograph at the bottom Hauptman Steiner, Adjutant of Stalag 18A speaking to the prisoners. Several civilians are to be seen in the photograph: Hauptman Steiner treated the British prisoners as well as he possibly could, even to the extent of warning our Sergeant Major of when a search was likely to take place. Photograph five:- snow can be seen falling heavily. Several of the prisoners obviously suffer severely from the cold. Number six:- two types of Russian caps can be seen in this photograph. A great many wore French caps coming down over their ears. In the foreground two men in the one coat. This phenomenon of two men in the one coat was a means of keeping warmer than they would otherwise be and the practice gave rise to the rumour that there were some babies among the Russians. Further back in the photograph there is one who could quite easily be a baby. Photograph number seven:- waiting for food. All kinds of old tins are in use and it is easy to see that many of the men are very poorly clad. Number eight:- two men on the right wearing Russian caps and a Mongolian type of face in the background. Number nine:- the man on the left was said to be a Russian airman but I think that he was almost certainly from the tanks. Number ten:- a common type of Russian cap is worn by the man in the foreground. He seemed to be a little better-clothed than some of the others. Number eleven:- another general view. Number twelve:- one of the men seems to have a Naafi spoon in his pocket, whether it is or not I do not know, but it looks rather like it. Number thirteen:- again, two men in the one coat. Number fourteen was a close-up of the same pair. Number fifteen; another two in one coat, a Russian cap on the left, spiked top and with red star. Number sixteen: another type of Russian cap, and close-up of one who needs a good wash; but he is not so badly starved as some of the others. Number seventeen: a very poor-looking man. Number eighteen: that pair does not look too well either. Number nineteen shows prisoner stripping under guard, before entering the delouser; the NCO is Obergefreiter Stahl. This was the lad who treated me very well when he thought that I had a head wound. Some time later he was sent to the Eastern front, because it was alleged that he treated the British prisoners too well. He is wearing the Austrian Alpine cap and the edelweiss in his sleeve. The other soldier was also very good. Number twenty-one shows the prisoners stripping outside the delouser. They stripped in the cold on a late October afternoon and then had a hot shower. They collapsed in their hundreds as they entered the showers. All afternoon British stretcher bearers carried them from the bath to their billets. Afterwards, those who cold stand queued for the smallest and dirtiest scraps of food. They were controlled largely by members of their number, chosen by the Germans, given more food and a cat of nine tails. I had a photograph of them standing there with their whips, but it has evidently been lost. They used their whips freely on their less fortunate comrades. Number twenty-two shows two who had died of exposure and starvation in the night. Those at the end of the queue who had not passed through the delouser by the time the guards were called for their evening meal were left in the open to make the best of it. Some of them did not survive. The two shown had attempted to cover themselves with some plants. When we had passed through the same compound in July, the high summer, we were given tents and a thick layer of straw. Those of our lads who helped to clean the wagons the Russians had travelled in, found them knee-deep in all kinds of filth, with some dead bodies underneath. Many of those who had been processed died in the barracks during the night and one body was found which had been opened and the liver removed.

Now back to Bodendorf – our first guard had written out an 'Order of the Camp'. It was pinned up on the notice board in his own room, and went like this:

1. Do not forget that you are a soldier.

2. Always show discipline.

3. Do not show indiscipline.

4. The soldier of the highest rank in the room will shout *achtung* on the entrance of a German soldier and also on the second entrance of the Commando Fuhrer, every morning.

5. When making a request, stand to attention.

6. If you have any complaints see the Commando *Fuhrer*, do not row amongst yourselves.

7. Keep to the timetable.

8. Do not say you are sick unnecessarily, or you may be treated as a malingerer.

9. Always obey a command; this is part of your discipline.

10. Make your bed orderly; always keep your room clean.

(signed) Mazourek Johann.

We had Jan Mazourek only a very short time before he was sent to the Russian front. He was an eccentric likeable character and no one paid attention to his 'Orders'. I thought that the orders would be a good souvenir so I used my key and removed them. They are still here somewhere.

Extract from letter from the Regimental Paymaster to my mother dated 4/8/41. 'In consequence of the soldier being posted as a prisoner of war, your allowance will not cease on 5/10/41 as previously notified, but will continue on the issue rate of 14/- per week, which was the issue before being posted missing'. The armchair army was very logical: if a soldier was missing, then any voluntary allowance was also missing. If a soldier was killed, then they killed the allowance. Everything was neat and tidy.

A card received with a Red Cross parcel said, 'This parcel, sent to you by the Red Cross and St John war organization, comes to you from the Whist Drive Committee, Corburton, Lincolnshire, supporter of the fund from which the cost of parcels is defrayed. The donor sends you at Christmas-time best wishes for your health and happiness'. I received the parcel on 23 October 1942 and at this time I would like to express my thanks to that committee and all other similar groups throughout the world who helped to keep thousands of men alive.

Contents of the parcel were: Best wishes and Christmas greetings from the Red Cross Packing Centres; Half-pound butter, half-pound chocolate biscuits, quarter-pound chocolate, six ounces sugar, small tin nestlés milk, one pound Christmas cake, one pound Christmas Pudding, one tin of sweets, two ounces of cheese, one tin of apricot and plum jam; one steak and tomato pudding; one tin braised steak and macaroni; two ounces tea.

There is some information on clothing and uniforms in the Buchanan Castle Booklet. Civilian outfit consists of: One hat, One suit – jacket, waistcoat, and trousers, or sports jacket and flannel trousers; one shirt and two collars, one tie, one pair socks, one pair shoes, one raincoat or mackintosh, two studs, one pair cufflinks. When you leave the army you will take with you into civilian life the following items: cap badge, kit bag, ankle boots, braces, identity discs, short cellular drawers (two pairs), woollen drawers (two pairs), knitted gloves, hussif (or housewife), Khaki flannel shirts (two), jersey pullover, socks (two pairs), two hand-towels, two woollen vests, button brush, button stick, hair brush, shaving brush, shoe brush, tooth brush, hair comb, safety razor, one suit battledress, one GS cap. If some unforseen national emergency arises and you are called up again within twelve months you will be expected to produce these articles, so take care of them.

While a prisoner I received regular letters from my mother, Reggie, and from Seonaid. I also received two letters from Donald. In addition there were several letters from Lydia and odd letters now and then from other friends. My art teacher asked my mother to send her best wishes and passed on a sum of money to buy something to send on to me. Some ten years ago everything I brought home was still here and easily available. Much appears to have disappeared but there is so much in the house that it is a major operation to find anything. Information on members of the company who escaped from Greece or who had not been to Greece came from Tommy Ross, with rather less from Tubby Johnson and Peter MacPherson.

Various Memorabilia

Now some information on the last section of photographs – Various Memorabilia. The first is the oldest photograph I have of myself, which was taken while I was at school at the age of nine. The second is another of myself, this time nineteen or twenty years old, and fishing at Oban Reservoir, at Glen a Beraidh. I have now found a postcard from Mrs Mellor (a dedicated worker and supporter of the Red Cross), the Argyll Branch of the Red Cross Society. It is not dated but it must have been August/September 1945. 'Dear Mr MacLean, I now return your book of photographs. It went up to the War Office and the contents have been noted by the Department. Many thanks for allowing us to see them. My regrets for the long period we have had the book. Yours sincerely, K Mellor. P.S. I hope you are now quite fit. I have acknowledged receipt of the book. KOM.

Photograph three: taken by the old gentleman from Murau, the engineer. Nearest the camera is Willie Hamilton from Peebles; immediately behind is myself and, in the distance (not much of him showing) is, I think, Ginger Buckley. It is an enlargement from a very small original. Number four is a photograph taken at the swimming bath at the guesthouse in Bodendorf. Back row, *left to right*, Guard A Granberger, from Linz. Everything he stole was divided equally between the prisoners and his wife. He took plenty of anything that was handy. This is the guard I was with when I met Countess Wassilie. He was really very good and we had him a long time. Next to him is Adolf Stock, one of Washhouse Nanna's boys. At that time he was twelve or thirteen and at fourteen he was sent with the Hitler Youth to build tank traps in the forward areas of Yugoslavia and was under attack from British aircraft. Next is Freida, one of the girls who worked in the guesthouse. She was a likeable girl and was the girl detailed to do our washing. Next was Frau Charles from Vienna, who spent a long summer there; for speaking to, and giving gifts to the prisoners, she narrowly escaped a severe sentence. She had a friend who was always with her, a younger girl of about twenty-five. She was 'Frau something or other'. She was a lovely swimmer and known to us by her first name, Erna. She was about at the time, although she is not in the picture. It may be from her camera. Beside Frau Charles is Carl (known as a kind of local stallion). We got on very well with him, although we did not work alongside him very often.

First on the second top row is Donald Fraser from North Shields; behind him is Bert Wheeler; next to him is Edwards from Birmingham, Trinaman, a cockney and a very likeable lad – from the KRRs; next is myself; then, in the next row, beside Donald Fraser, is Plato from New Zealand; then a smiling Willie Hamilton from Peebles; next to him is Poulson, the cockney of whom I had a very poor opinion; behind and to the right of him is Fred Cooper from Nottingham, a regular, from the tanks. This is the boy who was sent home to die, and he was likely to have been very ill when this photograph was taken. Next to Fred is John Joyce from Glasgow, whom I met twenty years later in a lift in Hamilton (Scotland). In the front row are Donald Greaves from Birmingham, Ginger Buckley from Oldham and Jack Feaver, the farmer's boy from Kent – three fine people.

Number five: this again is an enlargement from one of the engineer's snaps and was taken during the last springtime in Austria. The fact that Pouchy is wearing his summer trousers and his winter drawers indicated that it is either spring or autumn. The little piece of bread on the log beside the axe is slightly larger than the daily ration we received during the last four months of the war. *Left to right*: the first in the picture is Willie Hamilton; the man behind him is totally obscured; then comes Ginger Buckley – as usual he is almost naked. The next man is Ken Hibbert from Buckley, Chester, then myself, and Ernie(?) Plato, from New Zealand, at the back.

Number six: taken in the camp at Bodendorf; reading from the left the lads are: R Judd, Kiwi; Arthur Higginbotham, Kiwi; Fred Cooper, Nottingham; Leslie (Ginger) Buckley, Oldham; Donald Fraser, North Shields; W Hamilton, Peebles: G MacLean, Oban; John Joyce, Glasgow; K Hibbert, Buckley, North Wales: interior of the bughouse, Bodendorf, Winter 1942/3. The bugs would emerge from between the sheets, where one sheet overlapped the other. These photographs were hidden above John Joyce's head. They were simply slipped in between the sheets.

Numbers seven and eight: photographs of me in the snow. Number seven would be the winter of 1942/3. I have a very good uniform on and in deep winter snow. The date of the other I am not so sure about, but it shows the back of the guesthouse, with the older type of logs in that part; joints between those logs were filled with spagnum moss.

Number Nine: *Back row*: first, a young Englishman we had for a short time and whose name I have forgotten. All the short time he was with us he had a boil on the back of his neck and, appropriately, he was a pain in the neck; next was Alex Maver, from Dundee, who is mentioned in different parts of the book, and who eventually was sent home early; next was Len Bigmore from Sassafras, Australia. He was the very likeable chap with the gap in his spine; next was Willie Hamilton from Peebles; then Bob Baddock, a cheery cockney; then, Sam Copestick from Stoke. He had been in some kind of accident and had been told that he would permanently have two left legs. This defect could be seen if one looked for it, but he was in no way incapacitated and was far and away the best swimmer we had. In the next row first is Jimmie Swift whom I have mentioned several times. He was Copestick's mate, from the same company No. 292 R.E.; next is myself and you can see that I still wear the old Greek army hat, so it must have been 1942; next, Owen Davies from Bootle; then next is Alex Brown from Salford; the next man is Joe Frodsham, who is another man of whom I had a high opinion. He was, I think, from Bradford; next to him, and almost fading out, is Donald Fraser from North Shields; *front row*: Clem McLarty, an excellent Australian; next our man of confidence, *vertrauensman*, or *dolmitch*, or whatever: Ken Hibbert from Buckley; next Bob Judd, New Zealand Artillery; next another Kiwi, the well-known Leslie Michael James O'Sullivan, from Dunedin; next again is still another Kiwi, Arthur Higginbotham. I cannot really remember where he came from, but I connect him with the Canterbury Plains.

Number ten: I think that this one was also taken in the spring. The uniforms are in better condition and generally we are better-clad. There are five Frenchmen hanging about at the back. I can distinguish Marius, but the rest I have forgotten. Marius is the one immediately to the right of our lads, the little one with the moustache. Now the back row: Bert Wheeler from Leicester; Jack Feaver from Kent, self, and Donald Greaves from Birmingham. *Intermediate row*: Poulson fron London, Willie Hamilton from Peebles, Donald Fraser from North Shields, Fred Cooper from Nottingham. *Front row*: Ernie Plato, Kiwi; Ken Hibbert from Buckley Chester; John Joyce from Glasgow; Trinamin from London; Ginger Buckley from Oldham and Edwards from Birmingham.

Number eleven: This one was taken later on, I think, probably in winter 1943. *Back row*: Hibbert from Buckley; Buckley from Oldham; Higginbotham from New Zealand; Fred Cooper from Nottingham; John Joyce, Glasgow and Jack Feaver, Kent. *Front Row*: Bert Wheeler, Donald Fraser, Willie Hamilton, G MacLean, Bob Judd and I can't remember the other guy. He was a New Zealander. We had him only a short time. As you can see he was a handsome lad – all his numerous girlfriends must have been sending him knitted sweaters. He would wear on the road thirteen or fourteen sweaters, and no jacket. He liked his Macho image and Jack Feaver used to say, 'Humph, no jacket – thirteen sweaters – tough.'

Number twelve: photograph taken at Margate, after a month in the army. *Bottom row* – J H Carmichael, Tobermory; G C Jamieson, Selkirk; J R Sanderson, the borders somewhere; F Sinclair, Lochgilphead; T Pomphrey, Lochgilphead and A Campbell, Ardrishaig. *Middle Row*: A Stewart, Lismore; R Screeton, Manchester; C M Gibbs, Selkirk. *Back row*: G MacLean, Oban; T C Ross, Stirling; R Newall, Selkirk and A Cormack, Ardrishaig.

Number thirteen: Margate again. *Back row*: T J Scot, from Gala(?); A Stewart, Lismore; G Melvin, Hawick. *Front row*: R Jackson, Kippen; G MacLean, Oban; J Wemyss, Hawick; T J Ross, Stirling; the boys on each side of me did not come home.

Number fourteen: photograph taken on the steps of the billets opposite the roller-skating rink at Margate. *Back*: G MacLean, Hugh Carmichael. *Middle*: P McPherson, J Rose. *Front row*: A Cormack, T Pomphrey.

Next I come to the photographs of the Stalag entertainments. I did not know personally any of the people in these, so I have not numbered them along with the rest. All dresses were designed and made in the Stalag. Bottom photograph shows Padre John Ledgerwood, of the second New Zealand Echelon, with the white topper. The Stalag beauty Queen was one of the boys dressed-up. The rest were just pictures of the production.

Number Fifteen: the nearest picture I have of the camp; it is about a mile and a half to the spot where I saw the little Polish girl.

Number Sixteen: a posed photograph that was taken on my leave in December 1940 by a Frenchman who ran a photographic studio in Cairo.

Now a word about some of the souvenirs I brought home: first, from Columbo. Most of my souvenirs were lost in Greece, but I do have a little book and one or two postcards and there are two tiny elephants about somewhere. Fron the canal area I took some stones, fossilised plants – the largest and best are in Greece somewhere. From the Cairo area came a piece of the rock temple of the pyramids. This temple is cut out of the rock and the floor is partly damaged, with small pieces of it lying about – from these I took a piece about half-inch cube. There were also postcards, photographs and some leather wallets. From the Western Desert came a piece of the first bomb that fell on us – it has now disappeared. All the rest was in my kitbag and was lost in Greece. The only things I managed to take care of were those I carried on my person. From Greece came no material items, only memories, good and bad, but above all of a courageous generous people. From Austria came an SA Dagger, a decorative pipe, allied leaflets, paper bandage, paper string, some 'Window', which was used by the allies to confuse enemy radar, a badge from a French soldier's helmet, removed from a door in Austria. Some coral from Port Sudan, which is no longer a thing of great beauty. Italian shoulder badge, German badges used as we use paper flags for raising money. A most disgusting-looking old tooth, which was the only solid item in a bowl of 'soup'. Joe Frodsham nearly choked on it and I managed to rescue it as he was throwing it out of the window. A wooden small-toothed comb for removing nits. My German identity plate. British identity discs. A little pennon complete with swastika from a German staff car. That is about all.

Egypt and Libya

Entrance to Cairo Zoo.

Italian monument at Sidi Barrani.

Italian graves between Barrani and Buq-Buq.

Two of our company at an Italian kilo post. Ed Sweeney on left.

Lance Corporal Walker on right at another kilo post.

'He who hesitates is lost' – with picture of Mussolini.

An Italian
four-wheel-drive
vehicle.

Fort Capuzzo.

Gambert Road
House.

Bodies of Italian
troops killed by
British shell hit
on an
ammunition
truck. They were
buried by our
troops.

Russians Captured at Smolensk

Above: View of Stalag XVIIIA, Wolfberg. *Below*: Stalag XVIIIA, Guard's Section.

The French compound in background; Russians in foreground.

Hauptmann Steiner, Adjutant of Stalag XVIIIA, addressing prisoners.

General view of Russians.

Centre: two men sharing one coat, one way of keeping warm.

Waiting for food.

Close-up of a few Russians.

The man on the left was in the tanks.

Most of the Russians were very poorly clad.

An identity disc can be seen on the man on the right.

The man second from the left has what appears to be a 'NAAFI' spoon.

The men seem to know that they are being photographed.

This is the best example of two men in one coat.

Two pairs – each
pair in one coat.

Freezing and starving.

Some signs of malnutrition.

Stripping for delousing.

Centre:
Obergefreiter
Stahl, who treated
British prisoners
better than most
guards.

Stripping at the
'delouser'.

Two prisoners
who died during
the night of cold
and hunger.

Various memorabilia

The author, aged 9.

The author at Oban Reservoir.

Working on the road. W. Hamilton in foreground, author at rear.

The swimming bath at Bodendorf.

A work party in Austria, 1945.

In the camp at Bodendorf, 1942–43.

Two photographs of the author at Bodendorf, 1942–43.

Two photographs taken at rear of guesthouse, Bodendorf.

Photograph taken at rear of guesthouse, probably 1943.

Margate, one month after joining up.

Margate, March 1940.

As above – some of the
Argyll boys.

Stalag XVIIIA – camp entertainment.

Above: The camp at Bodendorf.

Posed photograph taken by a
Frenchman, Cairo, Christmas 1940.